Changing Orders in International Economic Law Volume 1

These two groundbreaking volumes look at complex legal issues in the changing global economy from the perspective of Asia and/or Japan. Contributors scrutinize the past, present, and future and discuss what the global legal order in economic fields could be like by navigating uncertain and turbulent times.

The books address six main themes: (1) Polarization and diversification of values, progress of regionalism and restructuring of multilateral rules, (2) Full-scale arrival of the digital economy and its impact, (3) Empowerment of private persons/entities, (4) Reconsideration of the concept of "territorial jurisdiction", (5) Law of national security and rule in emergency situations, and (6) Values of Sustainable Development Goals (SDGs) in trade and investment liberalization rules. The book also examines various legal problems under the COVID-19 crisis and suggests how the post COVID-19 global economic order will be from the perspective of Asia and/or Japan.

This comprehensive insight will shed light on the intertwined and complex phenomena of the world economy and allow readers of business law and international law to have a better understanding of this volatile era.

Dai YOKOMIZO is Professor of Private International Law at the Graduate School of Law, Nagoya University.

Yoshizumi TOJO is Professor of International Economic Law at the College of Law and Politics, Rikkyo University.

Yoshiko NAIKI is Professor of Public International Law at the Graduate School of Environmental Studies, Nagoya University.

Routledge Research in International Economic Law

The Legality of Economic Activities in Occupied Territories
International, EU Law and Business and Human Rights Perspectives
Antoine Duval and Eva Kassoti

International Investment Protection within Europe
The EU's Assertion of Control
Julien Berger

Trade, Migration and Law
Free Movement of Persons in the South African Development Community
Victor Amadi

The Americanization of the World Trade Order
Asif H Qureshi

Reform and Regulation of Economic Institutions in Afghanistan
Haroun Rahimi

The Freest Market in the World
The Constitutional Logic of Economic Liberty in Hong Kong
Gonzalo Villalta Puig and Eric C Ip

International Trade Regulation
Evolving Dynamics and Shifting Foundations
Zhiqiong June Wang and Jianfu Chen

For more information about this series, please visit https://www.routledge.com/Routledge-Research-in-International-Economic-Law/book-series/INTECONLAW

Changing Orders in International Economic Law Volume 1

A Japanese Perspective

Edited by
Dai YOKOMIZO, Yoshizumi TOJO, and Yoshiko NAIKI

Routledge
Taylor & Francis Group
LONDON AND NEW YORK

First published 2024
by Routledge
4 Park Square, Milton Park, Abingdon, Oxon OX14 4RN

and by Routledge
605 Third Avenue, New York, NY 10158

Routledge is an imprint of the Taylor & Francis Group, an informa business

British Library Cataloguing-in-Publication Data
A catalogue record for this book is available from the British Library

ISBN: 978-1-032-04412-5 (hbk)
ISBN: 978-1-032-04414-9 (pbk)
ISBN: 978-1-003-19309-8 (ebk)

DOI: 10.4324/9781003193098

Typeset in Times New Roman
by Apex CoVantage, LLC

Contents

Figures

Contributors

Yoshinori ABE is Professor of Public International Law at the Faculty of Law, Gakushuin University. He has also been affiliated with the International Trade and Investment Dispute Settlement Division, Ministry of Foreign Affairs of Japan, for ten years, where he served as a legal adviser on the WTO dispute settlement and investment arbitration. He is currently conducting a comparative analysis of dispute settlement systems and procedures in international economic law and public international law.

Shigeki CHAEN is Professor at the Law School of Osaka University. His research area is intellectual property law, and he is currently studying mainly industrial design protection. He has an ongoing research project regarding design protection in the digital world.

Kojiro FUJII is Partner at Nishimura & Asahi and specializes in competition and international trade laws. His expertise in these areas has been frequently recognized by international and domestic legal publications, such as Chambers and NIKKEI's most successful lawyer rankings. He graduated from the University of Tokyo, Faculty of Law and earned an LL.M. at NYU School of Law, where he was granted a Hauser Global Scholar and was awarded the Frank T. Diersen Prize and Betty Bock Prize in Competition Policy.

Yoshihisa HAYAKAWA is Professor of Law at Rikkyo University and teaches or conducts research at several foreign universities, including Columbia University, Cornell University, Queen Mary University of London, and the Australian National University. He also serves as a partner at Uryu and Itoga, Tokyo, as counsel in many cases of transnational litigation and international commercial arbitration and as an arbitrator in many arbitration cases. Moreover, he serves as a representative of Japan for several inter-governmental organizations, including UNCITRAL, APEC, ISO, and the Hague Conference on PIL, and as an Arbitrator for the Court of Arbitration for Sport.

Shuya HAYASHI is Professor of Law at the Graduate School of Law, Nagoya University. His main areas of research are competition law and telecommunications/broadcasting law. He is also actively engaged in policy recommendations and deliberations in the areas of competition and telecommunication/law and policy. For example, he serves as a Commissioner of the Radio Regulatory Council and as Deputy Chair of the Telecommunications Market Review Board, Ministry of Internal Affairs and Communications of Japan. He was the winner of the DOCOMO Mobile Science Award (in the Social Science category), Mobile Communication Fund 2020.

Takami HAYASHI is Professor of Private International Law at Doshisha University. She was a visiting scholar at the Institute for German, European, and International Family Law at the University of Bonn from 2009 to 2011. Her main areas of research are international family law and international succession law.

Keisuke IIDA is Dean and Professor at the Graduate School of Public Policy (GraSPP), the University of Tokyo. He previously taught at Princeton University and Aoyama Gakuin University. His areas of interest include the politics of international trade, the politics of international financial crises, and the nexus between security and economics. He is also President of the Japan Association of International Relations (JAIR). He holds a Ph.D. (Political Science) from Harvard University. He has been a visiting scholar at the University of California, Berkeley and Academic Associate at the US-Japan Relations Program at Harvard University.

Yurika ISHII is Associate Professor at the National Defense Academy of Japan, where she teaches the public international law course. She received a Ph.D. from the Graduate Schools for Laws and Politics, the University of Tokyo, with a dissertation on the international regulation of economic crimes, which was published as “International Regulation of Transnational Crimes” (Yuhikaku, 2017, awarded the 51st Adachi Mineichiro Award). Her latest work includes “Japanese Maritime Security and Law of the Sea” (Brill, 2022, awarded the 39th Ohira Masayoshi Memorial Award).

Tomoko ISHIKAWA is Professor at the Graduate School of International Development, Nagoya University. Her main research areas include foreign investment law, international human rights law, international environmental law, and corporate social responsibility. Her professional experience includes serving as an associate judge at the Tokyo District Court and holding the position of Deputy Director at the Ministry of Foreign Affairs of Japan.

Akiko KATO is Professor at the College of Law, Nihon University, Japan. Before coming to Nihon University, she worked as a research fellow at the Institute of Intellectual Property and as a faculty member at Kanto-Gakuen University. She holds a Ph.D. from International Christian University. Her research interests are the balancing between intellectual property rights (IPRs) holders’ private interests and the public interest using IPRs. Recently, she explored the global/domestic procurement of medical products in the face of the COVID-19 pandemic as a case study of access to medicine issues. Her research extends to the relationship between the protection of geographical indications and regional development.

Shiho KATO is Associate Professor at the Institute of Social Science, the University of Tokyo. Before joining the Institute of Social Science in 2023, she worked at Hiroshima University and Tokyo Metropolitan University. She specializes in Private International Law and obtained an LL.B., LL.M., and Ph.D. in Law from Nagoya University. A key theme of her research is the role of private international law in regulating private cross-border activities under globalization. She is currently conducting a funded research project that examines how to coordinate the relationship between national and non-national (e.g., religious) orders from the perspective of legal pluralism.

Tsuyoshi KAWASE is Professor at the Faculty of Law, Sophia University and Faculty Fellow at the Research Institute of Economy, Trade, and Industry. He has successively held several positions, including Associate Professor at Osaka University and Deputy Director of the Multilateral Trading System Department, Ministry of Economy, Trade, and Industry (METI) of Japan. He also served as Chairman of the Subcommittee on Trade Remedies, Industrial Structure Council, METI. His current research interests include the trade aspects of national security, global warming, and state capitalism. He holds an LL.B. and LL.M. from Keio University and an LL.M from the Georgetown University Law Center, United States.

Azusa KIKUMA is Principal Deputy Director of the Economic Dispute Settlement Division, International Legal Affairs Bureau, Ministry of Foreign Affairs of Japan. He has been engaged in many negotiations on investment agreements, including the Trans-Pacific Partnership (Investment Chapter) and the Japan-EU Economic Partnership Agreement (Investment and ISDS Chapters). He also represented the Government of Japan under the UNCITRAL Working Group III (ISDS reform). In his current post at the Ministry, he supervises litigation teams in cases of WTO Dispute Settlement and Investor-State Dispute Settlement. He teaches negotiation/litigation strategy of international economic law at Keio University Law School.

Kazumochi KOMETANI is Of Counsel at Nishimura & Asahi and Visiting Professor at the Graduate School of Public Policy, The University of Tokyo. He previously served as General Counsel for the International Legal Affairs, Trade Policy Bureau, Ministry of Economy, Trade, and Industry of Japan. He has been practicing international economic law in the Government of Japan, the World Trade Organization (WTO), and law firms for more than 30 years, in particular engaging in dispute settlement under the WTO, free trade agreements, and investment treaties. He has also published a number of articles and teaches in law schools and public policy schools on these topics.

Takashi KUBOTA is Professor of International Financial Law at the Law School of Waseda University (Ph.D. [Osaka], LL.M. [Harvard, Tokyo]). He previously worked at Nagoya University and the Bank of Japan. He conducted overseas studies at Harvard University, the University of Melbourne, KU Leuven, Queen Mary University of London, the Australian National University, and the University of Auckland. His research interests include global business transactions and electronic commerce. He is currently working on a funded project for digital currencies that focuses on the joint study of jurisprudence and cryptology to attain privacy and security simultaneously in global digital currency transactions.

Mari NAGATA is Professor of Private International Law at the Graduate School of Law and Politics, Osaka University. She received a Ph.D. from Osaka University and worked at Osaka University of Foreign Studies before taking her current position. Her main areas of research are international civil procedural law, international business law, and international family law. Her current research interests include comparative legal analysis of the U.S. Foreign Relations Law Restatement, empirical research on ADR, and enforcement issues in international family law cases.

Yoshiko NAIKI is Professor at the Graduate School of Environmental Studies, Nagoya University. Before coming to Nagoya, she worked at Osaka University, where she obtained a doctoral degree in international public policy. She has been examining the relationship between trade/business and other values in light of "trade and the environment", sustainable food governance, and soft-law aspects. She has two ongoing research projects: smart cities in Asia and global sustainable value chains.

Junji NAKAGAWA is Professor at the Faculty of Liberal Arts, Chuo Gakuin University. His major research field is international economic law. He has published monographs on international investment law, international harmonization of economic regulation, and the WTO. His current research project addresses the relationship between international trade/investment laws and sustainable development.

Kazuhiro NAKATANI has been Professor of International Law at the Graduate Schools for Law and Politics, the University of Tokyo since 1999. His research areas include international economic law, international air law, and international energy law. He is Secretary-General of the International Law Association's Japan Branch and President of the Air Law Institute of Japan. He joined the Tallinn Manual 2.0 on the International Law Applicable to Cyber Operations as a legal expert (2015–16). He was also a visiting scholar at the University of Oxford (1988–89).

Midori NARAZAKI is Professor of International Private Law and International Economic Law at the Faculty of Law, Chuo University. Her recent research focuses on judicial remedies for violations of property rights and human rights caused by transboundary environmental damage from the perspective of private international law.

Yuko NISHITANI is Professor of Private International Law at Kyoto University. She holds a Ph.D. from the University of Heidelberg. She is Vice President of the Hague Academy of International Law since May 2023. She has been a Visiting Professor at various universities in the United States and Europe, and most recently at the New York University in Spring 2023. She served on several legislative committees and represented the Japanese Government at the Hague Conference on Private International Law. She is currently working on global legal pluralism, cultural identity and family relationships, business and human rights, climate change, public interest in the international community, and transnational dispute resolution.

Takemasa SEKINE is Professor at the Graduate School of International Social Sciences, Yokohama National University. He received his legal education at Keio University (Ph.D. and LL.M.). He is currently a member of the Government Procurement Review Board. His recent research focuses on the relationship between the World Trade Organization (WTO) and free trade agreements (FTAs), subsidy regulation under FTAs, and procedural issues under the WTO dispute settlement procedures.

Hiroo SONO is Professor of Law at the Graduate School of Law, Hokkaido University. Before joining Hokkaido University, he taught at Kanazawa University and Kyushu University. His main fields of research are contract law and international commercial law. He approaches these fields from the perspective of the interaction between private ordering and the regulatory function of private law. His current research projects include the effectiveness of global harmonization of private law and sustainable food supplies.

Takao SUAMI is Professor at the Law School, Waseda University. He studied law at the University of Tokyo (LL.B.), Cornell Law School (LL.M.), and the University of Leuven (KU Leuven) (LL.M.). He was a visiting professor at Duke University Law School and the University of Pennsylvania Law School in the United States. He served as President of the European Union Studies Association, Japan, and is currently President of the Japan Association of International Economic Law. His teaching and research interests lie in EU law, international economic law, global constitutionalism, and judicial policymaking in Japan.

Masabumi SUZUKI is Professor of Intellectual Property (IP) Law at Waseda University. He was a professor at Nagoya University from 2002 to 2023. His research focuses on the international aspects of intellectual property law and policies related to industrial property law. Before becoming an academic, he was a government official at the Ministry of Economy, Trade, and Industry of Japan. He was admitted to the New York Bar in 1987 and is a member of the Management Boards of academic associations related to Japanese IP law and the Editorial Board of GRUR International.

Nozomi TADA is Professor of Conflict of Laws at the Faculty of Law, Seinan Gakuin University. He previously worked at Kumamoto University. He has been examining international civil procedure and transnational business transactions. His ongoing research projects include international judicial assistance using information technology and the principles of global ADR.

Koji TAKAHASHI is Professor at the Law School of Doshisha University. He started his full-time career in England, first as a researcher at the Institute of

Maritime Law (Southampton University) and then as a lecturer at the University of Birmingham. Since 2012, he has regularly taught intensive summer programs as an adjunct professor at Michigan State University in the United States.

Keisuke TAKESHITA is Professor at the Graduate School of Law, Hitotsubashi University. His main study fields are private international law and international civil procedure. He has engaged in many legislative projects concerning private international law in Japan. He was an associate member of various subcommittees of the Legislative Council, including those on jurisdiction (family law matters), the revision of the Code of Civil Procedure (Use of IT), and the revision of the Arbitration Act. Currently, he is also working as Chair of the Working Group on Jurisdiction at the Hague Conference on Private International Law.

Yoshizumi TOJO is Professor of International Economic Law at the College of Law and Politics, Rikkyo University. His research areas include the comparative study of competition law and policy, public utilities law, and international subsidy regulation. He is currently working on a research project on the digital economy, focusing on big-tech regulations and cross-border data flows.

Kazuhiro TSUCHIDA is Professor of Law at Waseda University where he has taught economic law and competition law for many years. He is the author of a recently published book, The Renaissance of Economic Law-Reorientation of Antimonopoly Law and Sector-Specific Regulation, and the co-author of a leading textbook, Antimonopoly Law-Text, Outline, and Cases. He is conducting joint research projects, particularly on digital platforms, AI, and algorithms with grants from the Japan Society for the Promotion of Science.

Osamu UMEJIMA is Professor at the International Division, Faculty of Economics, Takasaki City University of Economy (TCUE). He joined TCUE in 2017 and teaches international law, international economic law, and the introduction to legal systems in English. He also assumes the position of an advisor for the Special Custom Duty Investigation Office, Ministry of Economy, Trade, and Industry of Japan. Before joining TCUE, he practiced international trade law, including antidumping and countervailing measures, customs, WTO agreements and dispute settlements, and free trade agreements, at the White & Case LL.P. Tokyo and Washington, D.C. offices for 25 years.

Dai YOKOMIZO is Professor of Private International Law at the Graduate School of Law, Nagoya University. He previously worked at Kanazawa University and Hokkaido University. His research areas include transnational law, transnational business transactions, and arbitration. He is currently working on a funded project for digital platforms that focuses on coordination between national jurisdictions over the regulation of big-tech platforms.

Takuya YOSHIZAWA is Professor at the Faculty of Law, Kyoto Sangyo University. He is continuing his research on Japanese insurance contract law and insurance supervisory law and their international aspects. He is also currently conducting parallel research on InsurTech and metaverse insurance.

Table of International Treaties [Except for Bilateral Investment Treaties that Are Included in the References of Each Chapter]

Agreement between Japan and Mongolia for an Economic Partnership [Japan-Mongolia EPA], in force 7 June 2016.

Agreement between The European Union and Japan for an Economic Partnership [EU-Japan EPA], in force 1 February 2019.

Agreement between The United Kingdom of Great Britain and Northern Ireland and Japan for a Comprehensive Economic Partnership [UK-Japan EPA], in force 1 January 2021.

Agreement on Government Procurement (GPA), in force 1 January 1996.

Agreement on Investment under the Framework Agreement on Comprehensive Economic Cooperation between the Association of Southeast Asian Nations and the Republic of India [ASEAN – India Investment Agreement], in force 1 January 2010.

Basel Convention on the Control of Transboundary Movements of Hazardous Wastes and their Disposal [Basel Convention], in force 5 May 1992.

Berne Convention for the Protection of Literary and Artistic Works, in force 1 March 1989.

Budapest Convention on Contracts for the Carriage of Goods by Inland Waters [CMNI], in force 1 April 2005.

Bustamante Code, in force 25 November 1928.

Canada-Peru Free Trade Agreement [CPFTA], in force 1 August 2009.

Charter of the United Nations, in force 24 October 1945.

Comprehensive and Progressive Agreement for Trans-Pacific Partnership [CPTPP], in force 30 December 2018.

Comprehensive Economic Cooperation Agreement Between the Government of Malaysia and the Government of the Republic of India [Malaysia-India FTA], in force 1 July 2011.

Convention of 1 March 1954 on Civil Procedure, in force 12 April 1957.

Convention on Cybercrime, in force 1 July 2004.

Convention on International Civil Aviation [Chicago Convention], in force 4 April 1947.

Convention on International Interests in Mobile Equipment [Cape Town Convention], in force 1 March 2006.

Convention on Supplementary Compensation for Nuclear Damage [CSC], in force 15 April 2015.
Convention on the Contracts for the International Carriage of Goods by Road [CMR], in force 2 July 1961.
Convention on the Contracts for the International Carriage of Passengers and Baggage by Road [CVR] in force 12 April 1994.
Convention on the Liability of Hotel-keepers concerning the Property of their Guests, in force 15 February 1967.
Convention on the Prevention of Marine Pollution by Dumping of Wastes and Other Matter [London Convention], in force 30 August 1975.
Convention on the Service Abroad of Judicial and Extrajudicial Documents in Civil or Commercial Matters [Hague Service Convention], in force 10 February 1969.
Convention Relating to a Uniform Law on the Formation of Contracts for the International Sale of Goods [ULF], in force 23 August 1972.
Convention Relating to a Uniform Law on the International Sale of Goods [ULIS], in force 18 August 1972.
Digital Economy Partnership Agreement [DEPA], in force 7 January 2021.
Energy Charter Treaty [ECT], in force 16 April 1998.
European Convention on Compulsory Insurance against Civil Liability in respect of Motor Vehicles, in force 22 September 1969.
European Patent Convention [EPC], in force 13 December 2007.
EU-Canada Comprehensive Economic and Trade Agreement [CETA], in force 21 September 2017.
EU-Mercosur Trade Agreement, 28 June 2019, not in force.
EU-Mexico Trade Agreement, in force 1 July 2000.
Free Trade Agreement between Central America, the Dominican Republic and the United States of America [CAFTA-DR], in force 1 January 2009.
Free Trade Agreement between EFTA and Peru [EFTA–Peru FTA], in force 01 July 2011.
Free Trade Agreement between India and Malaysia [India-Malaysia FTA], in force 1 July 2011.
Free Trade Agreement between the Government of Australia and the Government of the Republic of Korea [Australia-South Korea FTA], in force 12 December 2014.
General Agreement on Tariffs and Trade [GATT], in force 30 October 1947.
Geneva Act of the Lisbon Agreement on Appellations of Origin and Geographical Indications, in force 26 February 2020.
International Convention for the Prevention of Pollution from Ships [MARPOL], in force 2 October 1983.
International Convention for the Protection of New Varieties of Plants, in force 10 August 1968.
International Convention for the Unification of Certain Rules of Law Relating to Bills of Lading, in force 2 June 1931.
International Convention on Civil Liability for Oil Pollution Damage [CLC], in force 19 June 1975.

International Covenant on Economic, Social and Cultural Rights, in force 3 January 1976.
International Convention on the Establishment of an International Fund for Compensation for Oil Pollution Damage [FC] [FUND], in force 16 October 1978.
Intra-MERCOSUR Cooperation and Facilitation Investment Protocol, in force 30 July 2019.
Korea-Australia Free Trade Agreement [KAFTA], in force 12 December 2014.
Malaysia-Australia Free Trade Agreement [MAFTA], in force 1 January 2013.
North American Free Trade Agreement [NAFTA], in force 1 January 1994.
Paris Agreement, in force 4 November 2016.
Paris Convention for the Protection of Industrial Property, in force 7 July 1884.
Paris Convention on Third Party Liability for Nuclear Energy [Paris Convention], in force 1 April 1968.
Patent Cooperation Treaty [PCT], in force 24 January 1978.
Peru-Australia Free Trade Agreement [PAFTA], in force 11 February 2020.
Regional Comprehensive Economic Partnership Agreement [RCEP], in force 1 January 2022.
Responsibility of States for Internationally Wrongful Acts, 3 August 2001, not in force.
Second Additional Protocol to the Convention on Cybercrime on enhanced co-operation and disclosure of electronic evidence, 17 November 2021, not in force.
Singapore-Australia Free Trade Agreement [SAFTA], in force 28 July 2003.
Trade Agreement between Japan and United States of America concerning Digital Trade [Japan-US Digital Trade Agreement], in force 1 January 2020.
Trans-Pacific Partnership Agreement [TPP] 4 February 2016, not in force.
Treaties of Montevideo, 1889.
Treaty of Lima, 1878, not in force.
Treaty on the Functioning of the European Union [TFEU], in force 1 December 2009.
United Kingdom-Japan Comprehensive Economic Partnership Agreement [CEPA], in force 31 December 2020.
United Nations Convention on Contracts for the International Sale of Goods [CISG], in force 1 January 1988.
United Nations Convention on International Settlement Agreements Resulting from Mediation [Singapore Convention on Mediation], in force 12 September 2020.
United Nations Convention on the Carriage of Goods by Sea [Hamburg Rules], in force 1 November 1992.
United Nations Convention on the International Effects of Judicial Sales of Ships ["Beijing Convention on the Judicial Sale of Ships"] 7 December 2022, not in force.
United Nations Convention on the Law of the Sea [UNCLOS], in force 16 November 1994.
United Nations Convention on the Use of Electronic Communications in International Contracts, in force 1 March 2013.
United States-Mexico-Canada Agreement [USMCA], in force 1 July 2020.

Vienna Convention on Civil Liability for Nuclear Damage [Vienna Convention], in force 12 November 1977.
Vienna Convention on the Law of Treaties, in force 27 January 1980.
World Trade Organization [WTO] Agreements, in force 1 January 1995.

- Agreement Establishing the World Trade Organization [Marrakesh Agreement]
- Agreement on Subsidies and Countervailing Measures [SCM Agreement]
- Agreement on the Application of Sanitary and Phytosanitary Measures [SPS Agreement]
- Agreement on Technical Barriers to Trade [TBT Agreement]
- Agreement on Trade-Related Aspects of Intellectual Property Rights [TRIPS]
- Dispute Settlement Understanding [DSU]
- General Agreement on Trade in Services [GATS]

Preface

It is a great pleasure to write a short introduction to the two volumes on international economic law in my capacity as a president of the Japan Association of International Economic Law (JAIEL). These two volumes are published to celebrate the 30th anniversary of JAIEL in 2021.

JAIEL was founded in 1991 as a national academic association for the legal study of international economic and business law. Before its foundation, in Japan, existing academic associations such as the Japanese Society of International Law, the Japan Association of Economic Law, and the Private International Law Association of Japan had covered various issues of international economic law. In the late 1980s, however, the international economic environment was challenging Japan in many respects. On the one hand, the trade imbalance with the United States and the European Community (EC) had become a difficult problem for Japan that it was forced to quickly resolve. On the other hand, the establishment of NAFTA and the completion of the internal market in the EC indicated the emergence of regionalism. Moreover, the ongoing negotiations under the Uruguay Round would presumably achieve major reform of the GATT. In addition, the former socialist countries in Eastern Europe were expected to join the international trade regime in the not-to-distant future, since they had already started the process of regime change towards a free economy. All in all, it was manifest at this moment that the framework of the international economy would suffer substantial changes in the near future. It was unfortunate that the state of affairs in Japan on international economic law study had not yet been well-developed and was generally considerably behind other developed countries. This was because such a study had been dispersively conducted in several different forums. Thus, with respect to overcoming such a defect, the founders of JAIEL had an idea to found an academic association specializing in international economic law in order to encourage all concerned scholars and practitioners to come together.

Thirty years after its foundation, JAIEL currently has some 400 members who are professors, researchers, practicing attorneys, graduate students, and government officials. The areas of law that are covered by JAIEL include international law, WTO law, economic law, private international law, international business law, tax law, and intellectual property law. JAIEL's main activity is to hold an annual study meeting once a year, which focuses on a couple of common themes (usually two).

For example, the last five years' common themes were "Revisiting the System of Investment Dispute Settlement" and "International Cartels and Extraterritorial Application of Competition Law of East Asian Countries" (2017); "Present and Future of the International Trade Law Order" and "Rethinking the Mandate of the WTO Appellate Body" (2018); "Current Issues of International Realization of Intellectual Property Protection" and "Legal Issues Concerning Crypto Assets (Virtual Currency) in International Economic and Trade law" (2019); "The Current State of the Formation of New Rules on Digital Trade" and "Legal Aspect of Digital Data in the Global Market" (2020); and "Brexit, Japan-UK EPA and Future of International Economic Law in the United Kingdom" and "Legal Order of Trade and Investment in 'Free and Open Indo-Pacific (FOIP)'" (2021). These themes demonstrate well where the major interests of JAIEL exist. JAIEL annually publishes its own journal, the *Yearbook of International Economic Law*, through its foundation. It has already so far published 30 issues. Furthermore, it published a set of two volumes to celebrate its 20th anniversary in 2012: one focuses on trade, investment, and competition, and another focuses on transactions, property, and procedure. As a consequence of these activities, JAIEL has made remarkable academic achievements thus far and has led discussions on many issues about international economic law in Japan. However, it is undeniable that as our journals and books were published in Japanese, people who do not have Japanese language proficiency have a practical problem getting access to our achievements. Needless to say, international economic law is a global subject that affects all peoples of the world. A well-balanced discussion based upon the input from every part of the world is indispensable to finding solutions to unremittingly emerging problems. In other words, every scholar and lawyer throughout the world has to participate in transnational discussions on how to find a solution to each issue. To be frank, we have to recognize the academic imbalance between Japan and other countries. Therefore, JAIEL decided to publish its 30th-anniversary work in English. Through this English publication, JAIEL aims at contributing to the transnational discussion on international economic law and encouraging its members to actively participate in such discussion.

Articles included in the two volumes have a couple of common features. Firstly, all of them are characterized by their Japanese perspectives. Since all lawyers cannot avoid bringing up their understanding of law including international law in their local contexts, it is unavoidable that approaches to international economic law are not identical in different places. These articles expose such non-Western perspectives to the world. Secondly, many of them deal with newly emerging issues. Japanese scholars are sensitive to change in a global society. Therefore, they deal not only with the digitalization of the global economy but also with the impact of COVID-19 or national security on the international economic order. Thirdly, they cover subjects concerning both public and private international laws (conflict of laws). Their combination constitutes a tradition of Japanese academic approaches. Japanese scholars understand that this combination has become more important than ever under the progress of globalization. All in all, all articles serve as a gateway to the Japanese scholarship of international economic law.

We sincerely hope that a number of scholars and practitioners in the world will read the two volumes and will give their comments back to us. Due to several recent happenings, the landscape of the international economy has changed, and the legal framework of international economic law has also become unstable to a certain extent at least. In order to advance our knowledge of the current system, all of us will need more collaboration. If this publication constitutes a starting point for further collaboration among international economic law scholars in the world, then the objective of this publication has been attained.

Lastly, JAIEL set up a special task force in charge of this publication project for the 30th anniversary in early 2019. Since then, the task force has expended a great deal of time, energy, and efforts to complete this project. On this occasion, we would like to express our sincere thanks to Prof. Yoshizumi Tojo (the former Managing Director), Prof. Dai Yokomizo (the current Managing Director), and Prof. Yoshiko Naiki (the Vice-Managing Director). We also thank our editors at Routledge, Ms. Yongling Lam, and Mr. Kendrick Loo for guiding us patiently through the review, editing, and production processes. Without their work and efforts, these volumes would have never appeared before us.

Takao Suami, Professor of Law
Waseda University

1 Introduction

Yoshizumi TOJO

Landscape of the Global Economy

The 1990s is not the age of "the End of History" as Francis Fukuyama told but the beginning of another history or just another swing of the pendulum of history. This is what we are compelled to recognize through these past few decades. A faith in the open global market that proliferated in the 1990s has been greatly undermined, and the liberal economic order appears to be in confusion.

Firstly, we realize that liberal capitalism and a "borderless economy" do not function well as an institutional model for global prosperity that benefits everyone. On the contrary, we have witnessed widening economic disparities and inequalities both between and within countries that evoke a strong criticism of capitalism on its unfair distributional effect. Compensation for economic losers has rarely materialized. In contrast, the diversity in values between countries has increasingly intensified in these past two decades with the rise of China and other emerging economies such as Brazil, Russia, India, China, and South Africa (BRICS). In this connection, global economic integration based upon a rule-based international governance has become stagnant. In the World Trade Organization (WTO), for instance, the rule-making function has fallen far short from what was expected in the 2000s, the appointment of new judges to the Appellate Body was blocked by the United States, and the dispute settlement mechanism is at the verge of collapse. Instead, bilateral or regional trade agreements have proliferated in the form of customization, reflecting a divergence of values among countries and the individual circumstances of each contracting party.

Secondly, the notion of national security has expanded dramatically into the sphere of economic policy, such as trade restriction measures for widely appointed "strategic" goods on the ground of national security, transborder data transfer restriction in cyberspace, intellectual property protection, and other measures that safeguard essential security interests. The challenge is that almost all international rules of trade and investment are not prepared for the modern security concerns that have recently been expanding and evolving. Their security clauses have been narrowly interpreted to legitimize only measures based upon essential national interests under military and defense situations. Moreover, the Covid-19 pandemic and geopolitical tensions have brought various unilateral restrictions on international

DOI: 10.4324/9781003193098-1

trade and investment. These unilateral measures are likely to be violations of international law.

Thirdly, non-trade issues such as the environment or human rights protection have become increasingly more important in the global economy. Until the 1990s, non-trade issues had only a marginal status in international economic law. After the WTO came into force, the Appellate Body has tried to develop case law that balances free trade and environmental protection by allowing WTO members to justify their restrictive trade measures for the purpose and effect of environmental protection under Article XX of the General Agreement on Tariffs and Trade (GATT) 1994; this is in response to the criticism that the case law of the GATT undermines the proper balance between free trade and environmental protection. Afterwards, the 2030 Agenda for Sustainable Development and the Sustainable Development Goals (SDGs) emphasized the role of trade and the WTO's contribution to the promotion of sustainable development. Thus, non-trade issues have obtained a more important status in the rules of the WTO. These changes should encourage and guide further reforms of the WTO laws in the future.

At the same time, each state keeps struggling to accommodate its legal system to the development of globalization, including efforts to unify or harmonize public regulations and private laws regionally and globally, in order to reap the benefits of globalization. Moreover, many problems facing the world increasingly require coordinated solutions and more interaction among states and other global entities. These problems include global climate change, transborder environmental pollution, human rights violations, and poverty. These sorts of problems cannot plausibly be addressed solely within one legal system. Despite the obvious needs, we witness resistance to forming global governance and promoting solutions. One reason for this situation is the shortage of accountability for such solutions.

The challenge facing the world is how to build governance mechanisms for engagement to cope with these global problems, recognizing certain shared global values such as the environment and human rights and promoting mutual respect, dialogue, and cooperation, without requiring diversified systems to be a system based upon homogeneous values.

Guide to the Volume I

Against this backdrop, this volume collects fifteen articles contributed by eminent Japanese scholars that address important legal phenomena widely, which are focused on the mid- to long-term changes in legal orders since the 1990s. The purpose is to scrutinize the past, present, and future of the world legal order in economic fields, and we set up three areas: polarization of values, national security and emergency, and non-trade concerns.

Part 1: Polarization of Values

Iida (Chapter 1) surveys the literature of the political science field to analyze why the number of preferential trade agreements (PTAs) and international investment agreements (IIAs) have dramatically increased. According to Iida, most political science literature has focused on either competition or diffusion as an explanation. However, the world has already witnessed new trends toward de-globalization or at least deceleration in globalization. Iida argues that power transitions, the growing influence of security concerns, and the rise of populism are propelling these new trends and concludes that we are entering a new age of trade and investment governance amid globalization fatigue.

Sono (Chapter 2) addresses regional efforts in the current and past two decades concerning the unification of private law in relation to its global unification by reviewing the historical development of the unification of private law and finds that the global unification effort was initially started as a regional effort of unification and that current unification efforts emphasize "modernization" and "harmonization" rather than rigid "unification". Sono also examines regional unification in Europe, Latin America, Africa, and Asia to demonstrate that regional unification is not necessarily connected to regional economic integration and finds parallel development of global and regional unification of private law.

Nishitani (Chapter 3) discusses various avenues of effecting corporate due diligence across the global value chain on which today's cross-border business activities of multinationals are largely built. In the global market, multinationals in the Global North are likely to take advantage of the scant regulatory framework, poor security standards, and low wages in the Global South. Through an analysis, *Nishitani* argues that in order to achieve global governance, judicial remedies before national courts and international private law often do not suffice and need to be complemented by substantive due diligence acts to clarify the extent and content of the obligations of parents and subsidiaries while the challenge is the extent to which the parent ought to control the entire global value chain. Other means such as trade regulations, environmental, social, and governance (ESG) investment, corporate governance, guidelines, and settlement agreements should also be sought.

Kato (Chapter 4) analyzes Islamic finance, which is becoming more popular around the globe, and examines various legal problems in a dispute resolution before a court in non-Islamic law influenced jurisdictions as an adjustment process in a world of the multi-polarization of value. *Kato* analyzes the law in Japan and argues that although the choice of Islamic law is likely to be denied, the courts should take into account the principles of *Shari'a* as ascertained by the parties and the opinions given by *Shari'a* boards when ruling on Islamic law questions as a matter of contract, which will contribute to the proper functioning of global Islamic finance and serve as a model of the accommodation of religious norms in the judicial system of states.

Suami (Chapter 5) addresses the Comprehensive and Progressive Agreement for Trans-Pacific Partnership (CPTPP) and the Regional Comprehensive Economic Partnership Agreement (RCEP), the two mega-free trade agreements (FTAs) in the Asia-Pacific region, and clarifies their multi-tiered structure as the unique feature of these Asia-Pacific FTAs. In the case of any inconsistency or contradiction among these existing FTAs, both CPTPP and RCEP provide a mutual consultation clause, and this mechanism is expected to be crucial in solving the dilemma of the choice of law for the parties of these agreements. He highly appreciates the coexistence of the two agreements and concludes that the recent experience in the region strongly suggests the importance of taking into account the interests of developing countries.

Kometani (Chapter 6) addresses the Appellate Body crisis in the WTO, which began with the US blockage of the appointment process for Appellate Body members and resulted in a dormant Appellate Body. *Kometani* assumes that this crisis is caused by perceptions as to its exercise of judicial discretion resulting in its perceived inability to discipline non-market economies such as China and argues that proposals to suppress judicial overreach by clarifying Article 3.2 of the Dispute Settlement Understanding would not resolve US concerns. Alternatively, *Kometani* proposes that the legitimacy of judicial discretion by WTO adjudicators should be assessed on the basis of Dworkin's "unity of value" to attain "sustainable development" as the common goal of the WTO Agreement with a view to upgrading the "rule of law" in the WTO framework.

Part 2: National Security and Emergency

Nakatani (Chapter 7) explores the legality of unilateral restrictions on international economic transactions because of the Covid-19 pandemic and the legality of unilateral embargoes, suspensions of air transport, and restrictions on foreign investment because of national security in relation to the relevant provisions of international treaties. He also analyzes the legality of unilateral restrictions on international economic transactions as economic sanctions in response to serious breaches of international law. Although economic sanctions on their face conflict with key provisions of the treaties of international trade and investment, they may be justified countermeasures when they meet certain requirements such as those of prior demand of redress and proportionality. *Nakatani* argues that international economic law experts must acknowledge the importance of general international law to the proper understanding of the interpretation of international economic law.

Kawase (Chapter 8) addresses the recent development of trade-restrictive measures allegedly necessary for national security purposes, which accompany the expansion of the notion of national security, that developed from traditional military concerns and various economic issues such as the resilience of global supply chains and emerging technologies. Because of the global Covid-19 pandemic, public health has also become an important national security concern. *Kawase* observes that international tribunals are cautious about broadening the scope of the term "essential security interests", while security concepts are expanding in the real world. This potentially undermines the legitimacy of international rules of trade and investment. *Kawase* argues that it is imperative for the WTO and other international trade and investment forums to update their security concepts and strike a proper balance between "new" quintessential functions of the state and free and non-discriminatory trade and investment.

Ishikawa (Chapter 9) examines recent developments of tightening the foreign direct investment (FDI) of Japan on the ground of national security concerns.

Japan's policy shift towards tightening FDI regulations raises a question of conformity between these regulations and the international obligations in international investment agreements (IIAs). In this regard, security exception clauses in IIAs are of particular relevance. Through analysis of their wording and function and of investment arbitration cases in which security exception defenses were invoked, *Ishikawa* argues that future IIA-making should treat security exceptions even more cautiously based on the clear recognition that textual differences in their clauses play a crucial role in the interpretation and outcome of disputes.

Suzuki (Chapter 10) examines the relationship between intellectual property (IP) and national security measures, presenting four types of measures that may affect it: (i) promoting IP protection to deal with security issues, (ii) weakening or limiting IP protection out of security concerns, (iii) controlling the exportation of sensitive goods and technologies that encompass IP, and (iv) 'forced' technology transfer. Suzuki focuses on some Japanese measures. Through the analysis, Suzuki makes clear that there are two directions for compliance: one is to demand stricter compliance with international economic law from the viewpoint of national security, and the other is to provoke security exceptions to justify deviations from specific disciplines under international law.

Umejima (Chapter 11) observes that importing Members are more likely to impose a countervailing duty (CVD) than to challenge prohibited subsidies and actionable subsidies in WTO dispute settlement because CVDs are a faster and easier measure to counteract harmful subsidies. However, CVDs cannot require subsidy-granting Members to withdraw or to remove adverse effects of harmful subsidies and are not the perfect means to discipline for harmful subsidies. *Umejima* reviews the recent movement among WTO Members toward the reform of the WTO subsidy rules and proposes that WTO Members work together to take concerted actions against harmful subsidies such as their own imposition of CVDs or on behalf of a third country pursuant to Article VI:6(c) of the GATT.

Part 3: Non-trade Concerns

Nakagawa (Chapter 12) reviews the development of non-trade issues, such as human rights, sustainable development, and environmental protection, in international trade law since the application of the GATT to the early days of the WTO and to the SDG era. The status of non-trade concerns shifted from their marginal treatment to a more conciliatory treatment in the WTO and entered a new state through the adoption of the 2030 Agenda for Sustainable Development and the SDGs in 2015. The challenge is that this development remains largely theoretical, and the WTO rules remain unchanged. *Nakagawa* argues that SDGs encourage the reforms of the WTO rules to attain their broad-based goals and targets, such as the elimination of agricultural export subsidies, the amendment to the Agreement on Trade-Related Aspects of Intellectual Property Rights (TRIPS Agreement), new fisheries subsidy discipline for the sake of conservation of fisheries resources, and new negotiations on trade liberalization of environmental goods and services.

Naiki (Chapter 13) addresses international standardization in relation to SDG implementation by focusing on two examples: smart cities and the circular economy. *Naiki* observes that countries are competing for international standardization to convert their own national standards into international standards as the political dynamics of the SDGs, while international standard-setting activity is becoming increasingly more complex and fragmented in the SDG era. *Naiki* concludes that, considering the complexity involved, it is necessary to discern high-profile international standardization cases and give sufficient attention to the standard-setting games over such cases.

Kikuma (Chapter 14) examines the relations between an investment treaty and an investor's involvement in human rights violations that take place outside the territory of the host state (human rights violation *outside*). When the host state takes measures against the investor as a sanction in the case of a human rights violation *outside*, this may constitute a breach of obligations under investment treaties. The question is whether a state can defend itself by relying on the fact that the investor is allegedly involved in a human rights violation *outside* and how it is addressed in Investor-State Dispute Settlement (ISDS) tribunals. Kikuma analyzes the legal tools that ISDS tribunals have developed to address investor misconduct and concludes the development of new rules and/or guidelines on the level of due diligence required by the investor are necessary to make the legal tools practically workable.

Narazaki (Chapter 15) addresses international jurisdiction and choice of law issues in civil litigation on transboundary environmental pollution by classifying cases into four modes, especially focusing on the cases in which the Japanese government and/or Japanese companies are involved. Among the modes, the difficult cases are Mode 3 (cases where foreign investment causes environmental damage to the host state) and Mode 4 (where damage spreads to many countries due to transboundary movement and the trading of goods and services) in which the jurisdiction for preventing transboundary pollution is not centralized in a specific state, and it is still not clear how the responsibility of companies controlling worldwide business relations will be determined in civil litigation. In addition, with respect to the governing law, acts of harm in Mode 3 or acts causing damage in Mode 4 are committed in more than one place. *Narazaki* argues that the law of the country that is granted regulatory jurisdiction according to international treaty should be chosen as the applicable law in order to realize the protection against intra- and extraterritorial damage.

Kato (Chapter 16) addresses various schemes for IP sharing, which are required to strike an appropriate balance between global public and private interests on global concerns such as public health, environment, or human rights. One has witnessed many IP sharing cases under the Covid-19 pandemic, while IP sharing is quite limited for Covid-19 vaccines. In fact, there is an extreme disparity between developed and developing countries on access to therapeutic medicines and vaccines. *Kato* analyzes the relationship between governments' legal obligation on compulsory licensing and the responses of IP holders and argues that concerted governmental action will be needed instead of discrete compulsory licensing by each country, which would result in a scramble for vital products.

2 Change in the International Economic Order

From the Perspective of Political Science

Keisuke IIDA

Introduction

This chapter reviews the literature on preferential trade agreements (PTAs) and international investment agreements (IIAs) from the perspective of political science. In international trade and investment governance, the most conspicuous trend over the past two or three decades has been a phenomenal increase in the number of PTAs and IIAs.[1] Accordingly, political scientists have been trying to identify the causal mechanisms behind this trend. The political science literature focuses on either competition – what may be called 'competitive liberalisation' – or diffusion – that is, dominant ideas spreading to the rest of the world.

However, the world has already witnessed a trend toward de-globalisation or at least deceleration in globalisation. How can one reconcile the theory of competitive liberalisation with de-globalization? This chapter argues that the structure of the world economy has shifted toward de-globalisation; hence, earlier theories of competitive liberalisation must be reassessed.

Competitive Liberalisation

Baldwin (1995, 1997) proposed the theory of competitive PTA making or the 'domino theory of regionalism'. Baldwin (1997, p. 871) argued that PTAs exert powerful pressures for inclusion (the first effect) or for the creation of new PTAs (the second effect). According to Baldwin (1995, 1997), the enlargement of the European Union from EU-12 to EU-15 in 1995 was an example of the first effect, whereas the proliferation of preferential arrangements in the Western hemisphere, such as Mercosur, was an example of the second effect.[2]

Baldwin's domino theory has been tested and confirmed repeatedly. Early tests of the domino theory concentrated on the existence of trade diversion arising from free trade agreements (FTAs) or customs unions (CUs). Using the standard gravity model, Sapir (2001) showed that European Free Trade Association countries may have suffered from European Communities (EC) integration in the late 1980s and the early 1990s and that trade and investment diversion may have prompted them to apply for EC membership. Manger (2006) and Egger and Larch (2008), using a very similar method called spatial lags, found that the domino theory is valid in the

DOI: 10.4324/9781003193098-2

sense that countries 'are more likely to sign preferential trade agreements (PTAs) when their neighbors are doing so' (Manger, 2006, p. 15). Baldwin and Jaimovich (2012) tested the domino theory by using what they call the 'contagion' index. This index measures how much export advantage a country loses by other countries' PTA formation. The authors found consistent and robust results showing that PTAs of other country pairs affect PTA signing. Baccini and Dür (2012) empirically tested the domino theory by examining whether the propensity of country pairs signing PTAs with each other is dependent on the degree to which they are discriminated against by the trade diversion created by previous agreements. The authors found very robust results that export discrimination accounts for the likelihood of a country pair forming a new PTA.

In the area of investment, Guzman (1998) laid the theoretical foundation for a competitive model of IIA making. The author explained that most modern IIAs go beyond the traditional Hull Rule (which mandates 'prompt, adequate and effective' compensation for 'takings'). The author also clarified the dynamic competitive pressure imposed on capital-starved developing countries to bid for more foreign direct investment (FDI) by signing IIAs to outbid other host countries.

Guzman's theory has been subjected to a variety of tests and has been confirmed. Simmons (2014) corroborated Guzman's theory by showing that when capital-importing developing countries experience low or negative growth, they are likely to sign IIAs with capital-exporting countries. That is, they are in a more disadvantaged bargaining position when the economy is in dire straits. Elkins, Guzman, and Simmons (2006) proposed and empirically tested the theory of competitive liberalisation. Their theory of competition among host countries to attract FDI is based on the idea of 'investment diversion' (Elkins, Guzman and Simmons, 2006, p. 825), which is analogous to trade diversion in the theory of FTAs. To test the idea that hosts compete to attract FDI by signing increasingly more IIAs, they devised a measure called 'spatial lags'. Broadly, these are the number of IIAs that a given host's potential competitors have signed by the time the host makes a decision on whether to sign an IIA, although this is weighted by some measures of how closely 'competitive' they are with one another. The authors found evidence that this competition drives the decision to sign IIAs.

The previous model assumes an informed, rational decision on the part of the parties to the treaties. However, this is not necessarily the case. Poulsen (2014, 2015) showed that governments, especially in developing countries, are only 'boundedly rational' when signing IIAs; they consistently overestimate the economic benefits of IIAs while ignoring their costs: 'It was not until a country was hit by a claim itself, the potency of the treaties became apparent' (Poulsen, 2014, p. 12). Poulsen and Aisbett (2013) showed the latter result statistically by demonstrating that developing countries begin reducing the number of IIAs that they sign as soon as they themselves are hit by investor claims.

Jandhyala, Henisz, and Mansfield (2011) noted that the motivations for signing IIAs have varied over time. Dividing the sample period from 1970–2007 into three, they showed that the first wave (from the early 1970s to the late 1980s) was characterised by resolving the time-inconsistency problem between capital-exporting and capital-poor countries. The second period (during the 1990s) was motivated by less rational (more social) emulation, while IIA signing in the third period (from 2000 onwards) was motivated by more rational calculations.

Diffusion

PTAs and IIAs may spread to the rest of the world through diffusion: some ideas are so attractive or persuasive that other countries may try to imitate them in order to replicate the successes of the pioneers. Then, the soft power of a dominant country may account for the mimicking of the contents of the country's agreements by other countries.

Recently, political scientists have used a method called 'text-as-data' analysis, that is, machine reading of textual language and the systematic comparison of contents. For example, Allee and Elsig (2019) compared the text of 378 PTAs signed between 1954 and 2013 and found extensive emulation (or 'copying and pasting', in their words) among these agreements. The authors reported that 'the median agreement takes 56 percent of its text verbatim from its closest treaty match'. (Allee and Elsig, 2019, p. 606) Allee and Lugg (2016a) compared the text of the Trans-Pacific Partnership (TPP) to that of previous agreements that the TPP parties had signed and found that the TPP closely matches the previous agreements that the US had signed more so than any other country. In particular, the authors found that as much as 80 percent of the language in the TPP investment chapters is taken from previous US agreements (Allee and Lugg, 2016a, p. 7). Lugg *et al.* (2019) generalised the findings of Allee and Lugg (2016a): using a method called a topic model, the former inferred the authorship of each trade agreement and found that the authorship proportions correlate with the size of the participating economies.

Allee and Lugg (2016b) replicated the same analysis with respect to IIAs. They compared 57 Model BITs with 768 BITs that the author countries of these Model BITs subsequently negotiated. The authors found that 75–95 percent of the text of actual BITs of powerful countries, such as the US and major European states, matches that of their Model BITs. This demonstrates that the ideas embodied in the Model BITs are diffused (in a copy-and-paste manner) to the rest of the world.

New Trends

However, the political science literature on competition and diffusion to explain PTAs and IIAs cannot account for some newer trends that have appeared over the past decade or so.

First, the number of PTAs and IIAs signed each year is declining. The annual number of IIA signings peaked in 1995, and since then, increasingly fewer agreements have been signed. The number of PTAs signed per year also peaked in the early 1990s. Since then, the annual number of PTAs being signed shows a similar decreasing trend (See Figure 2.1).

The theories of competitive liberalisation and that of diffusion were invented to explain why countries are signing increasingly more PTAs and IIAs. Hence, they

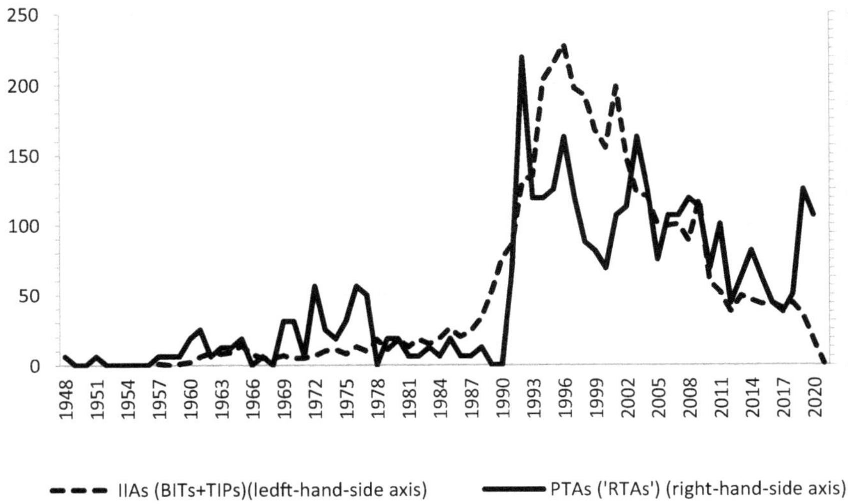

Figure 2.1 The number of PTAs and IIAs signed per year

Sources: WTO, UNCTAD

are inherently ill-suited for explaining why countries are signing fewer and fewer trade and investment agreements. The literature on domestic politics (e.g., Grossman and Helpman, 1995; Mansfield, Milner and Rosendorff, 2002) may be more suited to explaining why countries are signing fewer agreements if it is true that protectionist forces are getting stronger in many countries; however, no full explanations have been offered so far.

Another notable trend is the change in the content of trade and investment agreements. In particular, there is ongoing reform of IIAs, which is actively promoted by the United Nations Conference on Trade and Development (UNCTAD). Reflecting the preferences of many developing countries, UNCTAD has suggested reforms in IIAs (UNCTAD, 2012, 2015, 2018). Consequently, an increasing number of countries are renegotiating existing agreements or signing a new generation of IIAs. This trend has escaped notice in the political science literature, which tends to follow past trends rather than ongoing trends.

A related trend is an increase in attacks on the investor-state dispute settlement (ISDS) mechanisms embedded in BITs and trade agreements with investment provisions (TIPs). Europe is moving in the direction of signing a newer generation of economic partnership agreements (EPAs) with the investment court system. The US is disenchanted with ISDS and has removed it from the US-Canada side of the North American Free Trade Agreement (NAFTA) 2.0 (i.e., the US-Mexico-Canada Agreement). Japan is the only major country firmly attached to the idea of ISDS.

The political science literature has been silent on this question until very recently. Perhaps the first political science treatment of IIA renegotiations was Haftel and Thompson (2018), who statistically analysed the data on IIA renegotiations. They found what most analysts had known instinctively but not definitively: states are more likely to renegotiate existing IIAs after they become respondents in investor-state disputes.

If becoming respondents in investor-state claims is the key variable, then what explains the risk of becoming a respondent? This question was answered by Berge (2020), who conducted a quantitative analysis of the risks of investor-state disputes using the content of IIAs. The author found that the only treaty-design variable with statistically significant and robust effects is the number of substantive obligations in the agreements and that other aspects of IIAs do not matter. Thus, Berge (2020, p. 926) advises states seeking IIA reform to focus on what protections they give under IIAs rather than on how protections are written.

Haftel and Levi (2020) discussed an interesting anomaly in Argentina. After the 2001 financial crisis, Argentina became a respondent to as many as 60 investment arbitration claims. However, unlike some other countries such as Venezuela, Bolivia, and Ecuador, all of which denounced the World Bank's International Center for Settlement of Investment Disputes (ICSID), Argentina did not denounce ICSID or leave or renegotiate its IIAs. The authors examined why and concluded that external constraints combined with the effect of Argentinian identity as a 'responsible' 'European' member of the international community accounted for the lack of pushback against the IIAs or ISDS.

Backlash against ISDS may be merely a symptom of a broader trend against international adjudication. Voeten (2020) noticed backlashes against international courts in general, including investment arbitration, and traced some of them to the rise of populism. The author says that '[e]ighteen of the twenty-eight backlash episodes originated from populist leaders' (Voeten, 2020, p. 414). As mentioned, Bolivia (Morales), Ecuador (Correa), and Venezuela (Chavez) – all under left-wing populist governments – denounced ICSID. Bolivia and Ecuador went so far as to revise their constitutions to prohibit international investment arbitration (Voeten, 2020, p. 415).

Peinhardt and Wellhausen (2016) confirmed what has now become conventional wisdom: states prefer renegotiation (or recalibration) to outright withdrawal from their international commitments. They examined all the cases of withdrawals from international treaties and ISDS up to 2016 and found that despite states' attempts to partially withdraw from IIAs or ISDS, most have been unsuccessful and have switched their strategies to recalibration. The authors found that 'even highly frustrated states are not attempting to totally withdraw from modern international treaty law' (Peinhardt and Wellhausen, 2016, p. 574).

Regarding the content of IIA reform, seemingly contradictory results have been reported. Manger and Peinhardt (2017) measured the degree of precision in IIAs and found that precision increases over time and that the number of claims against the home country (capital-exporting country) accounts for the increase in precision. In contrast, Thompson, Broude and Haftel (2019), who analysed 247 renegotiated/terminated IIAs, found that the number of investment disputes involving both parties to IIAs has a statistically significant effect on IIA renegotiation to increase 'state regulatory space', that is, room to manoeuvre for state regulatory authorities.

Compared to the literature on IIA reform, there is less political science research on the revision or reform of PTAs. The only exception is Castle (2019), who reported the results of some preliminary analysis of their new dataset. Contrary to our impression of recent episodes of PTAs, such as the renegotiation of NAFTA into USMCA and the Comprehensive Economic and Trade Agreement or the EU-Canada Free Trade Agreement (CETA), the author argued that most renegotiations of PTAs are non-politicised and, hence, trade-promoting. This is because there is less political pushback from protectionist forces during renegotiation than at the initial signing of the agreement, which is much more politicised. The author found that revisions of PTAs are very common, but the proportion of what the author calls 'limiting' revisions – the sort that restrict market access compared to the original agreement – is small. In terms of independent variables that affect the probability of revision, Castle (2019) found that jointly democratic pairs, shared cultural similarities, and joint membership in the Organisation for Economic Co-operation and Development (OECD) raise the possibility of revision. Furthermore, the author found that only 'limiting' revisions reduce bilateral trade in the short and long run, while non-limiting revisions have the opposite effect.

There are three medium- to long-term trends in the global environment for trade and investment that may explain the previously discussed trends (i.e., a decrease in the number of PTAs and IIAs being signed and renegotiation/recalibration/partial withdrawal from various international commitments): (1) the relative decline of developed countries in the world economy; (2) the increasing importance of security in every issue-area of international relations; and (3) the rise of populism and the backlash against globalisation in both developed and developing countries.

First, there is a relative decline in the Group of Seven (G7) economies. The share of G7 economies in world GDP, world trade (exports), and outward FDI (stock) declined from 63 percent, 48 percent, and 74 percent in 1975 (1980 for FDI) to 45 percent, 33 percent, and 47 percent, respectively, in 2018.

In contrast, the share of BRICS[3] economies in world GDP, world trade (export), and FDI (stock) rose from 6.70 percent, 5.85 percent, and 2.63 percent in 1993 to 24.17 percent, 21.73 percent, and 9.36 percent (or 15.17 percent including FDI originating from Hong Kong), respectively, in 2018.

Haftel (2019) examined the policy of the BRICS countries toward the global investment regime, or the constellation of IIAs, and found that Brazil, India, and South Africa are pushing back against the regime, while China and Russia have continued to take a more subdued approach.[4] However, given the incoherence of attitudes among the BRICS countries, the author thinks that it is unlikely that BRICS will be the rule-maker of a new global investment regime.

The BRICS countries' approaches to PTAs are more diverse than those for IIAs, even though they are hubs for PTAs and other trade networks in their respective regions. In an unusual frank assessment of BRICS' PTA strategy, Cai (2020, p. 158) argued that '[i]n the long run, such difference(s) may produce a negative impact on the BRICS' mechanism of economic and trade cooperation and result in conflicts of economic and trade interests'.

Second, the increasing prominence of security concerns in various economic issue-areas may account for the trend toward decreasing enthusiasm for PTAs and IIAs. What Heath (2020, p. 1050) called the Cold War Settlement, where mutual restraint was used to enforce the boundary between security and economics, has quickly eroded due to the expansion of the scope of national security with the emergence of new actors and vulnerabilities. We need to reform the trade and investment regimes to handle this ever-increasing tension between security and economics.

The political science literature has hardly kept up with this new trend, which is unfortunate. In an earlier study on the effects of security on PTAs, Mansfield and Bronson (1997) showed that 'the combination of an alliance and a preferential trading agreement generates a greater impetus to trade than does either of these institutions' alone (p. 101). Therefore, when nations sign PTAs, they know that the trade-promoting effects of such agreements are greater when signed with an ally. This may result in more trade agreements signed with allies than with non-allies, although the authors did not show this effect directly. Later, this conjecture was affirmed by Martin, Mayer and Thoenig (2012, pp. 22–23), who showed that being in a military alliance together increases the likelihood of country pairs to sign a PTA.

A few studies have examined the relationship between PTAs and (militarised) disputes. For example, Mansfield and Pevehouse (2000) hypothesised that PTAs dampen disputes by providing a forum for bargaining and by promoting reciprocity, providing information, and constructing focal points by shaping states' expectations (p. 781). The authors analysed the impact of PTAs with dispute data and found that 'the likelihood that a pair of states will experience the outbreak of hostilities is about 50 percent lower if they belong to the same PTA than if they do not' (Mansfield and Pevehouse, 2000, p. 788). Assuming that nations know this law-like fact, they may enter into PTAs in part because they want to avoid disputes with PTA partners.

Martin, Mayer and Thoenig (2012) found that nations that faced wars in the past tend to have PTAs. The authors argued that the motivation for signing PTAs is two-fold: trade and security gains (in terms of reducing the incidence of war). For empirical estimation, they used the frequency of pre-1945 wars for each country pair. Not only does the frequency of pre-1945 wars have a positive effect on the probability that a given country pair signs a PTA, but also the interaction term between trade gains and the old war frequency has a positive coefficient. However, recent wars have a negative impact on the probability of signing PTAs (a more intuitive result), and the authors interpret this as increasing the political cost of negotiations.

The third trending variable, which is widely noticed but not sufficiently researched, is the increasing populist backlash against globalisation, which will affect both PTAs and IIAs. Broz, Frieden and Weymouth (2021) analysed the trends and sources of populist backlash against globalisation. They argued that the decline in manufacturing employment has affected particular communities, which turned populist and against globalisation. The authors showed in great detail that communities that experienced long-term economic and social decline have especially become the most enthusiastic supporters of populism.

Toward a New Theory of PTAs and IIAs

Perhaps it is high time that we reconsidered the theories of PTAs and IIAs. Existing theories are ill-equipped to explain the new trends in PTA and IIA making. The most important point is to return to the drawing board. Both PTAs and IIAs are creations of the height of globalisation from the 1990s and early 2000s. During this era, scholars and laypeople romanticised the great benefits of economic globalisation. Furthermore, to the extent that people were satisfied with the overall net benefits of globalisation, an increasing number of PTAs and IIAs were signed.

However, terrorism, the decline of the middle class in developed countries, massive immigration from poor countries, the Asian financial crisis (1997–1998), the global financial crisis (2008–2010), and most recently, the COVID-19 pandemic, took the sheen off globalisation. Now, we are in an age of globalisation fatigue, if not outright de-globalisation.

What kind of change should we expect from now on? The most likely scenario is increasing complexity, if not chaos. Some people call it 'G-zero' (Bremmer and Roubini, 2011), and some call it 'after hegemony' (Keohane, 1984). There is no longer a dominant country to lead the world toward greater openness in trade and investment. Japan and China, the number three and two economies in the world, respectively, may be willing to step forward as new leaders. However, we see few signs that they are ready to do so.

Notes

1 The political science literature generally uses the term PTAs to refer to any agreements signed under Art. XXIV and the Enabling Clause of the General Agreement on Tariffs and Trade (GATT), such as free trade agreements (FTAs) and customs unions (CUs). The terms PTAs and regional trade agreements (RTAs) are often used interchangeably, although not all PTAs are confined to a 'region'. The political science literature follows the United Nations Conference on Trade and Development (UNCTAD) convention to use the term IIAs, which include both bilateral investment treaties (BITs) and treaties with investment provisions (TIPs).
2 Solis, Stalling and Katada (2009) show that the same dynamics of competition existed in East Asia in the 2000s.
3 BRICS consists of Brazil, Russia, India, China, and South Africa.
4 The author attributes these differences to the position of China and Russia as capital senders, the role of state-owned enterprises (SOEs) in these two countries, and the greater susceptibility of democracies – that is, Brazil, India and South Africa – to pushback from civil society actors.

References

All subsequent websites were last visited on 17 August 2021.

Allee, T. and Elsig, M. (2019). Are the Contents of International Treaties Copied and Pasted? Evidence from Preferential Trade Agreements. *International Studies Quarterly*, 63(3), pp. 603–613. Available at: https://doi.org/10.1093/isq/sqz029

Allee, T. and Lugg, A. (2016a). Who Wrote the Rules for the Trans-Pacific Partnership? *Research and Politics*, 3(3), pp. 1–9. Available at: https://doi.org/10.1177/2053168016658919

Allee, T. and Lugg, A. (2016b). *Do Powerful States Write the Rules in Bits? Comparing Model and Negotiated Treaties*. The 2016 Annual Meeting of the American Political Science Association, Philadelphia. Available at: https://static1.squarespace.com/static/5d53eb6e9850140001239a8e/t/5d5423507b87210001ec7389/1565795153697/Allee+and+Lugg+APSA+2016.pdf

Baccini, L. and Dür, A. (2012). The New Regionalism and Policy Interdependence. *British Journal of Political Science*, 42(1), pp. 57–79. Available at: https://doi.org/10.1017/S0007123411000238

Baldwin, R. E. (1995). Domino Theory of Regionalism. In: Baldwin, R., Haaparanta, P. and Klander, J. eds., *Expanding Membership of the European Union*, 1st ed. New York: Cambridge University Press, pp. 25–53.

Baldwin, R. E. (1997). The Causes of Regionalism. *World Economy*, 20(7), pp. 865–888. Available at: https://onlinelibrary.wiley.com/doi/pdf/10.1111/1467-9701.00107

Baldwin, R. E. and Jaimovich, D. (2012). Are Free Trade Agreements Contagious? *Journal of International Economics*, 88(1), pp. 1–16. Available at: https://doi.org/10.1016/j.jinteco.2012.03.009

Berge, T. L. (2020). Dispute by Design? Legalization, Backlash, and the Drafting of Investment Agreements. *International Studies Quarterly*, 64(4), pp. 919–928. Available at: https://doi.org/10.1093/isq/sqaa053

Bremmer, I. and Roubini, N. (2011). A G-Zero World: The New Economic Club Will Produce Conflict, Not Cooperation. *Foreign Affairs*, 90(2), pp. 2–7. Available at: https://heinonline.org/HOL/Page?handle=hein.journals/fora90&id=212&collection=journals&index=

Broz, J. L., Frieden, J. and Weymouth, S. (2021). Populism in Place: The Economic Geography of the Globalization Backlash. *International Organization*, 75(2, Special Issue 2), pp. 464–494. Available at: https://doi.org/10.1017/S0020818320000314

Cai, C. (2020). Construction of Free Trade Zones in the BRICS Countries. In: Xiujun, X. ed., *The BRICS Studies: Theories and Issues*, 1st ed. London and New York: Routledge, pp. 149–162.

Castle, M. A. (2019). *Why Revise? Presenting a New Dataset on Renegotiations in the International Trade Regime*, p. 53. Available at: https://ssrn.com/abstract=3425591 or http://dx.doi.org/10.2139/ssrn.3425591

Egger, P. and Larch, M. (2008). Interdependent Preferential Trade Agreement Memberships: An Empirical Analysis. *Journal of International Economics*, 76(2), pp. 384–399. Available at: https://doi.org/10.1016/j.jinteco.2008.08.003

Elkins, Z., Guzman, A. T. and Simmons, B. A. (2006). Competing for Capital: The Diffusion of Bilateral Investment Treaties, 1960–2000. *International Organization*, 60(4), pp. 811–846. Available at: https://doi.org/10.1017/S0020818306060279

Grossman, G. and Helpman, E. (1995). The Politics of Free-Trade Agreements. *The American Economic Review*, 85(4), pp. 667–690. Available at: www.jstor.org/stable/2118226?seq=1#metadata_info_tab_contents

Guzman, A. (1998). Why LDCs Sign Treaties That Hurt Them: Explaining the Popularity of Bilateral Investment Treaties. *Virginia Journal of International Law*, 38(4), pp. 639–688. Available at: https://papers.ssrn.com/sol3/papers.cfm?abstract_id=2176003

Haftel, Y. Z. (2019). BRICS and the Global Investment Regime. In: Kim, S. Y. ed., *BRICS and the Global Economy (Vol. 2 of The Political Economy of the BRICS Countries)*. Singapore: World Scientific, pp. 181–205.

Haftel, Y. Z. and Levi, H. (2020). Argentina's Curious Response to the Global Investment Regime: External Constrains, Identity, or Both? *Journal of International*

Relations and Development, 23(4), pp. 755–780. Available at: https://doi.org/10.1057/s41268-019-00174-8

Haftel, Y. Z. and Thompson, A. (2018). When Do States Renegotiate Investment Agreements? The Impact of Arbitration. *The Review of International Organizations*, 13(1), pp. 25–48. Available at: https://link.springer.com/article/10.1007/s11558-017-9276-1 (last accessed 15 July 2021)

Heath, J. (2020). The New National Security Challenge to the Economic Order. *Yale Law Journal*, 129, pp. 1020–1098. Available at: https://papers.ssrn.com/sol3/papers.cfm?abstract_id=3361107

Jandhyala, S., Henisz, W. J. and Mansfield, E. D. (2011). Three Waves of BITs: The Global Diffusion of Foreign Investment Policy. *Journal of Conflict Resolution*, 55(6), pp. 1047–1073. Available at: https://doi.org/10.1177/0022002711414373

Keohane, R. (1984). *After Hegemony: Cooperation and Discord in the World Political Economy*. Princeton: Princeton University Press.

Lugg, A. *et al*. (2019). *Determining the Authorship of Preferential Trade Agreements: A New Technique Using a Supervised Author Topic Model v2.0*. Available at: www.peio.me/wp-content/uploads/2019/01/PEIO12_paper_108.pdf

Manger, M. S. (2006). *The Political Economy of Discrimination: Modelling the Spread of Preferential Trade Agreements*. Available at: https://citeseerx.ist.psu.edu/viewdoc/download?doi=10.1.1.584.5173&rep=rep1&type=pdf

Manger, M. S. and Peinhardt, C. (2017). Learning and the Precision of International Investment Agreements. *International Interactions*, 43(6), pp. 920–940. Available at: https://doi.org/10.1080/03050629.2017.1311258

Mansfield, E. D. and Bronson, R. (1997). Alliances, Preferential Trading Arrangements, and International Trade. *American Political Science Review*, 91(1), pp. 94–107.Available at: https://doi.org/10.2307/2952261

Mansfield, E. D., Milner, H. V. and Rosendorff, B. P. (2002). Why Democracies Cooperate More: Electoral Control and International Trade Agreements. *International Organization*, 56(3), pp. 477–513. Available at: https://doi.org/10.1162/002081802760199863

Mansfield, E. D. and Pevehouse, J. C. (2000). Trade Blocs, Trade Flows, and International Conflict. *International Organization*, 54(4), pp. 775–808. Available at: https://doi.org/10.1162/002081800551361

Martin, P., Mayer, T. and Thoenig, M. (2012). The Geography of Conflicts and Regional Trade Agreements. *American Economic Journal: Macroeconomics*, 4(4), pp. 1–35. Available at: www.aeaweb.org/articles?id=10.1257/mac.4.4.1

Peinhardt, C. and Wellhausen, R. L. (2016). Withdrawing from Investment Treaties but Protecting Investment. *Global Policy*, 7(4), pp. 571–576. Available at: https://doi.org/10.1111/1758-5899.12355

Poulsen, L. N. S. (2014). Bounded Rationality and the Diffusion of Modern Investment Treaties. *International Studies Quarterly*, 58(1), pp. 1–14. Available at: https://doi.org/10.1111/isqu.12051

Poulsen, L. N. S. (2015). *Bounded Rationality and Economic Diplomacy: The Politics of Investment Treaties in Developing Countries*. Cambridge: Cambridge University Press.

Poulsen, L. N. S. and Aisbett, E. (2013). When the Claim Hits: Bilateral Investment Treaties and Bounded Rational Learning. *World Politics*, 65(2), pp. 273–313. Available at: https://doi.org/10.1017/S0043887113000063

Sapir, A. (2001). Domino Effects in Western European Regional Trade, 1960–1992. *European Journal of Political Economy*, 17(2), pp. 377–388. Available at: https://doi.org/10.1016/S0176-2680(01)00032-5

Simmons, B.A. (2014). Bargaining over BITs, Arbitrating Awards: The Regime for Protection and Promotion of International Investment. *World Politics*, 66(1), pp. 12–46. Available at: https://doi.org/10.1017/S0043887113000312

Solis, M., Stalling, B. and Katada, S. (2009). *Competitive Regionalism: FTA Diffusion in the Pacific Rim*, 1st ed. New York: Palgrave Macmillan.

Thompson, A., Broude, T. and Haftel, Y.Z. (2019). Once Bitten, Twice Shy? Investment Disputes, State Sovereignty, and Change in Treaty Design. *International Organization*, 73(4), pp. 859–880. Available at: https://doi.org/10.1017/S0020818319000195

United Nations. Conference on Trade and Development (UNCTAD) (2012). *Towards a New Generation of Investment Policies*. New York: United Nations. Investment Policy Framework for Sustainable Development. World Investment Report. Available at: https://unctad.org/system/files/official-document/wir2012_embargoed_en.pdf

United Nations. Conference on Trade and Development (UNCTAD) (2015). *World Investment Report 2015: Reforming International Investment Governance*. New York: United Nations, especially pp. 120–171. Available at: https://unctad.org/system/files/official-document/wir2015_en.pdf

United Nations. Conference on Trade and Development (UNCTAD) (2018). *UNCTAD's Reform Package for the International Investment Regime*, 2018 ed. Available at: https://investmentpolicy.unctad.org/uploaded-iles/document/UNCTAD_Reform_Package_2018.pdf

Voeten, E. (2020). Populism and Backlashes Against International Courts. *Perspectives on Politics*, 18(2), pp. 407–422. Available at: https://doi.org/10.1017/S1537592719000975

3 The Impact of Regional Integration on Global Harmonisation of Private Law

Hiroo SONO

Introduction

Unification or harmonisation of private law is a concerted effort undertaken by sovereign states to unify or harmonise laws across national borders that govern the horizontal relationships of private parties. Unification or harmonisation is, by definition, international and primarily multilateral. The scope can be regional, or it can be global.

The 20th century witnessed the growth of global unification, which was, in a sense, development in tandem with the spirit of the General Agreement on Tariffs and Trade (GATT) and the World Trade Organization (WTO) system. However, at the turn of the century, regional economic integration began to flourish, fueled partly by disappointment towards the GATT and the WTO system. At the same time, we have witnessed active regional efforts to unify private law. The most conspicuous and successful example is the development of European Union (EU) private law. Will regional unification of private law be an impediment to global unification, or can they coexist?

In line with the theme of this volume, this chapter examines these questions by reviewing the historical development of the unification of private law. It reveals that the unification of private law in the late 19th century was initially a 'regional' exercise and that it became 'global' only in the 1970s. The revival of regional unification that we see today is, in one sense, a reversion to the past. This chapter examines three relationship patterns between regional integration and regional unification and the impact of regional economic integration on global unification of private law.

A few caveats apply. Apart from unification efforts undertaken by sovereign states, various private initiatives also set uniform rules. The International Chamber of Commerce (ICC)'s Incoterms and the Uniform Customs and Practices for Documentary Credits (UCP) are classic examples. This chapter does not deal with such private initiatives. Unification or harmonisation of law in the field of family law is also outside the scope of this chapter. This chapter primarily focuses on commercial law.

Lastly, the terms 'unification' and 'harmonisation' are interchangeable in the broad sense. In the narrow sense, however, 'harmonisation' entails elasticity, which is one feature of the present-day unification of private law, as is explained later.

DOI: 10.4324/9781003193098-3

The Transformation of Global Unification of Private Law

Global unification of private law today is promoted by three international organisations: the United Nations Commission on International Trade Law (UNCITRAL), the International Institute for the Unification of Private Law (UNIDROIT), and the Hague Conference on Private International Law (HCCH). Other entities produce uniform private law rules in specific fields, such as the International Maritime Organization (IMO), the International Civil Aviation Organization (ICAO), and the World Intellectual Property Organization (WIPO). However, unification of private law is not their primary mandate. Compared to the breadth of activities of UNCITRAL, UNIDROIT, and HCCH, the sector-specific organisations' unification activities are, although essential, limited in scope.

Unification of Private Law in the 19th Century: 'Regionalism in Disguise'

The international unification of private law began in the latter half of the 19th century when the movement of persons and goods across national borders increased with the development of means of transportation and communication. Such activities can be seen in Europe, Latin America, and Nordic countries. Still, the activities based in Europe eventually developed into global unification of private law. However, these European efforts were 'regionalism in disguise'.[1]

The Hague Conference on Private International Law (HCCH)

The HCCH is the oldest of the three organisations. The first conference was held in 1893 with the participation of 13 continental European countries (the HCCH became a permanent institution only in 1925, after World War I. Before that, it was a diplomatic conference held on an ad hoc basis). Japan was the first non-European country to participate in the conference, starting with the fourth meeting in 1904; until the 1950s, Japan was the only non-European participant (even the United States did not participate until the 1950s).

However, many countries that participated in the HCCH at the beginning of the 20th century were not necessarily positive about the participation of a country such as Japan, which is different from European countries (for details, see Sono, 2017, pp. 14–15). The direct purpose of Japan's participation in the conference was to conclude the Convention on Civil Procedure of 1896. In order to apply the Convention to territories outside Europe, each party was required to notify the depositary of such intention, and the Convention entered into force with respect to these territories only in relation to states that made an affirmative declaration. However, Japan was unable to obtain such cooperation and eventually gave up concluding the Convention. As can be seen from this, the HCCH at that time was basically an institution aiming to unify private international law in the European region. One commentator characterises that the HCCH has been a 'European Club' for over 50 years (Kono, 2005, p. 20).

International Institute for the Unification of Private Law (UNIDROIT)

The second-oldest organisation, UNIDROIT, was initially established in 1926 as an auxiliary organ of the League of Nations. Because it was an organ of the League of Nations, UNIDROIT is not a European institution. For example, Japan was a member of the League of Nations from the time of its establishment in 1927 and sat on the Governing Council until withdrawing from the League of Nations in 1933. However, the activities of UNIDROIT were suspended in 1937 due to the outbreak of World War II. It was eventually re-established as an independent inter-state organisation in 1940. However, the 20 member states of the re-established UNIDROIT consisted only of civil law countries in Western Europe and Latin America. More importantly, most of the work of UNIDROIT until around 1970 was in the nature of undertaking studies and providing drafts of uniform laws to the Council of Europe and later to the United Nations Economic Commission for Europe (UNECE). The end products include the European Convention on Compulsory Insurance against Civil Liability in respect of Motor Vehicles (1959) and the Convention on the Liability of Hotel-keepers concerning the Property of their Guests (1962) (see later for more examples. See also, Nishitani, Kozuka and Morishita, 2020, pp. 204–207; Sono and Takasugi, 2013, p. 48). In this way, until the middle of the 20th century, UNIDROIT's work was more regional than global.[2]

What could have been an exception was the Uniform Law on the International Sale of Goods (ULIS) and the Uniform Law on the Formation of Contracts for the International Sale of Goods (ULF) of 1964 (collectively, the 'Hague Uniform Sales Law'). However, the European nature of UNIDROIT in those days defined the fate of ULIS and ULF. In 1964, at a diplomatic conference held by the Dutch government, conventions relating to ULIS and ULF (collectively, the 'Hague Sales Law Conventions') were adopted, which obligated contracting states to incorporate these uniform laws into their legislation. The Hague Sales Law Conventions entered into force in 1972. However, only nine countries, among which seven were European, became parties to the Conventions (Belgium, Gambia, West Germany, Israel, Italy, Luxembourg, the Netherlands, San Marino, and the UK). Furthermore, seven of these countries later became parties to the 1980 United Nations Convention on Contracts for the International Sale of Goods (CISG) and denounced the Hague Sales Law Conventions. As a result, only two countries, namely, Gambia and the UK, are currently state parties to the Hague Sales Law Conventions.

The failure of the Hague Uniform Sales Law is often attributed to the facts that (i) it is more theory-oriented than practical; (ii) it was primarily developed by European civil law countries; (iii) and non-European countries, socialist countries, and developing countries were not included in the process (Goode, Kronke and McKendrick, 2015, pp. 216–217; Schwenzer and Muñoz, 2022, p. 37). As a result, the Hague Sales Law failed to obtain widespread global support.

Unification of Private Law since the Late 20th Century: Enter UNCITRAL

Based on these experiences, the United Nations General Assembly resolved to establish UNCITRAL in 1966. The first session of the Commission was held in 1968.

UNCITRAL's member states, which are elected by the General Assembly, are allocated among five geographic regions: Africa; Asia and the Pacific; Eastern Europe; Latin America and the Caribbean; and Western Europe and others. The composition of the Commission is structured so that the membership represents different legal systems (civil law and common law), economic systems (capitalist economies and socialist economies), and stages of development. Furthermore, in preparing uniform law instruments, consideration is given to the diversity of legal systems around the globe. The number of member states was 29 when UNCITRAL was established, but it gradually expanded to 60 by 2021. In 2021, based on Japan's proposal, it was decided to expand the number of member countries to 70. This is expected to result in a more diverse composition of member countries (UN General Assembly, 2021).

A good example of the inclusive character of UNCITRAL's work is the 1980 CISG. As it became already clear in 1969 that the number of its contracting states would not increase, UNCITRAL decided in 1969 to develop what would become the CISG with more global participation than the Hague Sales Laws. The CISG entered into force in 1980, and has become a *ius commune* in the field of international sales, and boasts 95 contracting states (as of 1 June 2023).

Another example is the 1978 United Nations Convention on the Carriage of Goods by Sea (the 'Hamburg Rules'). UNCITRAL developed the Hamburg Rules in response to criticism against the Brussels Bills of Lading Convention of 1924 (or the 'Hague-Visby Rules'). Developing countries, typically shipper countries, raised the criticism that the Convention favoured the carriers, typically from developed countries, over the shipper (Goode, Kronke and McKendrick, 2015, p. 276). Although the Hamburg Rules are not as successful as the CISG, they entered into force in 1992 and have 35 contracting states (as of 1 June 2023).

Thus, only after UNCITRAL entered the scene, international unification of private law became a global exercise. Today, 'globalisation' has also spread to the HCCH and UNIDROIT. Both organisations have a worldwide membership. As of 1 June 2023, the HCCH has as members 90 states and one regional organisation, while UNIDROIT has 65 member states (see Figures 3.1 and 3.2). However, it is still true that the countries in Africa and Asia are underrepresented in UNIDROIT and the HCCH.[3]

The Transformation of Unification of Private Law in the 21st Century

At the beginning of the 21st century, it seemed that the deepening of globalisation would make the unification of private law even more thorough. However, the transformation of the unification of private law today has become pronounced. The emphasis has shifted from 'unification of law' to 'harmonisation of law' and 'modernisation of law'.

Harmonisation of Law

'Harmonisation of law' is an approach aiming at approximating the laws so that the laws of different jurisdictions will share common principles rather than sharing

Figure 3.1 Geographic distribution of HCCH member countries

Source: https://assets.hcch.net/docs/fa2ded4d-0574-41d9-b749-289d44aef373.pdf (last accessed 18 May 2023)

Figure 3.2 Geographic distribution of UNIDROIT member countries

Source: www.unidroit.org/about-unidroit/members-states-2/ (last accessed 18 May 2023)

identical rules. Starting with the 1985 UNCITRAL Model Law on International Commercial Arbitration, non-binding instruments such as model laws and legislative guides have become prevalent. Instruments setting out 'principles of law' are also used (e.g., UNIDROIT Principles of International Commercial Contracts (first published in 1994; the latest version is 2016); 2015 Hague Principles on the Choice of Law in International Commercial Contracts). When domesticating these non-binding instruments, the recipient countries enjoy broad discretion. This approach aims at an 'elastic' unification of private law according to the circumstances of each country.

Modernisation of Law

There is also a shift in the centre of gravity from 'unification of law' to 'modernisation of law'. This shift often affects the scope of harmonisation. Instead of harmonising the law governing cross-border activities (i.e., *ius gentium* approach), recent harmonisation instruments also govern purely domestic activities (i.e., world law approach). In other words, the trend aims at 'domestic law reform'. The titles of recent model laws are indicative of this approach. Unlike the model laws in the early days, the first being the 1985 UNCITRAL Model Law on International Commercial Arbitration, the word 'international' is absent in recent model laws (e.g., UNCITRAL's Model Law on Electronic Commerce (1996), Model Law on Electronic Signatures (2001), Model Law on Secured Transactions (2016), Model Law on Electronic Transferable Records (2017), UNIDROIT's Model Franchise Disclosure Law (2002), and Model Law on Leasing (2008)).

One of the reasons for this shift is the pervasion of the 'Washington Consensus', which is a model of economic development based on the principles of a free market economy and the liberalisation of trade and investment (Williamson, 2008, p. 14). Based on this consensus, investment in development shifted from government official development assistance (ODA) to private sector investment that required domestic law reform in the recipient developing countries.

Second, the advancement of digital technology poses new legal challenges that cannot be solved within the confines of individual domestic law. For example, transactions of digital assets based on blockchain technology are not only new but also unimpeded by national borders. UNIDROIT's recent project on 'Digital Assets and Private Law' is an example.

Revival of Regional Unification of Private Law[4]

Classical Regional Unification of Private Law

As explained previously, the current global private law unification activities originated from European regional activities and have expanded to a global scale. However, other attempts at regional unification of private law have also been made. The reason why unification efforts that had their genesis in Europe have grown to become global is not just because of the economic superiority of Europe. Other regional unification efforts were genuinely regional.

Latin America

Beginning with the Treaty of Lima (1878; not in force), the Treaties of Montevideo (1889), and the Bustamante Code (1928), there was active promotion of regional unification of law in Latin America. These efforts predate the European efforts that began with the HCCH in 1893. However, in 19th-century Latin America, the challenge was establishing a unique international order in the Americas that was independent of and parallel to the European international order (Nakai, 2020, pp. 28–35). Therefore, the unification of private law in Latin America needs to be understood in the context of establishing a bulwark against European domination. This is perhaps a major reason why regional unification in Latin America did not expand globally (Basedow, 2003, p. 32; Kozuka and Takasugi, 2020, p. 203).

Since 1975, the development of private international law treaties in Latin America has been taken over by the *Conferencias Interamericanas sobre Derecho Internacional Privado* [Inter-American Specialized Conferences on Private International Law] (CIDIP) under the Organization of American States (OAS) framework (Kozuka and Takasugi, 2020, pp. 203–207; Takasugi, 2001, pp. 122–134).

Nordic and Benelux Countries

The unification of private law within the Nordic countries also began in 1872 when a meeting of Nordic jurists was convened with the participation of Norway, Denmark, and Sweden. Finland and Iceland joined in 1919. These countries shared not only the same legal tradition but also the same king, language, religion, and culture, and they are all relatively small in terms of population. These conditions led them to jointly embark on the unification of domestic laws in the form of 'legislative cooperation' (Backer, 2018; David, 1971, pp. 180–188; Letto-Vanamo and Tamm, 2016; Sono, Kozuka and Okino, 2020). Given this genesis, it is not surprising that this regional unification did not expand globally.

Similar efforts can be seen within the three Benelux countries (Belgium, the Netherlands, and Luxembourg), but their success seems limited (David, 1971, pp. 188–191).

Currently, all Nordic and Benelux countries are members of the EU or the European Economic Area (EEA), which does not permit national legislation that conflicts with EU law. The active unification of private law by the EU has therefore resulted in narrowing these regions' areas of private law unification.

Europe

Before the days of the EU, there were other attempts at regional unification. In addition to the initial activities of the HCCH and UNIDROIT, one must not forget the efforts of the Council of Europe and the UNECE in the European unification of private law (David, 1971, pp. 192–193; Nishitani, 2020, p. 196; Nishitani, Kozuka and Morishita, 2020, pp. 204–207). As we have seen previously, the Council of Europe, established in 1949, has been working on the unification of regional private law. The UNECE, established in 1947, is also working on the unification of private law, most notably in the field of carriage by road, railway, and inland navigation (e.g., the Convention on Contracts for the International Carriage of Goods by Road (CMR), 1956, the Convention on Contracts for the International Carriage of Passengers and Baggage by Road (CVR), 1973, and the Budapest Convention on Contracts for the Carriage of Goods by Inland Waters (CMNI), 2001). The work of both the Council of Europe and the UNECE reflects the dynamic nature of cross-border traffic and carriage within Europe. Private law has also been unified in other areas, such as patent cooperation, personal status relations, and nationality.

In contrast to the previous discussion, the unification of private law within the framework of the EU [and its predecessor, the European Communities (EC)] was widely implemented in the latter half of the 20th century. The purpose of such unification of private law is to integrate the European internal market, which should be distinguished from the earlier attempts at unification of private law in Europe.

Regional Integration and Regional Unification of Private Law

There are three relational patterns between regional integration and regional unification of private law in the latter half of the 20th century. They are (1) unification of private law for the purpose of regional integration, (2) regional integration without unification of private law, and (3) unification of private law without regional integration. We turn to them next.

Unification of Private Law for the Purpose of Regional Integration

In the latter half of the 20th century, the EU and the East African Community (EAC) are representative examples of utilising the unification of private law for the purpose of market integration.

EU private laws are formed within the scope of the powers conferred on the EU by the member states for the purpose of market integration (see generally, Basedow, 2021). Thus, EU private law began with areas that directly affect market integration. EU regulations and directives are used to unify substantive law in areas as diverse as competition, consumer protection, e-commerce, company, finance, transport, insurance, intellectual property, labour, and data protection. The EU is also active in making uniform rules in the area of judicial cooperation. Such instruments include the Brussels I Rules (2000) for civil and commercial cases and the Brussels II Rules (2000) for family law matters that provide uniform rules regarding jurisdiction and mutual recognition and enforcement of judgments. These instruments are vital as they facilitate the free movement of judgments and consequently create one judicial sphere. In the area of private international law, there are the Rome I Regulation (2008) on the law governing contractual obligations, the Rome II Regulation (2007) on the law governing non-contractual obligations, and the Rome III Regulation (2018) on the law governing divorce. In terms of the uniform interpretation and application of these EU private laws, the role of the European Court of Justice (ECJ) cannot be overlooked.

The current EAC (comprising Kenya, Tanzania, Uganda, Rwanda, and Burundi), established in 1999, aims to achieve regional economic integration based on the model of the EU (see generally, Agaba, 2011; Kozuka and Sono, 2020, pp. 214–216; Sono and Kozuka, 2015; Thorp, 2012). Specifically, (1) community legislation, such as in the field of customs, is enacted in the East African Legislative Assembly (EALA), and (2) private law is unified through an approach in which each country seeks 'approximation' of domestic laws. Such laws in the EAC include bankruptcy law, partnership law, labour law, employment law, and sale of goods law. Furthermore, (3) the establishment of the East African Court of Justice (EACJ), to which private disputes may be referred, is also noteworthy.

In Latin America, the *Mercado Común del Sur* [the Southern Common Market] (MERCOSUR) (established in 1991, with Argentina, Bolivia, Paraguay, and Uruguay as members) has achieved a certain degree of success in unifying private law in the area of judicial cooperation. Still, it has not been as successful in unifying substantive law. The *Comunidad Andina* [Andean Community] (CAN) (established in 1996 and now constituted by Bolivia, Colombia, Ecuador, and Peru) also sets the unification of private law as a policy objective and has a common intellectual property law. Still, it seems to be limited to unification in specific areas (Kozuka and Takasugi, 2020, pp. 207–208).

In addition, in Central Asia, the Eurasian Economic Union (EAEU), launched in 2015, is unifying private law with the aim of market integration (Yokomizo and Khakimov, 2020, p. 224).

Regional Integration without Unification of Private Law

Other regional integration bodies in Africa and Asia are missing from the regional integration explained previously. These regional integrations are generally not accompanied by unification of private law.

The African continent is undergoing gradual economic integration by initially being divided it into eight blocs, with a plan to integrate them into the African Union (AU) in the future (the EAC previously mentioned is one of these blocs) (Kozuka and Sono, 2015a).

Although it is often pointed out that the unification of private international law is an urgent issue for the promotion of trade between African countries (Oppong, 2006; Uka, 2020), among these regional integration bodies, only the EAC described previously has a mandate for the unification of private law. The launch in 2021 of the African Continental Free Trade Agreement (AfCFTA) similarly does not seem to have unification of private law on its agenda (Uka, 2020).

However, for intellectual property, there are two regional organisations. They are the *Organisation Africaine de la Propriété Intellectuelle* (OAPI), mainly consisting of former French colonies, and the African Regional Intellectual Property Organization (ARIPO), mainly consisting of common law countries (Kozuka and Sono, 2020, pp. 216–217). They are administrative cooperation organisations for the registration of patents and other rights, but OAPI also unifies substantive law rules.

The situation is similar in Asia, where various regional integration frameworks exist (e.g., CPTPP, RCEP, APEC, and ASEAN). For example, the ASEAN Economic Community (AEC), which aims at market integration, is also pursuing 'regional integration without unification of private law'. Only limited unification in areas of intellectual property, competition, consumer protection, and e-commerce is being pursued (Yokomizo and Khakimov, 2020, pp. 220–222; Nottage and Patterson, 2019, pp. 392–414).

The reasons for the lack of unification efforts in these regional integration bodies are unclear. However, it is interesting that these regions are also generally reluctant to accept global uniform law instruments. This attitude may indicate private law's minimal role in these regions and societies. One commentator suggests that the extremely limited interest in regional unification of private law in Asia is a result of the predominance of instrumentalism, which focuses heavily on policy-oriented rules (Kozuka, 2016, pp. 345–346). In fact, even in these regions, unification of private law with clear policy objectives, such as consumer protection law, competition law, and intellectual property law, is carried out.

Unification of Private Law Without Regional Integration

There is also the traditional regional private law unification without regional integration. Nonetheless, successful regional unification of private law will remove legal barriers to international trade within that region. Thus, it will facilitate regional economic integration, although not in the form of a constitutionalised regional economic integration organisation. CIDIP in Latin America is an example. In addition, regional unification of law is taking place within the Community of Independent States (CIS) of the former Soviet Union and in the Central Asian Republics (CARs) (Yokomizo and Khakimov, 2020, pp. 222–224).

Here, however, we focus on the *Organisation pour l'Harmonisation en Afrique du Droit des Affaires* [Organization for the Harmonisation of Commercial Law in Africa] (OHADA) (see generally, Kozuka and Sono, 2015a, 2015b, 2020). Founded in 1993, OHADA is an organisation of western African countries that were originally French colonies. The most striking characteristics of OHADA are that (1) OHADA's uniform acts immediately take effect and replace domestic laws in the member states (i.e., legislation is passed without going through the legislature of each country); (2) the *Cour Commune de Justice et d'arbitrage* [Common Court of Justice and Arbitration] (CCJA) was established to ensure uniform interpretation of the OHADA uniform acts; and (3) *l'Ecole Régionale Supérieure de la Magistratur* [Higher Regional School of Magistracy] (ERSUMA) was established as an educational institution of OHADA laws for the judges of each country.

In this way, OHADA has institutionalised a robust and unparalleled mechanism for unifying private law. So far, uniform acts on general commercial law, commercial companies, security rights, insolvency, execution, arbitration, business accounting, carriage of goods by road, cooperative societies, and mediation have been enacted.

The Dual Impact of Regional Harmonization

As previously described, regional unification is not necessarily connected to regional economic integration. But regional integration can be an impetus for regional unification of private law and *vice versa*. Whether related to regional economic integration or not, we see parallel development of global and regional unification of private law. The relationship between the two is intertwined. On the one hand, regional integration or unification can impede global unification. On the other hand, regional integration or unification may have the effect of facilitating global unification.

Regionalism as An Impediment to Global Unification of Private Law

Overriding of Global Unification by Regional Unification

Regional unification has the risk of driving out global unification. The controversy concerning the EU's Common European Sales Law (CESL) initiative and the CISG centred around this risk.

Although CESL eventually failed in 2014, the European Commission proposed in 2011 to establish an optional instrument for the sale of goods for small- and medium-sized enterprises (SMEs) and consumers within Europe (Basedow, 2021, pp. 70–72). Since most EU countries were already parties to the CISG then, CESL was considered a threat to the CISG. The CISG Advisory Council (CISG-AC) expressed concern that (i) CESL will trench upon the area occupied by the CISG; (ii) the resulting non-uniformity will increase legal costs due to the three-tier structure of domestic law, CESL, and the CISG; (iii) there is the likelihood that regional initiatives would not produce a better solution; (iv) states may become entrenched behind regional instruments at the expense of participating in the harmonisation of global contract law; and (v) the attractiveness of CISG to states that are not yet contracting states will be lessened to the extent that the universality of the CISG is compromised (CISG Advisory Council, 2012). The CISG-AC also pointed out that, in fact, among OHADA Member States, where the sale of goods provisions of the OHADA Uniform General Commercial Law is modelled on the CISG, only three have become parties to the CISG.

Disruption of the Law-making Process

Regional integration may also have the effect of disrupting the negotiation of global uniform laws. The following example concerns the EU (see Basedow, 2003, pp. 40–46; Basedow, 2021, pp. 681–684).

The EU has legal personality (the Treaty on European Union, Art. 47) and treaty-making powers in matters over which it has competence (Arts. 3(2) and 216(1) of the Treaty on the Functioning of the European Union (TFEU)). For the EU to conclude treaties, however, it is also necessary that respective treaties grant regional economic integration organisations status to become a member. The HCCH amended Article 3 of its Statute in 2005 to grant Regional Economic Integration Organizations (REIO) qualifications to become parties. Consequently, the EU is responsible for negotiations at the HCCH, as long as the legislative competence for private international law is vested in the EU rather than in EU Member States. Similarly, it has also become standard practice in treaties adopted by UNCITRAL and UNIDROIT after 2001 [e.g., UNIDROIT Convention on International Interests in Mobile Equipment ('Cape Town Convention'), 2001, Art. 8, and most recently, UNCITRAL's Convention on the International Effects of Judicial Sales of Ships ('Beijing Convention on the Judicial Sale of Ships'), 2022, Art. 18] to grant REIO's qualification to become parties. However, since the EU is not a member of UNCITRAL or UNIDROIT, negotiation at these organisations is undertaken by EU member states. This can cause complications.

For example, even if EU Member States negotiate and adopt a treaty, the conclusion of the treaty by each EU Member State may only be possible if the European Commission ultimately accepts it. In other words, non-EU countries will be negotiating with EU Member States that lacks flexibility, because their hands are tied. Furthermore, even if an agreement is formed between individual EU Member States and non-EU states, it may happen that the treaty will not be concluded if the European Commission decides against it.

Mutual Facilitation of Unification

However, regional unification may positively affect global unification and *vice versa*.

First, all the problems discussed previously concern 'treaties'. The picture is different if we bring non-binding unification instruments such as model laws into the scene. The recent emphasis on the 'harmonisation' and 'modernisation' of laws (explained previously) allows regional and national deviations. Thus, the increasing use of non-binding instruments can support the cooperative relationship between regional integration and global unification of private law.

Second, global standards can be incorporated into regional integration instruments. For example, the electronic commerce chapters of the Comprehensive and Progressive Agreement for Trans-Pacific Partnership (CPTPP) require the member states to adopt a legal framework consistent with the principles set out in the UNCITRAL Model Law on Electronic Commerce (1996) or the United Nations Convention on the Use of Electronic Communications in International Contracts, 2005 (e.g., TPP, Art. 14.5). Such incorporation will facilitate global harmonisation.

Third, China's massive Belt and Road Initiative (BRI), if seen from the perspective of unification of law, may facilitate global harmonisation. China established the China International Commercial Court (CICC) in 2018 to settle private disputes arising from the promotion of the BRI. It may proceed to promote the unification of private law in countries along the Belt and Road. For example, China is a Contracting State of the CISG, but geographically, a vast vacuum of CISG contracting states lies between China and Europe (see Figure 3.3). If the BRI triggers a rapid increase in the number of CISG Contracting States, then this will be conducive to the global unification of private law (Wolff, 2017, 2020).

Conclusion

As described previously, the relationship between global unification of law and regional unification of law is, in a sense, a love-hate relationship. However, there is less tension when the instrument used is non-binding (e.g., model laws, legislative guides, and 'principles of law') than when it is binding (i.e., treaty). This is a result

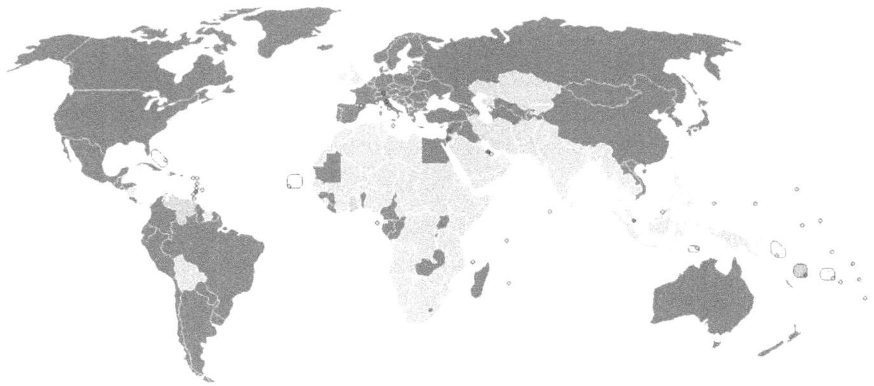

Figure 3.3 Geographic distribution of CISG parties

Source: Prepared by the author based on https://en.wikipedia.org/wiki/United_Nations_Convention_on_Contracts_for_the_International_Sale_of_Goods (as of 1 June 2022)

of the elastic unification allowed by non-binding instruments, combined with the recent shift to place more emphasis on 'harmonisation' and 'modernisation' than on 'unification'.

To achieve effective unification of private law in the future, it will be necessary to identify areas where reliance on treaties is essential from those where it is not.

Note: This work was supported by JSPS KAKENHI Grant Number JP20H00051.

Notes

1 The term 'regionalism in disguise' was coined by Basedow, 2003, p. 32.

2 Even today, UNIDROIT is involved in regional harmonisation. The 'Model European Rules of Civil Procedure' (2020) is a joint product of the European Law Institute (ELI) and UNIDROIT, which is an attempt at regional implementation of the more global American Law Institute (ALI)/UNIDROIT Principles of Transnational Civil Procedure (2006).

3 For studies analysing Asian countries' reluctance toward the unification of private law, see Kozuka, 2016; Kozuka, 2017; Kozuka, 2020.

4 This section is largely based on the results of the author's joint research: Kozuka and Sono, 2020; Kozuka and Takasugi, 2020; Nishitani, 2020; Nishitani, Kozuka, and Morishita, 2020; Sono, 2020; Sono, Kozuka, and Okino, 2020; Yokomizo and Khakimov, 2020.

References

All subsequent websites were last visited on 1 September 2022.

Agaba, S. (2011). The Future of International Commercial Law in East Africa. *European Journal of Law Reform*, 13(3–4), pp. 505–513.

Backer, I. (2018). *Styrket nordisk lovsamarbeid Muligheter og utfordringer*. Available at: www.norden.org/no/publication/styrket-nordisk-lovsamarbeid

Basedow, J. (2003). Worldwide Harmonization of Private Law and Regional Economic Integration. *Uniform Law Review*, 2003(1–2), pp. 31–49.
Basedow, J. (2021). *EU Private Law: Anatomy of a Growing Legal Order*. Cambridge: Intersentia.
CISG Advisory Council (2012). *The CISG and Regional Harmonization*. Available at: www.cisgac.com/cisgac-declaration-no1
Council Regulation (EU) No 1259/2010 in the Area of the Law Applicable to Divorce and Legal Separation (2007). Official Journal L343, pp. 10–16.
David, R. (1971). Chapter 5: The International Unification of Private Law. In: David, R. *et al.* eds., *International Encyclopedia of Comparative Law, Vol. II: The Legal Systems of the World: Their Components and Unification*. Tübingen: J.C.B. Mohr.
Goode, R., Kronke, H. and McKendrick, E. (2015). *Transnational Commercial Law*, 2nd ed. Oxford: Oxford University Press.
Kono, T. (2005). 100 Years of the Hague Conference of Private International Law and Japan-Past and Future. *Kokusai Shiho Nenpo [Japanese Yearbook of Private International Law]*, 7, pp. 20–31.
Kozuka, S. (2016). The Bifurcated World of Uniform Law: The Uniform Law of 'Islands' and of 'The Ocean'. In: Unidroit ed., *Eppur si muove: The Age of Uniform Law: Essays in Honour of Michael Joachim Bonell*, Vol. 1. Rome: International Institute for the Unification of Private Law, pp. 333–346.
Kozuka, S. (2017). The Selective Reception of Uniform Law in Asia. *Japanese Yearbook of International Law*, 60, pp. 86–112.
Kozuka, S. (2020). Idiosyncrasies of Japan and Asia Towards the Harmonization of Law. *Journal of Japanese Law* (Special Issue 13), pp. 153–169.
Kozuka, S. and Sono, H. (2015a). Afurika ni okeru Chiiki Togo to Ho Toitsu [Regional Integration and Unification of Law in Africa]. *Nihon Kokusai Keizaiho Gakkai Nenpo [Yearbook of the Japan Association of International Economic Law]*, 24, pp. 106–123.
Kozuka, S. and Sono, H. (2015b). OHADA (Afurika Shiho Chowaka Kiko) ni yoru Toitsu Keiyakuho no Chosen to Zasetsu [The Challenge and Failure of Uniform Contract Law for OHADA]. *Hokudai Hogaku Ronshu [The Hokkaido Law Review]*, 66(4), pp. 1250–1228.
Kozuka, S. and Sono, H. (2020). Afurika ni okeru Shiho Toitsu: 'Afurikaho' no Rinen to Genjitsu Shugi no Hazama [Unification of Private Law in Africa: Between the Ideal of 'African Law' and Realism]. *Ronkyu Jurist [Quarterly Jurist]*, 35, pp. 213–219.
Kozuka, S. and Takasugi, N. (2020). Raten Amerika ni okeru Ho Toitsu [Unification of Law in Latin America: Between the 'Americas' and 'Central and South America']. *Ronkyu Jurist [Quarterly Jurist]*, pp. 202–210.
Letto-Vanamo, P. and Tamm, D. (2016). Cooperation in the Field of Law. In: Strang, J. ed., *Nordic Cooperation: A European region in Transition*. Abingdon: Routledge, pp. 93–107.
Nakai, A. (2020). *Kokusaiho no Tanjo: Yoroppa Kokusaiho kara no Tenkan [The Birth of International Law: The Transformation from European International Law]*. Kyoto: Kyoto University Press.
Nishitani, Y. (2020). Oshu ni okeru Shiho Toitsu (Soron): Tayosei no naka no Toitsusei [Unification of Private Law in Europe (General Matters): Unity in Diversity]. *Ronkyu Jurist [Quarterly Jurist]*, 34, pp. 195–202.
Nishitani, Y., Kozuka, S. and Morishita, T. (2020). Oshu ni okeru Shiho Toitsu (Kakuron): Tayosei no naka no Toitsusei [Unification of Private Law in Europe (Specific Matters): Unity in Diversity]. *Ronkyu Jurist [Quarterly Jurist]*, 35, pp. 204–212.
Nottage, L. and Patterson, J. (2019). Consumer Contracts and Products Safety Law in Southeast Asia: Partly Trading Up? In: Hsieh, P. L. and Mercurio, B. eds., *ASEAN Law in*

the New Regional Economic Order: Global Trends and Shifting Paradigms. Cambridge: Cambridge University Press, pp. 392–414.

Oppong, R. (2006). Private International Law and the African Economic Community: A Plea for Greater Attention. *International and Comparative Law Quarterly*, 55(4), pp. 911–928.

Regulation (EC) No 593/2008 on the Law Applicable to Contractual Obligations (Rome I) (2008). Official Journal L177, pp. 6–16.

Regulation (EC) No 864/2007 on the Law Applicable to Non-Contractual Obligations (Rome II) (2007). Official Journal L199, p. 40.

Schwenzer, I. and Muñoz, E. (2022). *Global Sales and Contract Law*, 2nd ed. Oxford: Oxford University Press.

Sono, H. (2017). Going Forward with Uniform Private Law Treaties: A Study in Japan's Behavioral Pattern. *Japanese Yearbook of International Law*, 60, pp. 10–58.

Sono, H. (2020). Chiikiteki Shiho Toitsu no Yukue: Honkikaku no Shushi [The Future of Regional Private Law Unification: Introduction]. *Ronkyu Jurist [Quarterly Jurist]*, 34, pp. 194–195.

Sono, H. and Kozuka, S. (2015). Higashi Afurika Kyodotai (EAC) ni okeru Shiho Toitsu ni kansuru Oboegaki [Harmonization of Private Law in the East African Community (EAC)]. *Hokudai Hōgaku Ronshu [The Hokkaido Law Review]*, 66(4), pp. 1078–1061.

Sono, H., Kozuka, S. and Okino, M. (2020). Hokuo ni okeru Shiho Toitsu: Rippo Kyoryoku to iu Katachi [Unification of Private Law in the Nordic Countries: 'Legislative Cooperation']. *Ronkyu Jurist [Quarterly Jurist]*, 34, pp. 210–217.

Sono, H. and Takasugi, N. (2013). Haagu Kokusai Shiho Kaigi, UNIDROIT, UNCITRAL [The Hague Conference on Private International Law, UNIDROIT, and UNCITRAL]. In: Sono, H. *et al*., *Shiho Toitsu no Genjo to Kadai [The Current State and Challenges of Unification of Private Law]*. Tokyo: Shoji Homu, pp. 44–55.

Takasugi, N. (2001). Beishu no Toitsu Kokusai Shiho Joyaku [Uniform Private International Law Treaties in the Americas]. *Kokusai Shiho Nenpo [Japanese Yearbook of Private International Law]*, 3, pp. 119–146.

Thorp, T. (2012). The Rule of Law and the Implementation of an Economic Acquis Communautaire in Sub Saharan Africa: Legal Challenges for the East African Community. In: Herrmann, C. and Terhechte, J. eds., *European Yearbook of International Economic Law 2012*. Berlin: Springer, pp. 485–546.

Uka, O. (2020). Cross Border Dispute Resolution Under AfCFTA: A Call for the Establishment of a Pan-African Harmonised Private International Legal Regime to Actualise Agenda 2063. *Law Digest*, 2020, pp. 56–58.

UN General Assembly (2021). *Enlargement of the Membership of the United Nations Commission on International Trade Law, A/RES/76/109*. Available at: https://research.un.org/en/docs/ga/quick/regular/76

Williamson, J. (2008). A Short History of the Washington Consensus. In: Serra, N. and Stiglitz, J. eds., *The Washington Consensus Reconsidered*. Oxford: Oxford University Press, pp. 14–30.

Wolff, L. (2017). From a 'Small Phrase with Big Ambitions' to a Powerful Driver of Contract Law Unification? – China's Belt and Road Initiative and the CISG. *Journal of Contract Law*, 52, pp. 50–69.

Wolff, L. (2020). Legal Responses to China's 'Belt and Road' Initiative: Necessary, Possible or Pointless Exercise? *Transnational Law and Contemporary Problems*, 29(2), pp. 249–325.

Yokomizo, D. and Khakimov, A. (2020). Ajia ni okeru Shiho Toitsu: Tonan Ajia oyobi Chuo Ajia wo Chushin ni [Unification of Private Law in Asia: With Focus on Southeast Asia and Central Asia]. *Ronkyu Jurist [Quarterly Jurist]*, 35, pp. 219–224.

4 'Business and Human Rights' from Global and Asian Perspectives

Yuko NISHITANI

Introduction

Today's cross-border business activities of multinationals are largely built on the global value chain or supply chain. Multinationals headquartered in a developed country purchase goods, parts, or raw materials from their subsidiaries, suppliers, or contractors (hereinafter 'subsidiaries, etc.') situated or transacting in a developing country, which can cause human rights abuses or environmental damage in the developing country. Asia has often been the centre of such human disasters. Incidents include, for example, the Bhopal explosion in India (1984), Nike's child labour in Pakistan (1996), and Rana Plaza's collapse in Bangladesh (2013). In the global market, multinationals in the Global North are likely to take advantage of scant regulatory framework, poor security standards, and low wages in the Global South.

Notably, Asia has a diverse picture. It encompasses Japan and the Republic of Korea as the Global North, whereas most other countries belong to the Global South. The People's Republic of China, India, and Indonesia arguably have both elements of the Global North and the Global South, as their total GDP ranks high, but their GDP per capita is still relatively low (IMF, 2021). It is a challenging task for academics and policy makers in Asia to develop appropriate measures and legal frameworks to combat human rights violations and environmental damage across the global value chain.

A series of binding and non-binding international instruments have been adopted to provide for corporate due diligence. Although the United Nation (UN)'s Guiding Principles on Business and Human Rights (2011) and Sustainable Development Goals (SDGs) (2015) have shaped recent developments, other instruments, such as the Organisation for Economic Co-operation and Development (OECD) Guidelines (2011) and the International Labour Organization (ILO) Core Conventions (2022), also play important roles. It is an innovative construct that parent (or lead) companies as private parties, in addition to sovereign states, are held responsible for human rights violations committed by their subsidiaries, etc. Various states have acquiesced to the idea of corporate due diligence and started to take appropriate measures to implement the Guiding Principles. Likewise, the Japanese government adopted the 'Action Plan for Business and Human Rights' in October 2020 (Japan, Ministry of Justice, Human Rights Bureau, 2020). It was, however, not until May 2021 that Japanese industry became aware of the full scale of the impact of corporate due

DOI: 10.4324/9781003193098-4

diligence when the US authorities banned imports of UNIQLO shirts due to the reported use of cotton from Xinjiang, China. On 13 September 2022, the Japanese Ministry of Economy, Trade and Industry adopted the 'Guidelines on Respect for Human Rights in Responsible Supply Chains', which set forth only a general framework for corporate due diligence. It is a delicate question whether and the extent to which multinationals should control and be held liable for wrongful acts committed by their subsidiaries or subcontractors abroad within the global value chain.

In what follows, this study examines various ways of achieving corporate due diligence to protect human rights across the global value chain. After discussing judicial remedies for victims in view of European private international law (or conflict of laws) and substantive law, this chapter delineates the state of the discussion in Japan. To enhance sustainable corporate activities, other measures are studied in relation to trade law and soft law. Some final remarks conclude this chapter.

Although the notion and scope of human rights differ throughout various jurisdictions, this chapter refers to human rights that are universally acknowledged, such as the right to life, liberty, and security, non-discrimination, prohibition of slavery, and basic labour rights.

Judicial Remedies

Introduction

As for judicial remedies, the question is whether and the extent to which victims of human rights abuses in the Global South can claim damages against multinationals headquartered in the Global North. Local courts in developing countries are often feared dysfunctional, corrupt, and biased. Nor were they considered to provide an adequate forum for seeking remedies due to unfavourable substantive law or limited amounts of assets owned by the subsidiaries. Thus, the discussion has so far concentrated on whether the judiciary in the US or Europe, in which the parent company is located, can provide an appropriate forum.

The US used to offer remedies for victims of human rights violations that occurred overseas under the Alien Tort Statute (1948), but the US Supreme Court has restricted its causes of action and denied extraterritoriality since *Kiobel v. Royal Dutch Petroleum Co.* (2013). In *Nestlé USA v. Doe* (2021), the Supreme Court similarly dismissed the damages claims of six alleged child labour victims who were kidnapped from Mali and taken to Ivory Coast to work on a cacao plantation and who sued two US companies that purchased cacao. After the US closed its doors to victims in the Global South, Europe sees itself as a possible alternative forum.

EU Private International Law

International Judicial Jurisdiction

The courts of an EU Member State, in which a multinational is established or headquartered, are readily granted international jurisdiction based on the defendant's domicile (Brussels I *bis*, Arts. 4(1), 63). Yet, jurisdiction over her foreign subsidiaries, etc. that sit outside the EU and that directly commit human rights violations can be granted only under the EU Member State's domestic law when it provides for the joinder of parties, or accepts jurisdiction on the grounds of joint tortfeasors, *forum necessitatis*, or universal jurisdiction.

Notably, the Hague Court of Appeal decisions of 29 January 2021 in *Oguru et al. and Milieudefensie v. Shell Petroleum, Royal Dutch Shell and Shell Nigeria* also granted jurisdiction against the subsidiary, as per the UK Supreme Court decisions in *Vedanta Resources PLC et al. v. Lungowe et al.* (2019) and *Okpabi v. Royal Dutch Shell* (2021). The 2021 Dutch decisions concerned oil pipeline leaks in Nigeria. Four individual plaintiffs from the region and Milieudesensie, a Dutch environmental organization, sought damages against and removal of contaminants by the Shell parent companies and Shell Nigeria. Although jurisdiction over the parents was affirmed as the defendants' domicile under Brussels I (Shell Petroleum's incorporation and Royal Dutch Shell's registered office in The Hague), Shell Nigeria was also subject to jurisdiction based on the joinder of parties for closely connected claims pursuant to Dutch law. This result, however, was an exception, as jurisdiction over foreign subsidiaries outside the EU is often denied under the EU Member States' domestic law, such as in Germany (Dutta, 2020, pp. 55–57).

Applicable Law

Even if international jurisdiction is approved, applicable law remains an issue. Among different avenues, first, the law governing contracts (Rome I, Art. 3 ff) is usually not relevant due to a lack of contracts between the parent company or subsidiaries and the victims.

Second, unfair competition is governed by the law of the marketplace (Rome II, Art. 6(1)), which is usually the law of an EU Member State. In the *Lidl* case in Germany, the company was condemned for profiting from clothes that were advertised as being produced through 'fair trade' although the workers in Bangladeshi factories who produced these clothes were subject to abusive labour conditions. *Lidl* was held responsible for unfair competition (Weller, Hübner, and Kaller, 2018, p. 258). Yet, although the construct of unfair competition may pressure a company to comply, it cannot provide a remedy for victims of human rights abuses by aiming at market order and consumer protection.

Third, in corporate law, direct piercing of the corporate veil allows equating the subsidiary with the parent. This is determined by the *lex societatis* of the subsidiary, which is either the law of incorporation or the law of the main seat, depending on the EU Member State's conflicts rule. Yet, the applicable substantive law hardly allows direct piercing of the corporate veil of a subsidiary that is properly and independently doing business. Whether the CEOs of the parent company incur a supervisory duty, or command and order, over the subsidiary is also determined by the *lex societatis* of the subsidiary as a matter of corporate governance. Conventional corporate law, however, refutes such control over or involvement in a separate legal person within the corporate group (Mansel, 2018, pp. 452–453; Wagner, 2016, pp. 759–766).

Ultimately, the most likely construct in relation to third parties is tortious claims. Torts are principally governed by the *lex loci damni* (Rome II, Art. 4(1)), unless an escape clause or the parties' choice of law intervenes (Rome II, Arts. 4(2)(3), 14). This usually refers to the law of the subsidiary's place of business in a developing country. Conventional tort law typically establishes a tort of the acting subsidiary or other party but denies joint liability of the parent for its lack of duty of care and direct involvement in the subsidiary as a separate legal person (Mansel, 2018, pp. 453–454; Wagner, 2016, pp. 757–771).

The previously mentioned 2021 Dutch decisions, however, exceptionally granted remedies pursuant to Nigerian law designated by the Dutch conflict rules prior to Rome II. First, as for the oil leaks, the defendant Nigerian subsidiary alone was held liable and ordered to compensate for the damage pursuant to the Nigerian Oil Pipelines Act (1956), which provides for strict liability, after the subsidiary failed to prove third-party sabotage as the cause of the accidents. Second, the Nigerian subsidiary was denounced for negligence liability for breaching the duty of care by failing to install a leak detection system, and the parents in the Shell group were held jointly liable for being substantially involved in this matter. Because Nigerian law is embedded in English common law, the Shell group parents were denounced for having knowledge of the subsidiary's actions and incurring direct liability pursuant to the previously mentioned UK Supreme Court decision in *Vedanta Resources PLC et al. v. Lungowe et al.* (2019) and the Court of Appeal decision in *Okpabi v. Royal Dutch Shell* (2018). Thus, all the parties were ordered to install a leak detection system within one year.

Although such an outcome in favour of victims is rather an exception, the question is whether some reform is desirable to ensure remedies by establishing corporate due diligence.

Reform of EU Private International Law

For the sake of effective corporate due diligence, the EU first contemplated reforming private international law. The European Parliament Committee on Legal Affairs (2020) published a Draft Report on 11 September 2020, which proposed new rules on jurisdiction at the EU parent's domicile for the wrongs of her subsidiaries, etc. and *forum necessitatis* when access to justice is not guaranteed in third states (Brussels I *bis*, new Arts. 8(5), 26a). The Draft Report also sought to adopt a new tort conflict rule based on ubiquity like Article 7 Rome II on environmental damage, which allows the victim to unilaterally select, instead of the *lex loci damni*, the law of the parent company's seat or place of operation (Rome II, new Art. 6a). In its resolution of 10 March 2021, however, the European Parliament (2021) gave up these drafts and only recommended that member states ensure the application of the relevant due diligence act as overriding mandatory rules.

On 8 October 2021, the Groupe européen de droit international privé (GEDIP) (2021), as an academic organization, adopted a resolution in this respect. While reiterating the desirable overriding effect of the relevant due diligence act, the GEDIP recommended introducing jurisdiction rules grounded on joinder of parties and *forum necessitatis* and a tort conflict rule of ubiquity along the lines of Article 7 Rome II. To enhance private enforcement, these suggested rules will duly complement the current loopholes in jurisdiction for subsidiaries, etc. outside the EU and ensure the application of due diligence acts for parents domiciled outside the forum state.

The European Commission Proposal for a Corporate Due Diligence Directive of 23 February 2022 does not include any specific provisions on jurisdiction or applicable law but indicates instead that EU Member States ought to ensure that civil liability rules (Art. 22) have an overriding effect in relation to the applicable third-state tort law. The legislature may be afraid of reforming Rome II, as the respect for human rights may touch upon the delicate issues of infringement of personality rights, which had, after a lengthy debate, been excluded from the scope of Rome II (Art. 1(2)(g)). It would, however, be desirable that future due diligence directives be complemented with appropriate conflict of laws rules, with a view to ensuring application of the relevant due diligence act of the state closely related to the case.

Due Diligence Acts

For private international law to be functional and to ensure corporate due diligence across the global value chain, it is desirable that adequate substantive law rules be adopted to directly prescribe human rights due diligence on parent companies. This avenue has been taken by various legal systems. As Rühl (2020, pp. 67–72) points out, due diligence legislation can be classified into three groups: due diligence acts providing for obligations of multinationals (i) to report and disclose violations, (ii) to comply with due diligence and monitor and prevent violations, and (iii) to incur civil liability in the case of breaches of due diligence obligations.

The 2014 EU Non-Financial Reporting Directive, the 2015 UK Modern Slavery Act, and the 2022 EU Corporate Sustainability Reporting Directive belong to (i), whereas the 2017 EU Conflict Minerals Regulation and the 2019 Dutch Child Labour Due Diligence Act are classified as belonging to (ii). As Rühl (2023, *forthcoming*) discusses, Germany adopted in 2021 the Supply Chain Due Diligence Act, which belongs to (ii) and provides for a series of due diligence obligations of German parent companies to prevent, monitor, and mitigate human rights violations across the global value chain. The German Act, however, precluded civil liability following vigorous opposition from industry. Similarly, in Switzerland, the original bill, which explicitly provided for civil liability with a reversed burden of proof, was no longer approved in a referendum on 29 November 2020.

To date, only the 2017 French *Loi de vigilance* belongs to (iii). This act orders French parent companies or dominant companies to design a detailed due diligence plan and compensate for damage caused in breach of the plan across the global value chain. Notably, the *Loi de vigilance* is restricted in scope to large French companies with more than 5,000 employees in France alone or 10,000 employees worldwide. This covers less than 300 companies seated in France. Furthermore, French companies incur civil liability only for 'serious' human rights violations or environmental violations committed by themselves or subsidiaries, etc. with whom they have an 'established business relationship'.

Despite its narrow scope, the *Loi de vigilance* is pioneering legislation and a strong instrument to combat human rights violations and environmental damage with an overriding mandatory effect. On 15 December 2021, in the first case applying the *Loi de vigilance*, the French Court of Cassation confirmed jurisdiction of the civil courts, instead of the commercial courts, concerning Total's oil drilling plans in Uganda. The case is still pending for a decision on the merits, after the District Court of Paris dismissed the claims for adjusting Total's vigilance plans and remedying human rights violations in summary proceedings on formal grounds on 28 April 2023. Although its proper application in the context of the company's activities remains an issue, the French law could be a model for other EU Member States in implementing the future Corporate Due Diligence Directive.

Notably, the 2022 European Commission Proposal for a Corporate Due Diligence Directive provides for damages claims (Art. 22) and belongs to (iii). If the European Parliament and European Council decide to follow the proposal, then other EU Member States, including Germany, will have to go beyond their domestic due diligence act currently in force to adopt civil responsibility. Combined with the overriding effects of implemented due diligence acts and possibly with adequate conflict of laws rules, future legislation in the EU is expected to considerably advance human rights due diligence.

Japan

Private International Law

How should the Japanese courts proceed when a claim for damages is made against a multinational headquartered in Japan by victims of human rights violations caused by its subsidiaries, etc. in a developing country?

International judicial jurisdiction against the Japanese parent company will be affirmed based on the defendant's domicile (Code of Civil Procedure 'CCP', 1996, Arts. 3–2(3)) and against its subsidiaries, etc. on the ground of joinder of parties (CCP, Arts. 3–6, 2nd sentence). In this respect, the Japanese courts can more readily exercise jurisdiction than many EU Member States. Yet, the Japanese courts are allowed – as a kind of *forum non conveniens* – to dismiss the claim under special circumstances in light of fairness between parties and the proper and expeditious administration of justice. Thus, victims may be declined remedies in Japan when evidence is concentrated in a foreign state and is difficult to access by Japanese courts (CCP, Arts. 3–9) (Nishitani, 2013, pp. 270–271, 2022a, pp. 836–838; Yokomizo, 2021, p. 42).

Once international jurisdiction is granted, applicable law constitutes the next hurdle. To establish remedies for victims, the legal construct of contracts generally does not work due to a lack of contractual relationships between the multinational and victims (Act on General Rules for Application of Laws 'AGRAL', 2006, Art. 7 ff). Similarly, unfair competition governed by the law of the parent's headquarters, or the *lex societatis* based on the place of incorporation, will not justify victims' damages claims. The remaining avenue is tort. Tort claims are principally subject to the *lex loci damni* when the occurrence of damage was predictable (AGRAL, Art. 17). It is regularly the law of the developing country where victims incur damage that controls. Due to the 'double actionability' principle, however, Japanese law always applies cumulatively (AGRAL, Art. 22). Unless the parent and subsidiaries, etc. fulfill strict conditions of joint torts under Japanese law, remedies are ruled out (Nishitani, 2022a, pp. 839–841; Yokomizo, 2021, pp. 42–43).

Due Diligence and Remaining Challenges

For corporate due diligence, it would be desirable for Japan to enact a due diligence act to clarify the extent and content of obligations of parents and subsidiaries, etc. Yet, establishing civil liability of the parent is likely to encounter strong opposition from Japanese industry, like in Germany and Switzerland. The extent to which the parent ought to control the entire global value chain is also a difficult issue. In the UNIQLO case, Fast Retailing insisted that it was unaware of the use of Xinjian cotton, and it thought that cotton from Australia was being used instead. It may not be expedient to impose too high of a duty of care on the parent, who can hardly control all the actions of its subsidiaries, suppliers, and subcontractors.

Even if due diligence acts granting civil liability advance in the EU and Japan, there will be other crucial issues. First, it is unlikely that vulnerable victims in a developing country with limited means would take it upon themselves to bring a suit against a multinational in the courts in the EU or Japan, which is costly and time consuming. In the previously mentioned UK and Dutch court decisions, victims' remedies could only be achieved with the help of non-governmental organizations (NGOs) in financing litigation or collective redress. Japanese collective redress, however, is limited in its substantive and territorial scope of application and only covers the recovery of consumers' property damage arising out of their contracts (Yamamoto, 2018, pp. 171–188; Yokomizo, 2018, pp. 191–197). Thus, it does not apply to human rights violations occurring in a developing country.

Second, if multinationals have civil liability imposed by a due diligence act in the state of establishment, then they may decide to transfer the headquarters of the parent to another developed country or move their subsidiaries from a problematic developing country to another developing country. This may lead to a 'race to the bottom' that allows multinationals to circumvent strict regulations and liability and eventually lowers human rights standards globally. Moreover, when decent multinationals take responsibility and pay damages, they will have to add the costs onto the price of goods and may lose competitiveness. Strict regulations may ultimately eliminate decent enterprises from the market (Rühl, 2020, pp. 73–74).

To ensure human rights protection and fair competition in the global market, it is desirable to stipulate uniform due diligence standards in a binding instrument. The UN Human Rights Council (2016) has installed an Open-Ended Intergovernmental Working Group since 2016 to prepare a draft treaty on state obligations to ensure corporate due diligence. However, agreeing on such a treaty is a long way off. In this respect, it is worth contemplating other possible legal and non-legal measures to enhance corporate due diligence and human rights protection.

Other Relevant Measures

Trade Law

Notably, recent multilateral trade or investment-related agreements tend to insert clauses on human rights and labour standards. The Comprehensive and Progressive Agreement for Trans-Pacific Partnership (CPTPP) and EU-Japan Free Trade Agreement (FTA) provide for abiding by fundamental labour standards substantiated by the ILO Core Conventions (2022), for example, minimum labour conditions and the prohibition of forced labour and discrimination. Similarly, the G7 Summit in June 2021 and G7 Trade Ministers' Meeting in October 2021 agreed on realizing human rights due diligence across the global value chain.

As unilateral trade measures, the EU has enacted the 2012 Generalised Scheme of Preferences (GSP) Regulation and requires respect for core human rights and labour standards in granting tariff preferences. Cambodia was once refused entitlement for GSP.

In the US, the Office of Foreign Assets Control (OFAC) of the Department of Treasury administers and enforces economic sanctions. In July 2020, the OFAC froze all US property and banned business transactions of the Xinjiang Public Security Bureau (XPSB), together with four government officials from China, for their reported connection to mass arbitrary detention and severe physical abuse against Uyghurs pursuant to the 'Global Magnitsky Act' (2016). Regular reporting on human rights violations in Xinjiang is now required by the 'Uyghur Human Rights Policy Act' of 17 June 2020. Furthermore, the Customs and Border Protection (CBP) of the Department of Homeland Security issued in January 2021 a withhold release order (§307 Trade Act) for an import ban of all cotton and tomato products that allegedly use forced labour in Xinjiang, unless proven otherwise. This was applied to the UNIQLO case. The scope of the withhold release order was extended to 20 product categories in July 2021 and ultimately to all products from Xinjiang by the 'Uyghur Forced Labor Prevention Act' on 23 December 2021, which took effect on 21 June 2022. This act prohibits a series of Chinese companies from exporting goods or investing in the US market and allows implementing sanctions such as freezing US assets and enjoining travel to the US. These developments heavily affect Japanese companies, which now need to make sure that no company operating in Xinjiang is involved in human rights abuses among their direct contracting partners or the second and third suppliers upstream in the value chain (Nishitani, 2022b, pp. 93–95).

Although these unilateral measures by the EU and US can be effective, they may run counter to free trade under the auspices of the World Trade Organization (WTO). The compatibility of these measures with the principles of national treatment (Art. III) and elimination of quantitative restrictions (Art. XI) ought to be examined against the general exceptions (Art. XX). Some authors regard these measures as necessary to protect public morals or human life or health (Art. XX lit a, b) or prohibit products of prison labour (lit e) (Nemoto *et al.*, 2021 (No. 2), pp. 62–65). Other authors, however, opine that the general exceptions are not fulfilled due to their limited scope and reach of state jurisdiction to prescribe (Kawashima, 2022, pp. 150–153). Pursuant to Article XX, measures need to be appropriate, reasonable for the purpose, and ensure transparency. Arguably, trade restrictions with a general scope could be justified when also covering human rights abuses in Myanmar and other states but not when only targeting the alleged forced labour in Xinjiang. Such a result may insinuate a need to improve the WTO system, which has focused on free trade without duly acquiescing to non-trade issues, such as human rights, the environment, and public health (Ito, 2020, pp. 354–355).

Notably, as a retorsion to the US, China enacted the Export Control Act 2020 (CN) on 17 October 2020, followed by the Chinese Ministry of Commerce (MOFCOM) (2021) Rules on Counteracting Extraterritorial Application of Foreign Measures of 9 January 2021. According to these Rules, the Chinese State Council may issue a prohibition order and take necessary countermeasures against unjustified extraterritorial application of foreign measures. The MOFCOM Rules also oblige a person, who infringes upon the rights and interests of a Chinese citizen or entity by observing such foreign measures, to compensate for the latter's damage. Due to their unclear scope and content, the MOFCOM Rules may vex Japanese companies facing contradictory requirements from the US and China to stop using products from Xinjiang but compensate for the damage of Chinese suppliers operating there. Japanese companies have therefore started to separate supply chains for the US and China. Yet, even if companies change suppliers to ensure export to the US, they may face boycotts from Chinese consumers for stopping the use of cotton from Xinjiang and firing workers, as was the case with H&M, Adidas, and Nike. Ultimately, unilateral trade sanctions are often enforced at the cost of private parties (Nishitani, 2022a, pp. 850–852).

When a country imposes its unilateral trade sanctions extraterritorially, as in the case of US sanctions against Iran, other states may counter by enacting blocking statues, like the EU. This may sharpen conflicts of state interests. Arguably, the recent US trade measures for human rights due diligence have the hidden purpose of creating an encircling net around China in their trade war. In the longer term, the global value chains will be subject to a dynamic change by switching suppliers or possibly reviving traditional Japanese cotton.

Soft Law

With a view to materializing corporate due diligence, soft law may also play a cardinal role. The UN Guiding Principles and SDGs illustrate goals to be achieved and serve as guidance for further developments. As a way of self-regulation, the Corporate Governance Code and Stewardship Code indicate the importance of corporate due diligence. With an advancement of environmental, social, and governance (ESG) investment, the Japanese government finally decided in June 2021 to join the 1957 ILO Abolition of Forced Labour Convention in order to not lose foreign investments. Furthermore, the strict US trade measures against Xinjiang indirectly raised the awareness of companies and induced the shunning of products resulting from forced labour. This means that reputation risk may motivate corporations to voluntarily abide by human rights standards.

After the import of UNIQLO shirts was blocked by the US authority in May 2021, major Japanese companies started to check their supply chains on their own. Fifty apparel companies ascertained the use of cotton from Xinjiang and halted it. Kao investigated about 5,000 venues, including palm oil farms on Sumatra Island, to eliminate human rights violations. In the manufacturing industry, Nissan, Mazda, Toyota, Hitachi, and Mitsubishi started to examine the labour conditions of their employees and factories of their suppliers. To ensure due diligence, Japanese companies can request compliance when signing contracts with suppliers and contractors through shōsha, namely, commercial intermediaries specific to the Japanese business models.

In Asia, soft solutions have often been successful in realizing human rights due diligence. In the case of Nike's child labour, a massive boycott of consumers forced Nike to end this practice in Pakistan and Bangladesh. Rana Plaza was a large compound and accommodated factories belonging to 29 apparel companies. When it collapsed in 2013, it caused 1,132 deaths, and more than 2,500 people were injured. To ensure remedies for the victims and their family members, the ILO, NGOs, companies, and other stakeholders conducted settlement negotiations and established the Rana Plaza Trust Fund. Although the total amount of compensation was set as 30 million US dollars, Benetton calculated its contribution to be 550,000 US dollars and voluntarily paid 1.6 million US dollars in response to a massive boycott of its products in Europe with propaganda such as 'united victims of Benetton'. Furthermore, the ILO installed a labour security and healthcare system, which is now supported by the workers' accident compensation regime of the Bangladeshi government. Such soft measures, based on settlement agreements without determining rights and obligations in legal terms, can be useful to enhance dialogue and cooperation for the prevention of abuse recurrence. This may possibly yield transnational legal ordering (Backer, 2016, pp. 46–57).

Conclusion

In Japan, the concept of companies incurring social responsibility has a long tradition. Ōmi merchants in pre-modern times had the idea of seeking tripartite benefits for sellers, purchasers, and society. Thus, Ōmi merchants carried out fair trade, labour protection, and philanthropy. In the 1970s, when various companies caused environmental pollution and related illness, such as Minamata disease, corporate social responsibility was often addressed. Today, following models of Western countries, Japan ought to take necessary steps to institutionalize corporate due diligence by enacting a supply chain act or implementing trade regulations. Arguably, Japan can play a leading role in achieving a free and fair market in Asia. Yet, to advocate human rights in other Asian countries, Japan ought to first solve the long-standing issues of conscripted workers from Korea and China during WWII and improve the poor labour conditions of technical intern trainees from Vietnam, China, the Philippines, and Indonesia.

To achieve global governance, judicial remedies before the courts in the EU or Japan often do not suffice. Instead, other means such as trade regulations, ESG investment, corporate governance, guidelines, and settlement agreements ought to be sought. For effective judicial remedies, it is also worth considering how to empower the judiciary of Asian and African developing countries so that victims can seek remedies before the local courts. As in the case of the Nigerian oil pipeline leaks, monitoring by the local authority becomes necessary when victims seek not only compensation for the damage inflicted in the past but also restoration of the environment and injunctions for the future. Once duly institutionalized, local courts in the Global South are suited to secure access to justice, collect evidence, and implement injunctive relief (Oppong, 2021, pp. 210–212). This is proven by a recent decision of the Environment and Land Court at Mombasa in Kenya in *KM v. Attorney General* (2020). For effective protection of victims, it would be desirable that Europe and Japan provide legal support for developing countries. As discussions on the SDGs show, global solutions are necessary to achieve common values and public interest in the international community. In climate change litigation throughout various states, the appropriateness of government policies is questioned in view of human rights standards. Notably, on 26 May 2021, The Hague District Court rendered a decision in a collective redress brought by Milieudefensie, which also represented 17,379 individual claimants, with Greenpeace NL and other NGOs against Royal Dutch Shell. The plaintiffs sought a ruling that CO_2 emission attributable to the Shell group be reduced by at least 45% worldwide by 2030. In applying Dutch law pursuant to Article 7 Rome II, the court granted the collective claims and condemned Royal Dutch Shell accordingly. To combat climate change, the Japanese government is also contemplating policies to reduce CO_2 emission by means of corporate governance and sustainable financing.

To attain corporate due diligence, adequate measures encompassing public and private enforcement need to be taken in close cooperation with industry and government. It is hoped that creative solutions are found grounded on common interests and solidarity in the international community.

References

All subsequent websites were last visited on 22 July 2023.

Act on General Rules for Application of Laws 2006 (JP).

Alien's Action for Tort 1948 (US).

Backer, L. C. (2016). Are Supply Chains Transnational Legal Orders: What We Can Learn from the Rana Plaza Factory Building Collapse. *U.C. Irvine Journal of International, Transnational and Comparative Law*, 1, pp. 11–66.

Code of Civil Procedure 1996 (JP).

Directive 2014/95/EU Amending Directive 2013/34/EU as Regards Disclosure of Non-Financial and Diversity Information by Certain Large Undertakings and Groups Text with EEA Relevance (2014). Official Journal L 330/1.

Directive 2022/2464/EU Amending Regulation 2014/537/EU, Directive 2004/109/EC, Directive 2006/43/EC and Directive 2013/34/EU, as Regards Corporate Sustainability Reporting with EEA Relevance (2022). Official Journal L 322/15.

Dutta, A. (2020). Internationale Zuständigkeit für privatrechtliche Klagen gegen transnational tätige Unternehmen wegen Verletzung von Menschenrechten und von Normen zum Schutz der natürlichen Lebensgrundlagen im Ausland. *Bericht der deutschen Gesellschaft für Internationales Recht*, 50, pp. 39–70.

European Commission (2022). *Proposal for a Directive of the European Parliament and of the Council on Corporate Sustainability Due Diligence and Amending Directive (EU) 2019/1937. COM (2022) 71 Final*. Available at: https://eur-lex.europa.eu/legal-content/EN/TXT/?uri=CELEX%3A52022PC0071

European Parliament (2021). *European Parliament Resolution of 10 March 2021 with Recommendations to the Commission on Corporate Due Diligence and Corporate Accountability (2020/2129(INL))*. Available at: www.europarl.europa.eu/doceo/document/TA-9-2021-0073_EN.html

European Parliament Committee on Legal Affairs (2020). *Draft Report with Recommendations to the Commission on Corporate Due Diligence and Corporate Accountability (2020/2129(INL))*. Available at: www.europarl.europa.eu/doceo/document/JURI-PR-657191_EN.pdf

Gesetz über die unternehmerische Sorgfalts-pflichten in Lieferketten 2021 [Supply Chain Due Diligence Act 2021] (DE).

Global Magnitsky Human Rights Accountability Act 2016 (US).

Groupe européen de droit international privé (GEDIP) (2021). *Recommendation to the European Commission Concerning the Private International Law Aspects of the Future Instrument of the European Union on [Corporate Due Diligence and Corporate Accountability]*. Available at: https://gedip-egpil.eu/wp-content/uploads/2021/02/Recommandation-GEDIP-Recommendation-EGPIL-final-1.pdf

International Labour Organization (ILO) (2022). *Core Conventions*. Available at: https://www.ilo.org/global/standards/introduction-to-international-labour-standards/conventions-and-recommendations/lang--en/index.htm

International Monetary Fund (2021). *World Economic Outlook Database*. Available at: www.imf.org/en/Publications/WEO/weo-database/2021/October

Ito, K. (2020). Kokusai Keizai Chitsujo no Tenkan to Rikken Shugi: Kiki no Jidai ka Henka no Jiki ka [Transformation of the International Economic Order and the Constitutionalism: An Era of Crisis or Chance to Change]. In: Teraya, K. and Ito, K. eds., *Kokusaihō no Genzai: Henten suru Gendai Sekai de Hō no Kanousei wo Toinaosu [The Current State of International Law: Reconsidering the Possibility of Law in the Contemporary Changing World]*. Tokyo: Nihon Hyōron Sha, pp. 350–361.

Japan. Ministry of Economy, Trade and Industry (2022). *Sekinin aru Supply Chain tō ni okeru Jinken Sonchō no tameno Guidelines [Guidelines on Respect for Human Rights in Responsible Supply Chains]*. Available at: www.meti.go.jp/press/2022/09/20220913003/20220913003-a.pdf

Japan, Ministry of Justice, Human Rights Bureau (2020). *Ima Kigyō ni Motomerareru 'Business to Jinken' heno Taiō: 'Business to Jinken ni kansuru Chōsa Kenkyū' Hōkokusho ['Action Plan for Business and Human Rights' Required for Enterprises: Report of 'Research on Business and Human Rights']*. Available at: https://www.moj.go.jp/content/001376897.pdf

Kawashima, F. (2022). Beichū no Senryakuteki Kyōsō to Kokusai Keizai Chitsujo no Kōzō Henka. Kachi Takyokuka wo uketa Rule no Saikôchiku ni mukete [Strategic Competition

Between the United States and China and Structural Change of International Economic Order. Towards Redesigning Rules in Response to Value-Diversification]. *Nihon Kokusai Keizaihō Gakkai Nenpō [International Economic Law (Yearbook of the Japan Association of International Economic Law)]*, 2022, pp. 141–163.

Kiobel v. Royal Dutch Petroleum Co. (2013). US Sup. Ct., 569 U.S. 108.

KM v. Attorney General, Petition No 1 of 2016 (Environment and Land Court, Mombasa, 2020) [2020] eKLR.

Loi n° 399/2017 du 23 mars 2017 relative au devoir de vigilance des sociétés mères et des entreprises donneuses d'ordre, *J.O.* 28 mars 2017 (FR).

Mansel, H. P. (2018). Internationales Privatrecht de lege lata wie de lege ferenda und Menschenrechtsverantwortlichkeit deutscher Unternehmen. *Zeitschrift für Unternehmens- und Gesellschaftsrecht*, 2018, pp. 439–478.

Milieudefensie, Greenpeace NL et al. v. Royal Dutch Shell (2021). The Hague Dist. Ct., ECLI:NL:RBDHA:2021:5337. English translation: ECLI:NL:RBDHA:2021:5339. Available at: https://uitspraken.rechtspraak.nl/inziendocument?id=ECLI:NL:RBDHA:2021:5339

Modern Slavery Act 201 (GB).

Nemoto, T. *et al.* (2021). Jinken Mondai he no Tsūshō Seisaku teki Approach [Trade-Related Approaches for Issues on Human Rights Violations], No 1 and 2. *New Business Law*, 1192, pp. 39–47, 1194, pp. 57–66.

Nestlé USA v. Doe (2021). US Sup. Ct., 141 S. Ct. 1931.

Nishitani, Y. (2013). International Jurisdiction of Japanese Courts in Comparative Perspective. *Netherlands International Law Review*, 60, pp. 251–277.

Nishitani, Y. (2022a). Corporate Due Diligence and Conflict of Laws: 'Business and Human Rights' in Asia. *Korea Private International Law Journal [Liber Amicorum Kwang Hyun Suk]*, 28(1), pp. 829–856. Available at: https://doi.org/10.38131/kpilj.2022.6.28.1.829

Nishitani, Y. (2022b). Kokusai Torihiki ni okeru Kigyō no Shakaiteki Sekinin: 'Business to Jinken' wo megutte [Corporate Social Responsibility in Cross-Border Transactions: On 'Business and Human Rights']. *Kokusai Shōtorihiki Gakkai Nenpō [Annual Report of the Academy for International Business Transactions]*, 23, pp. 85–97.

OECD (2011). *OECD Guidelines for Multinational Enterprises*. Available at: www.oecd.org/daf/inv/mne/48004323.pdf

Oguru et al. and Milieudefensie v. Shell Petroleum, Royal Dutch Shell and Shell Nigeria (2021). The Hague Court of Appeal, ECLI:NL:GHDHA:2021:132 (also 133–134). English translation: ECLI:NL:GHDHA:2021:1825. Available at: https://uitspraken.rechtspraak.nl/inziendocument?id=ECLI:NL:GHDHA:2021:1825

Okpabi v. Royal Dutch Shell (2021). UK Sup. Ct., UKSC 3. On appeal from [2018] EWCA Civ 191.

Oppong, R. F. (2021). SDG 6: Clean Water and Sanitation. In: Michaels, R., Ruiz Abou-Nigm, V. and van Loon, H. eds., *The Private Side of Transforming Our World: UN Sustainable Development Goals 2030 and the Role of Private International Law*. Cambridge: Intersentia, pp. 189–216.

People's Republic of China, Ministry of Commerce (MOFCOM) (2021). *Order No. 1 of 9 January 2021 on Rules on Counteracting Unjustified Extraterritorial Application of Foreign Legislation and Other Measures*. Available at: http://english.mofcom.gov.cn/article/policyrelease/questions/202101/20210103029708.shtml

People's Republic of China Export Control Act 2020 (CN). Available at: http://www.npc.gov.cn/englishnpc/c23934/202112/63aff482fece44a591b45810fa2c25c4.shtml

Regulation (EC) No 593/2008 on the law applicable to contractual obligations (Rome I) (2008). Official Journal L 177/6.

Regulation (EC) No 864/2007 on the Law Applicable to Non-Contractual Obligations (Rome II) (2007). Official Journal L 199/40.
Regulation (EU) No 978/2012 Applying a Scheme of Generalised Tariff Preferences (2012). Official Journal L 303/1.
Regulation (EU) No 1215/2012 on Jurisdiction and the Recognition and Enforcement of Judgments in Civil and Commercial Matters (Recast) (2012). Official Journal L 351/1.
Regulation (EU) 2017/821 Laying Down Supply Chain Due Diligence Obligations for Union Importers of Tin, Tantalum and Tungsten, Their Ores, and Gold Originating from Conflict-Affected and High-Risk Areas (2017). Official Journal L 130/1.
Rühl, G. (2020). Towards a German Supply Chain Act? Comments from a Choice of Law and a Comparative Perspective. *European Yearbook of International Economic Law*, 2020, pp. 55–81.
Rühl, G. (2023, *forthcoming*). Cross-Border Protection of Human Rights: The 2021 German Supply Chain Due Diligence Act. In: Borg-Barthet, J. ed., *From Theory to Practice in Private International Law: Gedächtnisschrift for Professor* Jonathan Fitchen. Oxford: Hart.
Sherpa et al. v. Total (2021). France, Cour de cassation.
Tariff Act 1930 (US).
United Nations (2011). *Guiding Principles on Business and Human Rights*. Available at: www.ohchr.org/documents/publications/guidingprinciplesbusinesshr_en.pdf
United Nations (2015). *Transforming Our World: 2030 Agenda for Sustainable Development*. Available at: https://sdgs.un.org/2030agenda
United Nations. Human Rights Council, Since 2016 (2016). *Open-Ended Intergovernmental Working Group on Transnational Corporations and Other Business Enterprises with Respect to Human Rights*. Available at: www.ohchr.org/en/hrbodies/hrc/wgtranscorp/pages/igwgontnc.aspx
Uyghur Forced Labor Prevention Act 2021 (US).
Uyghur Human Rights Policy Act 2020 (US).
Vedanta Resources PLC et al. v. Lungowe et al. (2019). UK Supreme Court, UKSC 20.
Wagner, G. (2016). Haftung für Menschenrechtsverletzungen. *Rabels Zeitschrift für ausländisches und internationales Privatrecht*, 80, pp. 717–782.
Weller, M. P., Hübner, L. and Kaller, L. (2018). Private International Law for Corporate Social Responsibility. In: Schmidt-Kessel, M. ed., *German National Reports on the 20th International Congress of Comparative Law*. Tübingen: Mohr Siebeck, pp. 239–268.
Wet Zorgplicht Kinderarbeid, Staasblad 2019 [Child Labour Due Diligence Act 2019] (NL).
Yamamoto, K. (2018). Special Proceedings for the Collective Redress for Property Damage Incurred by Consumers: About so-Called 'Japanese Class Action'. *Japanese Yearbook of International Law*, 61, pp. 168–188.
Yokomizo, D. (2018). Consumer Collective Redress and Japanese Conflict of Laws. *Japanese Yearbook of International Law*, 61, pp. 189–204.
Yokomizo, D. (2021). 'Business to Jinken ni kansuru Shidō Gensoku' to Teishokuhō ['Guiding Principles on Business and Human Rights' and Conflict of Laws]. *Ronkyu Jurist [Quarterly Jurist]*, 1560, pp. 39–43.

5 Resolution of Islamic Financial Disputes under Private International Law in Japan

Shiho KATO

Introduction

Islamic finance, or the provision of financial services in accordance with Islamic law (International Monetary Fund, 2017), has been regarded as an interesting global phenomenon for the last few decades in the sense that it has brought 'cultural pluralism' (Bälz, 2001, p. 48) into international commercial law.

Since the 2000's, there has been rapid growth of the Islamic financial services industry in terms of its size and global coverage. At the end of 2019, the industry was estimated to be worth US$2.733 trillion, which is about three times greater than its size in 2008 (Global Islamic Finance Report, 2021, p. 43). Islamic finance has also spread in non-Muslim majority countries, such as the UK and Singapore. Japan is no exception – banking regulations were modified to accommodate Islamic banking in 2008, and a legal framework for Japanese Islamic bonds (J-*sukuk*) was established in 2011 (Yoshida, 2014, p. 215). Currently, some commentators are of the view that since Islamic finance is 'risk-adverse' or a 'profit-and-loss-sharing based' finance, it is considered an 'appealing option of financing global recovery' in the post-COVID-19 era (Transnational Dispute Resolution, 2020).

As Islamic finance becomes more popular around the globe, disputes within Islamic finance are more likely to have a cross-border dimension. What questions might then arise in a dispute resolution before a court in non-Islamic law influenced jurisdictions such as Japan? In which aspect does the religiousness of Islamic finance matter in such litigation? This chapter examines these questions from the perspective of Japanese law. Since there have been no cases on this topic in Japan, the analyses in this chapter are important preparation for potential disputes before a Japanese court in the future.

This chapter first briefly describes some features of Islamic finance and then illustrates what challenges it might pose to a secular court. Based on these introductory analyses, this chapter examines the characteristics of the law of Islamic finance and analyzes how Islamic financial disputes can be resolved in a Japanese court.

DOI: 10.4324/9781003193098-5

Some Features of Islamic Finance

Islamic Law as an Evolving Body of Law

First, as Vogel and Hayes put it, 'Islamic banking and finance seek to apply the Islamic religious law (*Shari'a*) to a sector of modern commerce' (Vogel and Hayes III, 1998, p. 23). According to them, in Islam 'all law must be ultimately rooted in the Qur'an and the Sunna', the latter of which refers to Prophet Muhammad's sayings and actions. Islamic jurisprudence is drawn from these two sources by way of interpretations given by qualified Islamic scholars. Strictly speaking, the term Islamic law denotes both the divine law as revealed in these two sources, called *Shari'a*, and the human comprehension of it, called *fiqh*.

Note that *fiqh*, as a subjective comprehension of *Shari'a*, can be 'faulty, multiple, uncertain, and changing' (Vogel and Hayes III, 1998, p. 32). The divergence in *fiqh* can be explained by different schools of thought in Islamic jurisprudence (e.g., the Hanafi, Maliki, Shafi'i, and Hanbali, which are the four influential schools of thought in Sunni Islam) and the changes experienced over time. As Maria Bhatti puts it, Islamic law may be better understood as 'an adaptable and evolving body of law in light of *fiqh*' (Bhatti, 2019, p. 22).

The Key Role of Shari'a *Boards in Islamic Finance*

Second, as Vogel and Hayes put it, Islamic scholars 'have a profound influence on the day-to-day practice of finance' (Vogel and Hayes III, 1998, p. 9). According to them, since only scholars are capable of knowing what the law is, Muslim laypeople, including finantioanl institutitons, are expected to seek a legal opinion (*fatwa*) on any issue in doubt from a juriscounsult who issues fatwas (*mufti*). In the modern practice of Islamic finance, financial institutions that provide Islamic financial services usually maintain their own *Shari'a* expert advisory committees, called '*Shari'a* boards'. A *Shari'a* board gives the financial institution advice based on Islamic law. It also authorizes, approves, and gives certificates, in the form of *fatwa*, to certify that each proposed transaction is '*Shari'a* compliant'. El-Gamal opines that a distinguishing feature of Islamic finance lies in the central importance of a *Shari'a* compliance certificate (El-Gamal, 2006, p. 7).

Global Standardization in Islamic Finance

Third, it is said that modern Islamic finance was born in the mid-1970's (El-Gamal, 2006, p. 32), and an international standard-setting movement began in the 2000's. For example, in 2002, the Islamic Financial Services Board (IFSB) was inaugurated in Kuala Lumpur as an international standard-setting body in the industry. This organization comprises various national regulatory and supervisory authorities, international intergovernmental organizations, and market players such as financial institutions. Similarly, the Accounting and Auditing Organization for Islamic Finance Institutions (AAOIFI), a Bahrein-based and bank-sponsored not-for-profit organization, has established its own *Shari'a* board and set general standards for Islamic financial contracts. As some researchers on Islamic finance point out, these international institutions have contributed toward the globalization of Islamic finance over the last two decades (Nagaoka, 2011, pp. 37–38; Yoshida, 2017, pp. 69–74).

An Example of Islamic Finance's Contractual Structure

Finally, concerning the substantive aspect of Islamic finance, the two prohibitions of *riba* (usury forbidden in the Qur'an) and *gharar* (risk, uncertainty) have played a key role in shaping the Islamic law on contract and finance (Eisenberg, 2020, p. 45). Several contractual concepts or schemes have been formed to observe such *Shari'a* principles. One of them is the *murabaha*, which 'is probably the most commonly used Islamic finance structure in modern Islamic financing' (Nethercott, 2020, p. 180). Craig Nethercott explaines its basic form as follows:

> the seller buys goods at the request of a customer (hereafter, the purchaser). The seller takes title to such goods. In turn, the seller enters into a sale contract with the purchaser to buy such goods at an agreed (and disclosed) profit in addition to the purchase price (which is also disclosed). The seller and the purchaser agree [to] deferred payment terms and title to the goods is transferred from the seller to the purchaser.

Two contracts of sale are involved here: one is concluded between the intermediary seller (e.g., a bank) and the vendor (e.g., a manufacturer), and the other is between the intermediary seller and the purchaser (e.g., a customer of a bank). In the latter contract, the purchaser pays the purchase price of the former contract *plus* the make-up to the intermediary seller. As Kilian Bälz puts it (Bälz, 2001, p. 41),

> [e]conomically speaking, therefore, the intermediary (nowadays a bank) grants the [purchaser] a short-term loan which is remunerated by the make-up. In so doing, the *murâbaha* is turned into a credit vehicle that does not conflict with the Islamic ban on *ribâ* as – from a legalistic perspective – the transaction consists of two contracts of sale and does not involve the granting of a loan.

The Choice of *Shari'a* as the Governing Law of a Contract

As shown previously, Islamic finance follows several modes of financial structures to provide financial services in a *Shari'a* compliant manner. If a contractual dispute arises out of such dealings and the compliance with *Shari'a* becomes an issue, then how should a secular or civil court respond? This is exactly what English courts faced in the case of *Shamil Bank v. Beximco* (2004), a leading case that dealt with the issue of the choice of *Shari'a* as the governing law of a contract.

Factual Background

Beximco Pharmaceuticals and others entered into *murabaha* financing agreements with Shamil Bank of Bahrain (the Bank), an Islamic financial institution. The agreements contained a choice of law clause, which read '[s]ubject to the principle of the Glorious Sharia'a, this Agreement shall be governed by and construed in accordance with the laws of England'. As Baximco and others failed to pay the amounts due under the agreements, the Bank instituted proceedings in English courts. The defendants claimed that the agreements were void because they were disguised loans at interest, which are unlawful under Islamic law. Since this defense relied on the application of *Shari'a* principles, the main issue in this case was construction and the effect of the choice of law clause in the agreements.

The Court of First Instance's Decision

Morison J., the judge of the first instance court, construed the clause as designating only English law as the governing law of the agreements (*Shamil Bank of Bahrain EC v. Beximco Pharmaceuticals Ltd and others*, 2003). First, the judge found that the application of two separate legal systems to one contract is not allowed. This finding was based on the doctrine that a contract cannot be governed by two systems of law and the singular wording of 'law' of Art. 3(1) of the Rome Convention on the Law Applicable to Contractual Obligations 1980 (which was enacted into English law by the 1990 Contract (Applicable Law) Act). Second, the judge held that the choice of a non-national system of law as the governing law of a contract was inappropriate because Art. 1(1) of the Convention refers to 'a choice between the laws of different countries'.

Last, the judge held that the application of the principles of *Shari'a* to matters of commerce and banking was controversial, especially because there is a dispute as to the strictness in the interpretation and application of *Shari'a*. Regarding the parties' intent, Morrison J. concluded that it was improbable that the parties truly asked the English court to decide any dispute under such controversial religious principles, and this is especially true when the Bank had its own religious board to monitor *Shari'a* questions.

The Court of Appeals' Decision

The Court of Appeals affirmed the conclusion of the court of first instance (*Shamil Bank of Bahrain EC v. Beximco Pharmaceuticals Ltd and others*, 2004). The Court by itself examined the incorporation of the principles of *Shari'a* into the agreements governed by English law, which might require the Court to discuss the *Shari'a* defense as a matter of contractual obligations. However, it held that the clause was not specific enough for the purpose of incorporation. In arriving at this decision, the Court reasoned that

> [t]he doctrine of incorporation can only sensibly operate where the parties have by the terms of their contract sufficiently identified specific 'black

> letter' provisions of a foreign law or an international code or set of rules apt to be incorporated as terms of the relevant contract

and '[t]he general reference to principles of Sharia in this case affords no reference to, or identification of, those aspects of Sharia law which are intended to be incorporated into the contract'.

Summary

As shown in this section, two private international law questions arose in the *Shamil Bank* case: whether a choice of Islamic law as the governing law of a contract is valid or not and under what conditions the incorporation of principles of *Shari'a* into a contract is allowed. Before discussing these questions, it is important to analyze the character of Islamic law and finance in more detail. Although the court of first instance was concerned about its capability to deal with controversial religious law questions, in what sense is the religious nature of Islamic finance challenging for secular courts?

The Characterization of Islamic Finance

The Religious Nature of Islamic Law

Regarding the characterization of Islamic law and finance, Ralf Michales' idea of 'post-secular comparative law (*Postsäkulare Rechtvergleichung*)' is an important reference. Michaels argues that religious law, including Islamic law, can be included in comparative law studies as a good example of transnational law that is not territorially restricted and that has been developed with a long history in existing societies (Michales, 2016).

In his article, Michales discusses the relevance of the religious nature to comparative law studies. He claims that religious law cannot be reduced to its religiousness because rules comparable with secular law do exist in religious law (e.g., a usury ban under Jewish law). Michaels also observes that even inside religious law communities, there is a movement to reinterpret religious law as secular (e.g., the secularization of Islamic law). He, however, notes that one should not consider the religiousness as irrelevant as doing so would make it impossible not only to understand the law in a social context but also to capture the symbolic meaning of the law. Therefore, the religious aspect of Islamic law should not be understood as a factor preventing a secular court from dealing with disputes that touch on religious law questions.

Islamic Finance as a Developed Field in Transnational Islamic Law

Even if the religiousness can be relativized, one cannot ignore the ambiguity of religious law. As mentioned previously, ambiguity is one of the characteristic features of Islamic law in general. However, as far as the specific law on Islamic finance is concerned, the situation might be slightly different.

Islamic finance has been developed not only on the basis of precedent and analogy in classical Islamic law (El-Gamal, 2006, p. 33) but also through global business practices influenced by international standards, such as those published by the IFSB or the AAOIFI (Bälz, 2008, pp. 25–26). In this regard, Michales cites Nicholas Foster's argument that similar norm-creating mechanisms also exist in the West, for example, standard-setting under the auspice of private organizations such as the International Swaps and Derivatives Association (Foster, 2007, pp. 186–187). Considering such an influential global standardization movement, it is reasonable to regard the law on Islamic finance as a relatively standardized and elaborated field in transnational Islamic law.

Shari'a *Boards as Private Financial Supervisory Authorities*

Last, it is crucial to address the functions of *Shari'a* boards. As Michales puts it, their functional meaning can be found in private authorization and supervision of Islamic financial institutions (Michales, 2016, pp. 93–94). However, he emphasizes that unlike other secular certifications, *Shari'a* compliance certification is unique in the sense that such religious certification is essentially beyond the competence of states.

In fact, Malaysian legislation clearly distinguishes between the roles of the court and the *Shari'a* authority in the context of dispute resolution (Trakic, 2019). Under the Central Bank of Malaysia Act 2009, the court or arbitrator is obliged to refer *Shari'a* questions in Islamic finance to the *Shari'a* Advisory Council (SAC), which is the national *Shari'a* board in Malaysia (Sec. 56), and the rulings made by the SAC shall be binding on the court or arbitrator (Sec. 57). The idea presumably behind this provision is shown in the Court of Appeals' decision in *Bank Islam Malaysia Berhad v. Lim Kok Hoe & Anor (and 8 Other Appeals)* (2009), which stated that

> judges in civil court should not take upon themselves to declare whether a matter is in accordance to the Religion of Islam . . . [such an issue] needs consideration by eminent jurists who are properly qualified in the field of Islamic jurisprudence.

As shown here, Malaysian law, which leaves Islamic law questions to the national *Shari'a* board, intends to discharge secular judges from making decisions on these questions. Arguably, such 'recognition' of religion (Michales, 2016, p. 60) appears to be necessary for a better coexistence between the secular world and the religious world in contemporary society.

Summary

As examined in this section, the law on Islamic finance can be better captured as a relatively standardized field in transnational Islamic law, and in this field, the religious nature and ambiguity of Islamic law is relativized to a certain extent. However, considering the incapability and unsuitability of a secular state to decide on its own which opinion in religious law is legitimate or not, the role of *Shari'a* boards should be seriously taken into account by states. Having this in mind, the next section examines how the questions that arose in the *Shamil Bank* case would be dealt with in Japan.

Resolution of Islamic Financial Disputes in Japanese Courts

Islamic Law as the Governing Law of a Contract

In Japan, Article 7 of the Act on the General Rules for Application of Laws (AGRAL) 2006 provides that a contract shall be governed by 'the law of the place which was chosen by the party/parties'. Most authors consider this provision as open to interpretation on whether non-state law, including Islamic law, can be chosen as the law to govern a contract. No court decision has so far recognized non-state law as the applicable law to a contract or other legal relationships.

Commentators have been divided on this issue. The majority do not accept the choice of non-state law because of its lack of legal validity in a territorial jurisdiction. In their opinions, a reference to non-state law, such as *lex mercatoria* or the UNIDROIT Principles of International Commercial Contract, can only mean an incorporation (Nakanishi, 2011, p. 189). In contrast, some argue that a certain category of non-state law can be chosen as the law to govern a contract. This argument is in line with The Hague Principles on Choice of Law in International Commercial Contracts 2015, which provide that the parties can choose 'rules of law generally accepted on an international, supranational, or regional level as a neutral and balanced set of rules' (Art. 3) (Nishitani, 2021, pp. 542–543). Nonetheless, even a supporter for the latter view doubts the applicability of the law of Islamic finance due to its divergent nature (Morishita, 2008, pp. 30–31).

In light of the brief overview of the previous discussions, it is fair to tentatively conclude the following as a matter of the current law, practices, and discussions in Japan: where legislation does not explicitly allow the choice of non-state law and academic opinions have not been elaborated enough for courts to follow, the courts are likely to take a conservative approach that allows only the choice of state law. Therefore, the validity of choice of Islamic law as the law to govern a contract is likely to be denied in Japan, unless it is part of the governing state law (e.g., Saudi Arabian law).

Islamic Law as Incorporated into a Contract

The Effect of a Reference to the Principles of Shari'a

If the principles of *Shari'a* are not applied, then they may be taken into account as contractual terms within the framework of the applicable state law. As mentioned previously, most authors acknowledge such a possibility, but there has been no investigation as to under what circumstances a reference to non-state law can be construed as an incorporation in Japan.

In this respect, the Court of Appeals in the *Shamil Bank* case demanded a specificity, and a general reference, such as '[s]ubject to the principle of the Glorious Sharia'a', was considered to be 'plainly inadequate'. In contrast, as Jason Chuah states, where a contract is explicitly governed by state law but requires the parties to observe *Shari'a* in their transactions, the court would be 'required to interpret the contract and decide whether the parties have acted in accordance with Sharia as ascertained by expert evidence' (Chuah, 2010, p. 196).

It is doubtful whether there is a significant difference between a general reference to *Shari'a* and a clause saying that each transaction must be *Shari'a* compliant. As mentioned previously, the notion of *Shari'a* compliance is an essential normative feature of Islamic finance, and therefore, giving no meaning to a reference to *Shari'a* does not properly reflect the intention of the parties involved in Islamic finance. It then follows that even where there is only a general reference to *Shari'a*, which was the case in the *Shamil Bank* case, the courts should construe it in a meaningful way as much as possible and if required to do so by the party/parties, should decide as a matter of contract whether the transaction at issue was *Shari'a* compliant or not.

How to Confirm the Contents of the Principles of Shari'a

When a court touches upon Islamic law issues as a matter of contract, the question that arises is how to confirm its contents. Unlike in a case of the application of foreign law, the court is under no obligation to ascertain *ex officio* the contents of the principles of *Shari'a* because *Shari'a* compliance is considered to be a matter of contractual obligation under the state law that governs the contract. Thus, it is the parties that need to submit documents on Islamic law or reports of Islamic law experts as the evidence supporting their arguments. Note that 'expert witnesses, inquiries to an expert or expert institutions' are rarely utilized by Japanese courts, even for the ascertainment of foreign law (Nakano, 2017, p. 532). Similarly, the courts are not likely to consult by themselves Islamic law experts or institutions to confirm the contents of Islamic law.

Therefore, the documents or expert reports submitted by the parties play a crucial role in aiding the courts to decide the *Shari'a* compliance question as a matter of contract. In this regard, two issues become critical: how contradictory expert reports should be treated and the influence of *Shari'a* boards.

CONTRADICTORY ISLAMIC LAW EXPERTS' OPINIONS

In this respect, it is helpful to rely on an analogy with the treatment of foreign law: the submission of contradictory expert opinions resembles a failure to establish foreign law in the sense that the content of the law is too uncertain to an extent that courts cannot apply/confirm it and decide the dispute at hand.

In instances where courts find it impossible to ascertain foreign law, they declare it unidentified and often opt for *lex fori* (law of the forum, which in this case, is Japanese substantive law). Some commentators have justified this giving up of the application of uncertain foreign law from the perspective of procedural justice – that is, the duty of the court to administer a fair and speedy trial within a reasonable time (Sawaki and Dogauchi, 2018, p. 54).

As shown previously, a secular court is presumably incapable of deciding religious law questions by itself. Therefore, if the contents of the principles of *Shari'a* are considerably divergent among the documents submitted by the parties, then the courts, being incapable of determining which argument is legitimate, cannot help but resolve the dispute according to the state law applicable to the contract. Similar to a failure to establish foreign law, such a situation is justified from the perspective of procedural justice.

THE MEANING OF THE *SHARI'A* BOARDS' AUTHORIZATION

A Japanese court might also face a challenge on how to treat *fatwa* or a certificate or approval given by a *Shari'a* board of an Islamic financial institution (Chuah, 2010, pp. 196–197). In this regard, the English Court in *The Investment Dar Company KSCC v. Blom Developments Bank SAL* (2009) presented a deferential attitude to the decisions of *Shari'a* boards. It stated that

> [a claimant company] points to the undoubted fact that the Sharia committee of (I shall assume) respected scholars had authorised and approved of this form of contract which is a strong indication that the contract was indeed Sharia compliant.

As shown previously, opinions given by *Shari'a* boards play a presumably significant role for Islamic financial institutions and their clients – in the sense that both parties follow such opinions to be sure that they have observed the principles of *Shari'a*. Considering this influential role together with the states' incapacity to decide religious law questions, which was noted previously, it is appropriate for a Japanese court to regard a *Shari'a* compliance certificate, given by the *Shari'a* board of an Islamic financial institution, as a strong presumption that the contract in question is indeed *Shari'a* compliant. This solution is justified because it seems that this presumption does not generally contradict the parties' expectations about whether their contract complies with *Shari'a*.

Summary

This section argues that although the choice of Islamic law would probably be denied in Japan, a court should, if so requested by the party/parties, determine the issue of *Shari'a* compliance as a matter of contractual obligations under the applicable state law by relying on a *Shari'a* compliance certification issued by *Shari'a* boards and the principles of *Shari'a* ascertained by the evidence submitted by the parties. In this manner, the court can serve the expectations of the parties involved in Islamic finance, which is not only necessary for the proper functioning of global Islamic finance but also essential for a better accommodation of religious law in the judicial system of states.

Conclusion

This chapter, while attempting to find how to better handle Islamic financial disputes in Japanese courts, concludes that the courts will experience challenges in adjudicating them. Due to these challenges, arbitration has become a more feasible and attractive option for the resolution of Islamic financial disputes. Some arbitral institutions have introduced *Shari'a* compliant arbitral rules, such as the Asian International Arbitration Centre's *i-Arbitration Rules*, which were first launched in 2012 and revised in 2013, 2018, and 2021 (Bhatti, 2019, pp. 34–35). Although the choice of Islamic law might be unproblematic in arbitration, Islamic financial arbitration poses another set of questions to a secular court, such as the issue of discrimination on the grounds of religion or belief concerning the selection of arbitrators (*Jivraj v. Hashiwani*, 2010). Therefore, further research is required to examine the role of religious norms in arbitration, which is an important field to be examined under international commercial law.

References

All subsequent websites were last visited on 16 September 2022.

Bälz, K. (2001). Islamic Law as Governing Law Under the Rome Convention – Universalist Lex Mercatoria v. Regional Unification of Law. *Uniform Law Review*, 6(1), pp. 37–49.

Bälz, K. (2008). *Sharia Risk? How Islamic Finance Has Transformed Islamic Contract Law*. Available at: https://pil.law.harvard.edu/occasional-papers/

Bank Islam Malaysia Berhad v. Lim Kok Hoe and Anor (and 8 Other Appels) (2009). 6 CLJ 22.

Bhatti, M. (2019). *Islamic Law and International Commcerical Arbitration*. Abingdon, Oxon and New York: Routledge.

Chuah, J. (2010). Impact of Islamic Law on Conmmercial Sale Contracts – A Private International Law Dimension in Europe. *European Journal of Commercial Contract Law*, 2(4), pp. 191–204.

Eisenberg, D. (2020). Sources and Principles of Islamic Law. In: Nethercott, C. and Eisenberg, D. eds., *Islamic Finance: Law and Practices*, 2nd ed. New York: Oxford University Press, pp. 19–58.

El-Gamal, M. (2006). *Islamic Fiance: Law, Economics, and Practice*. New York: Cambridge University Press.

Foster, N. (2007). Islamic Finance Law as an Emergent Legal System. *Arab Law Quarterly*, 21(2), pp. 170–188.

Global Islamic Finance Report (2021). *The 11th Edition of Global Islamic Finance Report 2020–21*. Available at: www.slideshare.net/RepublikaDigital/gifr-2021-global-islamic-finance-report

International Monetary Fund (2017). *Islamic Finance and the Role of the IMF*. Available at: www.imf.org/external/themes/islamicfinance/

The Investment Dar Company KSCC v. Blom Developments Bank SAL (2009). EWHC 3545 (Ch).

Jivraj v. Hashiwani (2010). EWCA Civ 712.

Michales, R. (2016). Religiöse Rechte und postsäkulare Rechtsvergleichung. In: Zimmermann, R. ed., *Zukunftsperspektiven der Rechtsvergleichung*. Tübingen: Mohr Siebeck, pp. 39–102.

Morishita, T. (2008). Kokusai Shō-Torihiki ni okeru Hi-Kokkahō no Kinō to Tekiyō [Non-State Norms in International Commcerical Transactions]. *Kokusaihō Gaikō Zassi [The Journal of International Law and Diplomacy]*, 107(1), pp. 15–43.

Nagaoka, S. (2011). *Gendai Isurāmu Kin'yūron [A Study on Islamic Finance in the Modern World]*. Nagoya: Nagoya Daigaku Shuppan [Nagoya University Publishing].

Nakanishi, Y. (2011). Article 7 of the AGRAL. In: Sakurada, Y. and Dogauchi, M. eds., *Chūshaku Kokusaishihō II [Commentary on PIL, Vol. 2]*. Tokyo: Yūhikaku, pp. 179–198.

Nakano, S. (2017). Japan. In: Nishitani, Y. ed., *Treatment of Foreign Law – Dynamics Towards Convergence?* Cham: Springer International Publishing AG, pp. 529–540.

Nethercott, C. (2020). Murabaha and Tawarruq. In: Nethercott, C. and Eisenberg, D. eds., *Islamic Finance: Law and Practice*, 2nd ed. New York: Oxford University Press, pp. 179–200.

Nishitani, Y. (2021). Japanese Perspective on the Hague Principles. In: Girsberger, D., Graziano, T. and Neels, J. eds., *Choice of Law in International Commcerical Contracts: Global Perspectives on the Hague Principles*. New York: Oxford University Press, pp. 537–555.

Sawaki, T. and Dogauchi, M. (2018). *Kokusai Shihō Nyūmon [Introduction to Private International Law]*, 8th ed. Tokyo: Yūhikaku.

Shamil Bank of Bahrain EC v. Beximco Pharmaceuticals Ltd and Others (2003). 2 All ER (Comm) 849.

Shamil Bank of Bahrain EC v. Beximco Pharmaceuticals Ltd and Others (2004). EWCA Civ 19.

Trakic, A. (2019). Settlement of Islamic Fiance Dispute in Malaysia. In: Trakic, A., Benson, J. and Ahmed, P. eds., *Dispute Resolution in Islamic Finance: Alternatives to Litigation?* New York: Routledge, pp. 95–119.

Transnational Dispute Resolution (2020). *TDM Call for Papers for a Special Issue on 'Islamic Fiance and Dispute Resolution'*. Available at: www.transnational-dispute-management.com/news.asp?key=1832

Vogel, F. and Hayes III, S. (1998). *Islamic Law and Finance: Religion, Risk, and Return.* The Hague: Kluwer Law International.

Yoshida, E. (2014). Japan: A Comprehensive Picture of Islamic Finance. In: Thiagaraja, S. *et al.* eds., *The Islamic Finance Handbook: A Practitioner's Guide to the Global Markets*. Singapore: Wiley, pp. 213–226.

Yoshida, E. (2017). *Gurōbal Isurāmu Kin'yūron [The Global Financial Theory]*. Kyoto: Nakanishiya Shuppan [Nakanishiya Publishing].

6 Regional Economic Integration in the Asia-Pacific in the Era of Disintegration

Takao SUAMI

Introduction

The proliferation of bilateral and multilateral trade agreements has been a major characteristic of international economic law in the last three decades. The Asia-Pacific has not been an exception to this trend. Many countries have devoted a lot of energy and resources to conclude bilateral and multilateral agreements for regional economic integration in the region during this period. Several recent incidents, including the economic confrontation between China and the United States (US), the America-first policy of the US administration, Brexit, and the malfunction of the World Trade Organization (WTO) Appellate Body have aroused unfavorable conditions for the further development of international economic integration. Thus, people do not discuss 'integration' because they are rather anxious about 'disintegration' of the international economic order (Montanaro and Violi, 2020; Petersmann, 2020). However, disintegration is only one aspect of the present situation, and progress toward integration is still visible in the Asia-Pacific. The landscape in this region is complex. Even after the withdrawal of the US from the Trans-Pacific Partnership Agreement (TPP) by the Trump administration, this region retained the impetus for moving forward with economic integration. As a consequence, two major regional agreements, namely, the Comprehensive and Progressive Agreement for Trans-Pacific Partnership (CPTPP) and the Regional Comprehensive Economic Partnership Agreement (RCEP), were recently concluded and have already come into force. The relationship between 'universalism' and 'regionalism' has always been an issue for discussion (Potter, 1943). However, in the field of international trade law, regional or bilateral initiatives have complemented multilateral initiatives under the WTO, and both have reinforced each other until the present. Therefore, the significance of Asia-Pacific regional integration for the international economic order is worth examining.

This chapter presents an overview of the regional integration in the Asia-Pacific and specifies its distinguishing features. Furthermore, it presents implications for the international economic order as a whole.

DOI: 10.4324/9781003193098-6

Recent Developments of Multilateral Agreements in the Asia-Pacific

The History of FTAs before CPTPP and RCEP

In the 1990s, most Asia-Pacific countries began efforts to conclude free trade agreements (FTAs; often called an 'economic partnership agreements' (EPAs)) with countries in or outside the region. The point of departure was the establishment of a free trade area among the member states of the Association of South East Asian Nations (ASEAN), namely, the ASEAN Free Trade Area (AFTA). Since then, most countries in this region have promoted FTAs with ASEAN members with a view to strengthening economic relationships with them (METI, 2021, pp. 507–514; Suami, 2009, pp. 169–170). As a consequence, a dense network of regional FTAs gradually extended, and almost all countries in this region had taken part in the FTA network through several FTAs by 2010. In particular, ASEAN had become a network hub through a series of the ASEAN+1 agreements with many countries in this region. The landscape of regional economic order further progressed in the 2010s. Against the backdrop of the stalemate of the Doha Round, Asian-Pacific countries started negotiations for regional mega arrangements for trade and investment and arrived at the two major FTAs: CPTPP, effective in December 2018, and RCEP, effective in January 2022. The region is now covered by these agreements, which are examined hereafter.

The Renovation from TPP to CPTPP and Its Expansion

CPTPP is the successor of TPP and has extensive geographical coverage by 11 member states (Australia, Brunei, Canada, Chile, Japan, Malaysia, Mexico, New Zealand, Peru, Singapore, and Vietnam). After the withdrawal of the US from TPP, which made the coming into effect of TPP impossible, the remaining 11 members continued negotiations and concluded a new agreement named CPTPP. CPTPP has taken over most of the provisions of TPP. However, it suspends some of the TPP provisions (for example, several provisions in the intellectual property chapter, most of which are Trade-Related Aspects of Intellectual Property Rights (TRIPS)-plus provisions requested by the US; CPTPP, Art. 2). TPP was often regarded as a new model for future twenty-first century trade agreements. This is because TPP was more advanced than other FTAs in terms of membership, the level of trade and investment liberalization, and the intervention in domestic regulatory policies. Certainly, CPTPP has lost some of its advantages due to the US withdrawal, but it has taken over the rest of TPP's advantages by incorporating most of its provisions (CPTPP, Art. 1, Para. 2).

As a consequence, CPTPP aims at the high standards of trade liberalization by establishing a free trade area for both goods and services, along with responding to various non-trade issues affecting trade and investment that have emerged in the progress of free trade. To level the playing field, CPTPP has introduced a number of provisions that regulate or influence domestic laws in a variety of policy fields such as telecommunications, electronic commerce, competition policy including consumer protection, state-owned enterprises, intellectual property, labor, the environment, anti-corruption, and regulatory coherence. Regulations on state-owned enterprises are new for this region (except for the European Union (EU)-Japan EPA). Although the rest of these policy fields were covered by existing FTAs, their disciplines in CPTPP are more advanced, specified, and/or detailed than those in former FTAs. CPTPP has gone beyond the existing model of FTAs and reached a new stage of regional integration. Therefore, CPTPP is often called a model for trade agreements in the new generation, and some of its provisions actually serve as references for other agreements including RCEP.

Furthermore, the potential to expand its membership is one of CPTPP's features. Notably, after its entry into force, CPTPP attracted attention from several parties. In 2021, both China and Taiwan officially applied for their accession to CPTPP. Particularly, the application from China was unanticipated because of its stringent requirements. For instance, China was expected to have difficulties in imposing regulations on state-owned enterprises (Kawase and Ambashi, 2018; Lee, 2016, pp. 486–487), and hence, China was not supposed to join CPTPP (Ajibo *et al.*, 2019, p. 428; Lewis, 2012, p. 235). However, China's intent to join CPTPP seems serious. It should be recalled that China already expressed its interest in TPP in 2013 (Lewis, 2013, pp. 372–374). In addition, South Korea also started examining its accession. Furthermore, it is remarkable that the United Kingdom (UK) formally applied for CPTPP membership in early 2021. The UK's application means the expansion of CPTPP to outside the Asia-Pacific. The internationalization process of CPTPP is thus expected to begin. After the membership of all of these countries, CPTPP will likely acquire more power to influence the design of future trade arrangements at the global level.

RCEP and the ASEAN Centrality

RCEP is the largest FTA with about 30% of the global economy (Ajibo *et al.*, 2019, p. 427). Seven states out of its 15 member states are CPTPP members (excluding Canada, Chile, Mexico, and Peru); the other eight states (China, Cambodia, Indonesia, Laos, Myanmar, Philippines, South Korea, and Thailand) are not members of CPTPP. In other words, RCEP covers ten ASEAN states and five other states that have concluded the 'ASEAN plus 1 FTAs' with ASEAN states. As a result, RCEP has wider coverage than CPTPP, though India decided not to join RCEP in the last stage of negotiations.

RCEP differs significantly from CPTPP with respect to its trade liberalization aspirations. The goal of RCEP is more modest and less ambitious than CPTPP (Ajibo *et al.*, 2019, p. 432; Lewis, 2013, p. 367). Although RCEP holds up a high target for economic integration, it is more friendly towards developing countries than CPTPP (Cohen, 2019, p. 568). The emphasis on developing countries was essential in RCEP negotiation. The Joint Declaration on the Launch of Negotiations for RCEP in 2012 not only confirmed 'ASEAN Centrality in the regional economic integration process' but also expressed that the negotiations would be based upon the principles adopted by the ASEAN Economic Minsters (ASEAN, 2012a, 2012b). One of these principles was to ensure flexibility for developing countries.[1] Therefore, many provisions in RCEP attribute importance to developing countries (ASEAN, 2012b).[2]

To achieve coexistence with developing countries, RCEP imposes relatively modest requirements on its membership. First, RCEP has less sectoral coverage than CPTPP in terms of non-trade issues. RCEP does not stipulate anything about labor, the environment, or state-owned enterprises. This is a major contrast between RCEP and developed country-oriented agreements such as CPTPP and the EU-Canada Free Trade Agreement (CETA) (Cohen, 2019, pp. 567–569). Since CPTPP provisions on these issues provide for high-level legal obligations on its members, their removal made RCEP's membership less burdensome. Second, subjects such as investment, intellectual property, electronic commerce, and competition are common to both CPTPP and RCEP in terms of non-tariff barriers. However, RCEP lags behind CPTPP in their substance. For instance, CPTPP provides investor-state arbitration for investment disputes (Arts. 9.19, 9.20). In contrast, RCEP lacks a system for investor-state dispute settlements (Art. 10.18). In RCEP, this issue has not been agreed to by the parties and is still under discussion. Likewise, unlike CPTPP (Art. 14.17), RCEP does not prohibit the transfer of source code as a condition for electronic commerce (Art. 12.16). In brief, RCEP generally imposes less obligations than CPTPP on its members. Thus, it is often mentioned that RECP's regulations are not as rigorous as those of CPTPP.

No Contradiction between CPTPP and RCEP

The previously mentioned RCEP's features are appealing to developing countries that do not want to strongly commit to legal obligations that cause domestic law reforms. However, RCEP is not an agreement oriented primarily towards developing countries. RCEP also shares many things common with CPTPP. For many subjects, the substantive and procedural frameworks of RCEP are not fundamentally different from those of CPTPP (Ajibo *et al.*, 2019, pp. 433–438). It is easy to find that many RCEP provisions were influenced by CPTPP.

Hence, RCEP is less ambitious than CPTPP but more ambitious than the ASEAN plus one FTAs. Most differences between the two (RCEP and CPTPP) are not in the matter of quality but in the matter of degree. Both of them have the effect of promoting intra-trade among their members. For example, as both apply uniform rules of origin to intra-trade, the risk of trade distortion by the spaghetti bowl effect will commonly diminish. The major difference of quality is chiefly caused by the wider coverage of non-trade issues by CPTPP. Although controversial issues for developing countries are excluded, RCEP has succeeded in achieving a high level of regional integration through liberalization of trade and investment. It is worth noting that some RCEP provisions (Arts. 11.11–11.17, 12.4, 12.7–12.8, 12.11) impose higher or more detailed obligations than the CPTPP provisions, and there is no explicit contradiction between them about their courses of action. In terms of common subjects, both CPTPP and RCEP have the same direction. This non-contradiction can be explained by the reason that a majority of CPTTP members can also participate in RCEP.

The Multi-Tiered Structure of FTAs in the Asia-Pacific Region

Accumulation of FTAs and Their Mutual Relationship

As aforesaid, before the formation of CPTPP and RCEP, their members were already involved in a dense network of existing FTAs, and many of them overlapped one another (e.g., the ASEAN-Japan EPA and the Singapore-Japan EPA). The addition of two mega-regional FTAs (CPTPP and RCEP) has made the structure of this network more complex. Therefore, it was an issue how the relationship between the existing FTAs and the new regional FTAs would be organized. It is worth exploring the current relationship between the existing and the newly concluded agreements.

The unique feature of the Asia-Pacific FTAs is that any new agreement does not legally substitute or supersede the existing agreements at all (Elms and Lim, 2012, pp. 35–38). This feature was explicitly mentioned in the ASEAN Guiding Principles in 2012 (ASEAN, 2012b). As a consequence of all agreements existing in parallel, in many cases, several agreements are applicable to the same trade between the two parties. In case of trade between Singapore and Japan, for example, four FTAs are applicable at the same time. They are (1) the Singapore-Japan EPA (2002), (2) the ASEAN-Japan Comprehensive EPA (2008), (3) CPTPP (2018), and (4) RCEP (2020). Each of the four agreements is independent from the others, and there is no hierarchical relationship among them. However, only one of them will in fact be applied to a particular trade. For example, after making a comparative analysis of these four FTAs, a Japanese company wishing to export its products from Japan to Singapore usually chooses one of them based upon advantageous conditions of tariff rates, rules of origin, customs procedures, and so on. In accordance with this course of practice, when exporting goods to Malaysia, Japanese electronic and electrical appliance companies have actually utilized not the Malaysia-Japan EPA but the ASEAN-Japan EPA. This is because the latter is more favorable to them than the former (Hiratsuka *et al.*, 2008, p. 317). In brief, the present arrangements of these FTAs allow 'whatever agreement gives them the greatest benefit' to be applied (Elms and Lim, 2012, p. 35).

In the case of any inconsistency or contradiction among the existing FTAs, CPTPP, and RCEP that leads to the dissatisfaction of and dilemma of choice of law for the parties of these agreements, both CPTPP and RCEP provide mutual consultation 'with a view to reaching a mutually satisfactory solution' (TPP, Art. 1.2; RCEP, Art. 20.2). Similar provisions are found in the existing bilateral FTAs in this region (e.g., Malaysia-Japan EPA, Art. 11). It may seem that after the formation of CPTPP and RCEP, mutual consultation has become more crucial to solve such a dilemma than before. However, any state that is a member of both agreements is unlikely to face such a dilemma. This is because as stated before, both agreements move towards the same or similar direction without any fundamental contradiction. Therefore, fulfilling CPTPP requirements would generally also result in meeting the requirements of RCEP. In conclusion, CPTPP and RECP can coexist with other existing agreements currently.

Until around 2020, it had been understood that because of the withdrawal of the US from TPP, RCEP would provide the major framework in this region (Ajibo *et al.*, 2019, p. 440). However, if all current candidates, including China, successfully join CPTPP, then the center of gravity will likely move from RCEP to CPTPP. Furthermore, it is anticipated that CPTPP may replace existing FTAs 'in the practical sense', though they would not be legally revoked (Elms and Lim, 2021, p. 35). Even if this change of gravity takes place, RCEP will not lose its importance. This is because all ASEAN member states have joined RCEP, while only part of them have joined CPTPP. To ensure its centripetal force for the ASEAN Community, ASEAN will be forced to continue to keep its commitment to RCEP (Fukunaga and Isono, 2013, p. 3). The coexistence of CPTPP and RCEP is often explained by the US-China rivalry in this region (Oba, 2016, pp. 105–110), but the realities surrounding both agreements are not so simple. The coexistence of these two frameworks reflects the economic reality within ASEAN. Since the level of economic development is still widely diverse among ASEAN member states, it is a challenge to find 'one size which fits all' of them. CPTPP and RCEP are mutually complementary from the ASEAN viewpoint.

Future of the Current Coexistence Arrangement

The two frameworks of CPTPP and RCEP currently exist in parallel. Assuming that the current arrangement continues for some time, the next question is the sustainability of this coexistence in terms of whether or not this state of affairs is expected to continue in the current way or would be undergoing any transformation. To examine this point, the concept of a Free Trade Area of the Asia-Pacific (FTAAP) is important.

The official discussion of FTAAP arose within the Asia Pacific Economic Cooperation (APEC) in the 2000s. APEC started its study of FTAAP in 2006 (APEC, 2006). Then, the 'Pathways to FTAAP' adopted in 2010 made clear that FTAAP should be pursued by all ongoing regional undertakings. Finally, the APEC Leaders' Lima Declaration in 2016 again reaffirmed their commitment to FTAAP and demonstrated that possible pathways to FTAAP would include TPP and RCEP (APEC, 2016). In APEC's idea, both TPP and RCEP will jointly contribute to the eventual realization of FTAAP, and they will finally converge under the umbrella of FTAAP in the long run. Since each of them has been regarded as a potential pathway of realizing FTAAP, APEC seems to pay equivalent attention to both of them, but the relationship between the two in the context of FTAAP is unclear. How will they finally converge into FTAAP? APEC's goal of regional integration is ambitious. Therefore, the Lima Declaration not only reconfirms the eventual realization of FTAAP but also reveals that FTAAP 'should do more than achieve liberalization in its narrow sense' but 'be high quality and comprehensive and incorporate and address "next generation" trade and investment issues'. Taking account of this high target, CPTPP seems to be more appropriate to the model of FTAAP than RCEP. This conclusion is consistent with the history that TPP was considered a forerunner to FTAAP in the late 2000s (Oba, 2016, p. 103). Meanwhile, the greatest obstacle for a CTPPP-based FTAAP was the prospect that China would never join CPTPP (Lewis, 2012, pp. 235–236). FTAAP without China is unthinkable. However, this obstacle was resolved by the Chinese application to CPTPP. It is still worth exploring how FTAAP should promote the development of developing countries, in particular the least-developed members within ASEAN. Assuming that CPTPP constitutes a foundation for FTAAP, more discussion will be necessary to make improvements to CPTPP (Lee, 2017, pp. 922–931). Therefore, many scholars have highlighted that FTAAP will not be a short- or medium-term project (Oba, 2016, p. 112).

Regional Integration in the Asia-Pacific and the International Economic Order

Disintegration or Integration?

Firstly, the recent inception of mega-regional trade agreements in the Asia-Pacific can be considered regional counter-evidence to the global decline in economic integration. It helps to suggest the current status of the international economic order in the context of integration-disintegration. As aforesaid in the introductory part of this article, many incidents indicating economic disintegration have recently taken place. The ongoing war in Ukraine is also making the Russian market separate from the global market. However, these incidents show one aspect of the international economic order. In the Asia-Pacific, international society still needs more integration. The state of affairs in the international economic order is not straightforward but complicated, because it has contradictory policy directions. How can we understand the whole order? From the author's perspective, the whole international society needs further economic integration. However, an adequate level of integration cannot yet be uniform and depends on each region or state. It is notable that this variety does not necessarily mean disintegration, because most of them share the same or similar directions, though they need different levels of integration. In other words, their differences exist in the degree of integration. This is revealed by the coexistence of CPTPP and RCEP.

The current dividing line on economic integration still exists between developing and developed countries, though as Brexit demonstrates, tensions about the level of integration often arise even among developed countries. The WTO was established in the 1990s as a universal framework that would be equally applied to all parties against the background of trade policy convergence between developing and developed countries (Ito, 2012, pp. 124–125). Unfortunately, irrespective of the expectations of developing countries, the WTO-centered international order has not fully succeeded in narrowing the economic gap between developing and developed countries. The principle of 'special and differential treatment' (S&D) means that trade disciplines allow differentiated treatment for developing countries. This principle had a long history in the General Agreement on Tariffs and

Trade (GATT) from the 1950s and has been taken over by the WTO Agreements that include many S&D provisions, which give various types of assistance to developing countries (Tempone, 2014). However, it has been demonstrated that these provisions are generally ineffective and that their review and reinforcement are still necessary. In this context, it is notable that arguments for global constitutionalism are paying attention to developmental issues (Yoo, 2018).

Incorporation of Non-trade Issues

Secondly, another sign of integration is a holistic approach to both trade and non-trade issues. As aforesaid, labor, environment, and consumer protection provisions are incorporated into CPTPP, in the same manner as other recent FTAs (LSE Consulting, 2021). Developing countries consider such provisions as disguised protectionism and do not generally agree to the inclusion of such provisions in their trade agreements (Elliott, 2012, p. 201; Kaufmann, 2014; Scherrer, 2020, pp. 291–292). In contrast, trade unions in developed countries support these provisions as instruments that protect their employment. After all, these provisions have usually been discussed from trade law perspectives such as affecting conditions of competition (Banks, 2021, pp. 647–650).

It is notable that these provisions fundamentally challenge the presupposition hitherto in international economic law. International economic law including EU law started its development on the presupposition of the separation between the economy and society (Suami, 2012, pp. 30–31). On the basis of this separation, international trade law concentrates on the economy. However, since the economy and society are mutually entangled, trade law must be connected with social issues for the purpose of striking a balance between the economy and society. The WTO normally finds such a balance in the framework of GATT's and the General Agreement on Trade in Services (GATS)'s exceptions (GATT, Arts. 20, 21; GATS, Arts. 14, 14bis). Under this framework, however, free trade structurally takes priority over non-trade issues. In essence, there is no hierarchy between free trade and the social values (e.g., public morality, the environment, and the health and life of humans) to be protected in each society. Nevertheless, under the WTO framework, non-trade issues cannot be treated equally with free trade. Although trade liberalization is always a fundamental principle, social values are only allowed as exceptions in the case of meeting stringent requirements (Montanaro and Violi, 2020, pp. 310–312). As a result, social values have to be undermined. When the level of free trade is low, such inequality does not go beyond a permissible limit. However, when any trade agreement becomes more liberalized and effective, it is more difficult to keep an equilibrium between free trade and social values within the principle-exception paradigm. This is demonstrated by the European Court of Justice (ECJ)'s preliminary ruling in the Viking case (*International Transport Workers' Federation v. Viking*, 2011), which made the freedom of establishment have priority over the right to collective labor action (Suami, 2012, pp. 270–274). Hence, the incorporation into CPTPP of independent chapters for labor and the environment, which aims at a high level of integration, is inevitable. Such provisions in trade agreements have the potential to achieve a better balance between free trade and social values if they are well drafted (Banks, 2021, pp. 667–671; Wang, 2019, p. 17). The ILO Resolution also suggests that governments should 'consider to include fundamental principles and rights at work in trade agreements' (ILO, 2016, 2017).

Dispute Settlements under Regional Trade Agreements

Third, another concern about disintegration is the development of divergent interpretations of equivalent obligations in the current overlapping arrangements. In terms of the texts of both CPTPP and RCEP, there is no explicit contradiction between them. If any member satisfies a higher obligation in one of them, usually CPTPP, then it will meet the requirements of the other, usually RCEP. However, the exact meaning of legal texts always has to be clarified through formal interpretation by dispute settlement procedures (DS). FTAs including CPTPP and RCEP usually rely upon WTO interpretation. When their obligations are equivalent to the WTO obligations, consistency can be maintained among them. However, most FTAs are equipped with their own DS that are similar to the WTO DS. Therefore, the operation of the FTA DS is likely to engender a risk of fragmenting international trade law jurisprudence by rendering not only constructions inconsistent with the WTO jurisprudence but also conflicting decisions (Lewis, 2015). Fortunately, this theoretical risk of fragmentation has not yet been realized, because the FTA DS have been rarely used so far. This is because, in terms of equivalent obligations, most of the parties have chosen to bring their cases before the WTO DS rather than their FTA DS. Unfortunately, the WTO DS have been in crisis because of the malfunction of the Appellate Body caused by the recent refusal of the US to appoint new Appellate Body members, and it is not expected to return to normal operations in short course (Maruyama, 2021; Pauwelyn, 2019). Even now, it is argued that the FTA DS cannot be an alternative to the WTO DS (Salazar and Ihl, 2020). However, a couple of recent examples show that the FTA DS have recently become more active than before. The EU brought four cases before the FTA DS after 2018.[3] This reveals the EU's radical policy change. These cases target not only a non-trade issue (worker's rights) that is outside the WTO but also traditional trade issues (safeguard measure, export ban, and restrictive trade measures) within the WTO (The Arbitration Panel, 2020). In addition to the EU, the US also brought an issue on worker's rights before the FTA DS in the early 2010s (Claussen, 2020, pp. 33–39).

Therefore, non-reliance on the FTA DS may gradually change in the near future in view of these cases. If the FTA DS become more popular, then international economic law will likely face fragmentation problems.

Concluding Remarks

Irrespective of the apparent disintegration in the world, the existence of CPTPP and RCEP suggests that demand for trade and investment liberalization is still strong in the Asia-Pacific region. This region has vast territory and comprises both developing and developed countries. Developing countries' interest must be different from developed countries' interest, and this difference exists within ASEAN. Any regional trade arrangement in the Asia-Pacific is required to address these different interests, and the current duplicate arrangement consisting of CPTPP and RCEP is suitable and provisionally justified for the current state of affairs in this region.

From a future perspective, Asia-Pacific countries are considered to have taken one step further towards FTAAP by adopting these agreements. Although the final goal of FTAAP is not clear, there is no doubt that future discussion will be based upon the direction of these two agreements. Therefore, their implementation has to be carefully observed. The greatest concern is the malfunction of the WTO DS. The WTO has consistently constituted the legal foundation of all regional trade agreements. It is not certain whether or not it can work well without effective WTO DS.

Note: This article is part of the achievements by a scientific research project funded by the Japan Society for the Promotion of Science (JSPS; Grant No. 18H03617). On this occasion, the author expresses his sincere thanks to the JSPS.

Notes

1 According to this principle, RCEP includes 'appropriate forms of flexibility inclusion provision for special and differential treatment plus additional flexibility to the least-developed ASEAN Member States'.

2 For example, unlike CPTPP, RCEP's provision of intellectual property takes 'different levels of economic development' and 'an appropriate balance between the rights of intellectual property right holders and the legitimate interests' into consideration (Art. 11.1, Para. 1).

3 The four cases are 'Korea labour commitments', 'Southern African Customs Union poultry safeguards', 'Ukraine wood export ban', and 'Algeria trade restrictive measures' (European Commission, n.d.)

References

All subsequent websites were last visited on 6 April 2022.

Ajibo, C. *et al.* (2019). RCEP, CPTPP and the Changing Dynamics in International Trade Standard-Setting. *Manchester Journal of International Economic Law*, 16(3), pp. 425–440.

APEC (2006). *2006 Leaders' Declaration.* Available at: www.apec.org/meeting-papers/leaders-declarations/2006/2006_aelm

APEC (2016). *Leaders' Declaration, Annex A: Lima Declaration on FTAAP.* Available at: www.apec.org/meeting-papers/leaders-declarations/2016/2016_aelm/2016_annex-a

The Arbitration Panel (2020). *Restrictions Applied by Ukraine on Export of Certain Wood Products to the European Union: Final Report of the Arbitration Panel.* Available at: https://trade.ec.europa.eu/doclib/docs/2020/december/tradoc_159181.pdf

ASEAN (2012a). *Joint Declaration on the Launch of Negotiations for the Regional Comprehensive Economic Partnership.* Available at: https://asean.org/wp-content/uploads/2016/10/SEOM-AFPs-Bali-Annex-4-Joint-Declaration-on-the-Launch-of-Negotiations-for-the-RCEP.pdf

ASEAN (2012b). *Guiding Principles and Objectives for Negotiating the Regional Comprehensive Economic Partnership.* Available at: www.mofa.go.jp/mofaj/press/release/24/11/pdfs/20121120_03_03.pdf

Banks, K. (2021). Fit for Purpose? The Extent and Enforcement of International Trade Agreement Labor Obligations After the Guatemala-Labor Obligations Decision. *Georgetown Journal of International Law*, 52(3), pp. 639–678.

Claussen, K. (2020). Reimagining Trade-Plus Compliance: The Labor Story. *Journal of International Economic Law*, 23(1), pp. 25–43.

Cohen, A. (2019). Trading Places: With the United States in Retreat, Who Writes the International Rules for Trade? *Georgia Journal of International and Comparative Law*, 47(2), pp. 539–573.

Elliott, K. (2012). Labour Standards and the TPP. In: Lim, C. L., Elms, D. K. and Low, P. eds., *The Trans-Pacific Partnership, a Quest for a Twenty-First-Century Trade Agreement*. Cambridge: Cambridge University Press, pp. 200–210.

Elms, D. and Lim, C. (2012). An Overview and Snapshot of the TPP Negotiations. In: Lim, C. L., Elms, D. K. and Low, P. eds., *The Trans-Pacific Partnership, a Quest for a Twenty-First-Century Trade Agreement*. Cambridge: Cambridge University Press, pp. 21–44.

European Commission (n.d.). *Bilateral Disputes (4)*. Available at: https://policy.trade.ec.europa.eu/enforcement-and-protection/dispute-settlement/bilateral-disputes_en

Fukunaga, Y. and Isono, I. (2013). Taking ASEAN+1 FTAs Towards the RCEP: A Mapping Study. *ERIA-DP-2013-2*, pp. 1–31. Available at: www.eria.org/ERIA-DP-2013-02.pdf

Hiratsuka, D. *et al*. (2008). Escaping from FTA Trap and Spaghetti Bowl Problem in East Asia: An Insight from the Enterprise Survey in Japan. In: Soesastro, H. ed., *Deepening Economic Integration – The ASEAN Economic Community and Beyond*, ERIA Research Project Report 2007-1-2, IDE-JETRO, pp. 304–327. Available at: www.eria.org/uploads/media/Research-Project-Report/RPR_FY2007_1-2_Chapter_16.pdf

ILO (2016). *Resolution Concerning Decent Work in Global Supply Chains*. Available at: www.ilo.org/wcmsp5/groups/public/-ed_norm/-relconf/documents/meetingdocument/wcms_497555.pdf

ILO (2017). *Handbook on Assessment of Labour Provisions in Trade and Investment Arrangements*. Geneva: International Labour Office. Available at: www.ilo.org/wcmsp5/groups/public/-dgreports/-inst/documents/publication/wcms_564702.pdf

International Transport Workers' Federation v. Viking (2011). Case no. C-438/05. European Court Reports 2007 I-10779.

Ito, K. (2012). WTO Taisei to Hatten-Tojokoku, Sabetsu-Shugi to Hi-Shijokeizaikoku Ga Motarasu Eikyo No Bunseki [WTO System and Developing Countries – Analysis of Influence from Discrimination Policy and Non-Market Economy Countries]. In: Nihon Kokusai-Keizai-Ho-Gakkai [The Japan Association of International Economic Law] ed., *Kokusai-Keizai-Ho Koza I – Tsusho, Toshi, Kyoso [International Economic Law I: Trade, Investment and Competition]*. Kyoto: Horitsubunka-sha, pp. 122–141.

Japan. Ministry of Economy, Trade and Industry (2021). *2021 nen ban Fukosei Boeki Hokokusho [The 2021 Report on Unfair Trade Practices]*. Available at: www.meti.go.jp/shingikai/sankoshin/tsusho_boeki/fukosei_boeki/report_2021/honbun.html

Kaufmann, C. (2014). Trade and Labour Standards. In: *Max Plank Encyclopedias of International Law*. Oxford: Oxford University Press. Available at: https://opil.ouplaw.com/home/MPIL

Kawase, T. and Ambashi, M. (2018). *Disciplines on State-Owned Enterprises Under the Trans-Pacific Partnership Agreement: Overview and Assessment*, ERIA-DP-2017-13, pp. 1–29. Available at: www.eria.org/uploads/media/ERIA-DP-2017-13.pdf

Lee, Y. (2016). The Eagle Meets the Dragon – Two Superpowers, Two Mega RTAs, and So Many in Between: Reflections on TPP and RCEP. *Journal of World Trade*, 50(3), pp. 475–496.

Lee, Y. (2017). Future of Trans-Pacific Partnership Agreement: Just a Dead Trade Initiative or a Meaningful Model for the North-South Economic and Trade Integration? *Journal of World Trade*, 51(5), pp. 907–932.

Lewis, M. (2012). Achieving a Free Trade Area of the Asia-Pacific Does the TPP Present the Most Attractive Path? In: Lim, C. L., Elms, D. K. and Low, P. eds., *The Trans-Pacific Partnership, a Quest for a Twenty-First-Century Trade Agreement*. Cambridge: Cambridge University Press, pp. 223–241.
Lewis, M. (2013). The TPP and the RCEP (ASEAN+6) as Potential Paths Toward Deeper Asian Economic Integration. *Asian Journal of WTO and International Health Law and Policy*, 8(2), pp. 359–378.
Lewis, M. (2015). The TPP and the RCEP (ASEAN+6) as Potential Paths Toward Deeper Asian Economic Integration. *Social Science Japan*, pp. 11–13, March.
LSE Consulting (2021). *Comparative Analysis of Trade and Sustainable Development (TSD) Provisions for Identification of Best Practices to Support the TSD Review*. London: LSE Enterprise. Available at: www.lse.ac.uk/business/consulting/assets/documents/TSD-Final-Report-Feb-2022.pdf
Maruyama, W. (2021). Can the Appellate Body Be Saved? *Journal of World Trade*, 55(2), pp. 197–230.
Montanaro, F. and Violi, F. (2020). The Remains of the Day: The International Economic Order in the Era of Disintegration. *Journal of International Economic Law*, 23(2), pp. 299–322.
Oba, M. (2016). TPP, RCEP, and FTAAP: Multilayered Regional Economic Integration and International Relations. *Asia-Pacific Review*, 23(1), pp. 100–114.
Pauwelyn, J. (2019). WTO Dispute Settlement Post 2019: What to Expect? *Journal of International Economic Law*, 22(3), pp. 297–321.
Petersmann, E. (2020). Economic Disintegration? Political, Economic, and Legal Drivers and the Need for 'Greening Embedded Trade Liberalism'. *Journal of International Economic Law*, 23(2), pp. 347–370.
Potter, P. B. (1943). Universalism Versus Regionalism in International Organization. *The American Political Science Review*, 37(5), pp. 850–862.
Salazar, N. G. and Ihl, J. T. (2020). Dispute Settlements at the World Trade Organization, the Comprehensive and Progressive Agreement for Trans-Pacific Partnership, and the Pacific Alliance. *Journal of International Dispute Settlement*, 11(4), pp. 638–658.
Scherrer, C. (2020). Novel Labour-Related Clauses in a Trade Agreement: From NAFTA to USMCA. *Global Labour Journal*, 11(3), pp. 291–306.
Suami, T. (2009). Regional Integration in East Asia and Its legalization, Can Law Contribute to the Progress of Integration in East Asia? In: Nakamura, T. ed., *East Asian Regionalism from a Legal Perspective, Current Features and a Vision for the Future*. London and New York: Routledge, pp. 169–189.
Suami, T. (2012). EU Shijo-Togo No Shinka to Hi-Boekiteki Kanshinjiko [Deepening of EU Market Integration and Non-Trade Issues]. In: Nihon Kokusai-Keizai-Ho-Gakkai [The Japan Association of International Economic Law] ed., *Kokusai-Keizai-Ho Koza I – Tsusho, Toshi, Kyoso [International Economic Law I: Trade, Investment and Competition]*. Kyoto: Horitsubunka-sha, pp. 254–274.
Tempone, E. (2014). Special and Differential Treatment. In: *Max Plank Encyclopedias of International Law*. Oxford: Oxford University Press. Available at: https://opil.ouplaw.com/home/MPIL
Wang, H. (2019). The Future of Deep Free Trade Agreements: The Convergence of TPP (and CPTPP) and CETA? *Journal of World Trade*, 53(2), pp. 317–342.
Yoo, H. S. (2018). Development Issues in the Discourse of Global Constitutionalism. In: Suami, T. *et al.* eds., *Global Constitutionalism from European and East Asian Perspectives*. Cambridge: Cambridge University Press, pp. 351–376.

7 Judicial Overreach Should Be Guided Rather than Suppressed in Order to Resolve the Appellate Body Crisis

Reflecting on Dworkin's View on Judicial Discretion

Kazumochi KOMETANI

Introduction – US Concerns Are Essentially about the Appellate Body's Interpretations that Restrict the US's Ability to Address Imports from Non-market Economies

There is yet to be any real prospect of a solution to the Appellate Body crisis. It began in 2017 with the US blockage of the appointment process for Appellate Body members. Since then, no appointment process has been initiated, resulting in a dormant Appellate Body.

In February 2020, the United States Trade Representative (USTR) published a report justifying its continued blockage (hereinafter referred to as 'the 2020 USTR Report'). The US has placed great emphasis on jurisdictional oversteps, for example, certain members remaining in office beyond the four-year term pursuant to Rule 15 of the Working Procedures of the Appellate Body, while the discussion in the WTO has chiefly focused on jurisdictional issues (e.g., World Trade Organization, 2019). However, US trade experts agree that judicial overreach by the Appellate Body is a 'major systemic concern' of the US (e.g., Payosova, Hufbauer, and Schott, 2018, p. 8). Section III of the 2020 USTR Report includes the following interpretations as being of concern to the US:

- (i) The 'erroneous' interpretation of the term 'public body' in relation to Chinese state-owned enterprises (SOEs);
- (ii) The interpretation of the non-discrimination obligation under the Agreement on Technical Barriers to Trade (TBT Agreement) and the General Agreement on Tariffs and Trade (GATT) 1994 that focuses on the trade effects of measures;
- (iii) The prohibition on the use of 'zeroing' methodologies in the determination of dumping margins;
- (iv) The stringent and unrealistic test for using out-of-country benchmarks in assessing the benefit of a subsidy;

DOI: 10.4324/9781003193098-7

(v) The interpretation of Article XIX of the GATT 1994 and the Safeguards Agreement requiring the finding of 'unforeseen development'; and
(vi) The restrictive interpretation on the simultaneous imposition of dumping and countervailing duties on imports from non-market economies such as China.

This list reveals that the US's concerns concentrate on the Appellate Body's interpretations that restrict its ability to counter imports from non-market economies such as China. When the US first defended its blockage in its 2018 NTE Report, it referred to two interpretations by the Appellate Body in disputes unrelated to China as examples of judicial overreach: one was adopted in the long-standing 'border tax adjustment' dispute with the EU, and the other was in the 'Byrd Amendment' dispute with the EU, Japan and other market economies. They are no longer referred to in the 2020 USTR Report.

The 2020 USTR Report states that '[t]he United States and other free-market nations established the World Trade Organization . . . in 1995 as a forum for negotiating and implementing trade agreements' (p. 1). Unsurprisingly, the WTO Agreement might not have as carefully elaborated the expected code of conduct for non-market economies as it does for market economies. Thus, US criticism on judicial overreach implies that resulting ambiguities have led to the favorable exercise of judicial discretion towards non-market economies and, therefore, that resolving such ambiguities should be at the discretion of WTO Members in their efforts to achieve fair treatment. This is a legitimate systemic concern that WTO Members should take seriously.

Hirsh's Overreach Proposal to Suppress Judicial Overreach

Numerous proposals and analyses have been propounded to resolve the Appellate Body crisis not only within the WTO but also outside WTO fora, i.e., by non-governmental entities (e.g., Lo, Nakagawa and Chen, 2020). Among them, this chapter specifically discusses a proposal to suppress judicial overreach tabled by Bruce Hirsh, former Chief International Trade Counsel for the US Senate Committee on Finance (Hirsh, 2019, hereinafter referred to as the 'Overreach Proposal'). Essentially, it seeks to 'clarify' Article 3.2 of the Dispute Settlement Understanding (DSU) in a way that *requires* judicial restraint. Article 3.2 states the following:

> The dispute settlement system of the WTO is a central element in providing security and predictability to the multilateral trading system. The Members recognize that it serves to preserve the rights and obligations of Members under the covered agreements, and to clarify the existing provisions of those agreements in accordance with customary rules of interpretation of public international law. Recommendations and rulings of the DSB [Dispute Settlement Body] cannot add to or diminish the rights and obligations provided in the covered agreements.

The Overreach Proposal (p. 6) analyzes the differences in the views of the US and the other Members on judicial overreach, with reference to the relationship between the second and third sentences of this provision, as follows:

> Discussions of whether the Appellate Body has engaged in overreach often devolve into a debate about whether the Appellate Body should be seeking to read meaning into 'ambiguous' WTO provisions, in particular provisions reflecting negotiators' decisions to employ 'constructive ambiguity' in order to reach agreement on controversial issues. The United States has argued that Members did not intend that WTO adjudicators would read meaning into such ambiguous provisions that was not intended. Against this, others have argued that under customary rules of interpretation of public international law, it is the responsibility of treaty interpreters to identify the meaning of even ambiguous provisions.

Accordingly, the Overreach Proposal (pp. 5–7) recommends that Members clarify Article 3.2 of the DSU as follows:

> DSU Article 3.2, including its reference to 'security and predictability,' does not justify expanding or narrowing the reach of WTO provisions or filling gaps in WTO coverage; and
>
> . . . customary rules of interpretation of public international law do not justify gap-filling or expanding or narrowing the reach of WTO provisions, in particular by narrowing or expanding the scope of general terms or broadly worded provisions.

Such limitations on judicial discretion find support in how the Appellate Body regards the WTO Agreement. The Appellate Body appears to presuppose that the WTO Agreement rests on the subjective value judgement by Members on what may be the proper balance between trade and non-trade interests that should conflict with each other. In one case, the Appellate Body interpreted Article III:4 of the GATT 1994 as prohibiting restrictive trade measures, regardless of their policy objectives and, in turn, interpreted Article XX as providing exceptions for certain legitimate policy objectives (EC – Seal Products, 2014, Paras. 5.117, 5.124–5.129). This indicates that the Appellate Body recognizes that Members have agreed to prioritize their trade interests over non-trade interests except for those enumerated under Article XX, crucially, on the premise that their trade interests should be in conflict with non-trade interests. Therefore, the judicial decision on any indeterminate textual aspect of the WTO Agreement unavoidably involves subjective value judgement independent from that of sovereign Members, because such textual indeterminacy suggests the absence of the Members' subjective value judgement. Since the Appellate Body's interpretation is final in a given dispute under the adverse consensus rule prescribed in Article 17.14 of the DSU, that is, without consent of the parties, it is legitimate to doubt whether the view on judicial discretion should be taken for granted in the WTO context that 'under customary rules of interpretation of public international law, it is the responsibility of treaty interpreters to identify the meaning of even ambiguous provisions'. This is the essence of the US argument.

Nevertheless, I submit that it is doubtful that the Overreach Proposal truly addresses US concerns, although other Members should be rather concerned that it may render the dispute settlement mechanism ineffective for dispute resolution. At first glance, the Overreach Proposal is responsive to US concerns. If Article 3.2 of the DSU is interpreted as requiring judicial restraint on 'constructive ambiguity' in the relevant text, then the Appellate Body would reconsider, among other things, the interpretation of the term 'public body' and consequently, might refrain from finding as WTO-inconsistent the US treatment of a Chinese SOE as a 'public body' pursuant to the US interpretation, that is, that a 'public body' encompasses any entity – whether it is an SOE or not – that is 'controlled' by the state.

However, such proposed clarification of Article 3.2 of the DSU is a double-edged sword. Specifically, it engenders the risk of limiting the US's right to seek a Part III remedy available under the Agreement on Subsidies and Countervailing Measures (ASCM) to uproot certain subsidizations by other Members. Let us suppose that the US becomes able to impose lawful countervailing duties on imports benefitting from input subsidies by an SOE that is 'controlled' by the government of another Member, by treating such an SOE as a 'public body'. This may be good news for the US. However, in response to a US complaint seeking a Part III remedy on the same subsidy, the respondent Member could argue that its SOE is not a 'public body', or even might be able to argue for a more restrictive interpretation of this term, precisely because the relevant text of the ASCM is ambiguous. Such responding Member could then request judicial restraint under Article 3.2 of the DSU, along the lines sought within the Overreach Proposal.

If the suppression of judicial overreach actually fails to address US concerns, then the possibility should be explored of guiding WTO adjudicators to enable Members to adequately counteract subsidization by SOEs (including via Part III remedies). Rather, this may be the realistic option available to the US to upgrade international trade rules as treating equally all trading partners including non-market economies. The EU, Japan and the US, for example, have been trying to develop disciplines for non-market economies (e.g., the US, EU, Japan Joint Statement, 2019), but even if additional rules are successfully created, it is uncertain whether China will accept them in addition to the commitments that it had already assumed at the time of its accession. Furthermore, the recent exchange of actions and reactions between the US and China on the 'forced technology transfer', as indicated in a recent USTR Report (2021, pp. 101–102), may be suggestive of the limits of US unilateralism, for example, Section 301 measures, to extract concessions from China. Despite the US's consistent opposition underlying the Appellate Body crisis, judicial rule-making in the WTO might be the sole viable path to serious rule-making (re-)negotiations on the part of WTO Members.

Alternative Proposals to Guide Judicial Overreach

I agree with Hirsh that on the premise that insofar as the WTO Agreement rests on the subjective value judgement of its parties, judicial discretion should generally be limited. However, I suggest a re-examination of this premise to elaborate an alternative proposal to guide judicial overreach.

For this purpose, Dworkin's 'unity of value' is instructive. Dworkin presented this thesis to oppose the value pluralism that was widely espoused, most prominently by Berlin (1969). Dworkin argued the 'unity of value' to mean that various values should be constructively interpreted such that 'each supports the others in a network of values' (2013, p. 101), or such that they are 'organized . . . in the fashion of a geodesic dome' (2008, p. 160). Furthermore, denying judicial discretion, Dworkin (1986, Chs. 7, 9) requires adjudicators to adopt a definitive interpretation on any ambiguous legal text to the extent that it has such effect, in criticizing Hart's widely supported legitimation of judicial discretion (Hart, 2012).

Such an approach supposes that all trade and non-trade interests should be interpreted as being coordinated with each other to thus mutually support a 'dome' housing the WTO Agreement. Referring to the state of such integrated interests as the notional 'zenith' of such a dome, I suggest construing the WTO Agreement as standing on the decision by Members to strive for the zenith of the dome and furthermore, construing Members as having elaborated the text of the WTO Agreements as the optimal (albeit non-exhaustive) code of conduct to follow in the quest for this zenith. These assumptions not only *provide* legitimacy for WTO adjudicators to 'interpret' any indeterminate text of the WTO Agreements, that is, to adopt a definitive interpretation, to attain the zenith, but also actually *require* them to do so. This judicial exercise involves no new subjective value judgement and entirely relies on the text of the WTO Agreement, specifically in accordance with customary rules of treaty interpretation (as mirrored in the Vienna Convention on the Law of Treaties, Arts. 31, 32). The examination of all WTO Agreements will help clarify how trade and non-trade interests are mutually supporting the dome housing the WTO Agreement.

My view is that 'sustainable development' should be located at the zenith of the dome as the principle of coordinating various values and interests. The first paragraph of the preamble of the Marrakesh Agreement Establishing the WTO states the following:

> Recognizing that their relations in the field of trade and economic endeavour should be conducted with a view to raising standards of living, ensuring full employment and a large and steadily growing volume of real income and effective demand, and expanding the production of and trade in goods and services, while allowing for the optimal use of the world's resources in accordance with the objective of sustainable development, seeking both to protect and preserve the environment and to enhance the means for doing so in a manner consistent with their respective needs and concerns at different levels of economic development.

'Sustainable development' was first proposed by the World Commission on Environment and Development (1987) and gradually recognized as a common interest for the international community. My view is that for the WTO, this is not a mere factor that needs to be given due regard in pursuit of trade liberalization but should be a principle of coordinating various values and interests. The concern for the sustainability of humanity's use of the ecosystem requires humanity's full dedication to sustainability. Sustainability should by no means be taken for granted. There are no guarantees against global natural catastrophes, or against emerging or recurrent epidemics that can pose risks to human security and even survival; similarly, it is not guaranteed that we will always find ways to survive such critical situations. Since the risk of extinction is too grave for any one generation to face, every generation should assume the responsibility as if it were its own to maximize sustainability. However, since it is incognizable how to maximize sustainability, we must develop a variety of cognizable values and interests that mutually support sustainability maximization. Thus, WTO Members should be construed as having sought trade liberalization in coordination with non-trade interests under the 'sustainable development' principle.

In what specific direction will this 'sustainable development' principle guide the interpretation of WTO Agreements? My view is that at the very least, all WTO provisions concerning the domestic market of Members, for example, the national treatment requirements under Article III of the GATT 1994, should be interpreted in a manner such that the proper functioning of the market mechanism is ensured in each Member's domestic economy, because this is a prerequisite for trade liberalization to help maximize sustainability. Governmental intervention in the domestic market can and should exclusively aim at ensuring the proper functioning of the market mechanism, because the WTO Agreement leaves border measures including trade remedy measures available to normalize cross-border trade flows. This interpretative approach supposes that trade expansion, as referred to in the preamble of the WTO Agreement, supports 'sustainable development' in harmony with the regulatory autonomy of WTO Members.

The market *alone* cannot address sustainability objectives, and it is not directly engaged in increasing sustainability. Sustainability building is beneficial to all future generations and current generations, and, thus, current generations have insufficient incentives to pay adequately for activities that increase sustainability. Therefore, sustainability building, for example, the establishment and operation of educational institutions, must be undertaken by the non-profit sector, i.e., the society or government. Nevertheless, sustainability maximization indirectly depends on the functioning of the market mechanism, since sustainability building needs a variety of goods and services that are produced and allocated in the economic sector. Thus, sustainability maximization requires the proper functioning of the market mechanism – not merely in the sense of letting it ensure contemporary market equilibrium but also taking into proper consideration the needs of future generations – in the Members' domestic economy, which optimizes, from a long-term perspective, the production and allocation of goods and services.

In this vein, WTO adjudicators should interpret any WTO provision concerning the domestic market of WTO Members. With respect to any ambiguous provision that permits more than one possible interpretation, adjudicators are not only legitimately allowed but also required to choose the one that best serves to ensure the proper functioning of the market mechanism.

Changes in Interpretations Expected from Guiding Judicial Overreach by Dworkin's 'Unity of Value'

This section discusses what interpretations could be adopted by WTO adjudicators to ensure the proper functioning of market mechanisms in the Members' domestic economy, to the extent that the relevant texts permit. The focus is on provisions related to subsidization by SOEs.

'Public Body'

The discussion starts with the term 'public body', which is the primary concern of the US. The Appellate Body has interpreted this term to mean an entity vested with a governmental authority, with reference to the state responsibility rule (US – Anti-Dumping and Countervailing Duties (China), 2011, Paras. 304–317). My view is that this reference is a misdirection to the attributability of SOEs' actions to their government, which fails to capture the distinct nature of Chinese SOEs. In the 'socialist market economy' of China, the managerial independence of SOEs is prescribed in Article 16 of the Constitution of the People's Republic of China (1982, as amended). As discussed in the following, the focus should be exclusively on the objective structure of SOEs that directly determines whether they are qualified to participate in the market.

For markets to operate properly, it should be ensured that all market participants act in a profit-oriented manner. For example, if an entity endlessly keeps selling products at a price causing financial loss, then it may muscle out from the market all competitors that may be producing the same products even more efficiently, which results in suboptimal outcomes for the entire economy.

Private business entities naturally act in a profit-oriented manner. This tendency is institutionalized by various governmental measures. For instance, the Companies Act of Japan (2005, e.g., Arts. 105, 355) provides for the mandatory corporate governance mechanism, requiring that stock corporations be established for a profit-seeking objective, and that management act in good faith and with due care in decision-making. Furthermore, the Bankruptcy Act of Japan (2004), Article 15, provides that if a business becomes insolvent, then it will be forced to go bankrupt, that is, to exit the market. The Company Act of Japan, Article 440, provides for the mandatory disclosure of accounting information, which helps creditors file a petition for bankruptcy. These measures jointly establish a governance regime that prevents businesses from continuing activities without seeking profit, thereby providing assurance of their qualification as market participants.

In contrast, governments, whether national or municipal, are not subject to this regime as their role is to conduct nonprofitable activities. Governments are structurally enabled to continue activities without seeking profit; for example, they are vested with mandatory revenue-raising powers through taxation or other means and are not subject to the bankruptcy laws applicable to private business enterprises. Using such prerogatives, governments, through, for example, regulations, subsidization, or other means, ensure the proper functioning of the market mechanism in which market participants seek profit and, consequently, the production and allocation of goods and services is optimized.

Such considerations require that the term 'public body' be interpreted as referring to entities that are structurally enabled to continue activities without seeking profit. Activities that cannot be continued without such ability should be 'governmental', even if they do not involve coercing private entities to do or refrain from doing something. Thus, for example, if the financial base of an SOE is fully supported by the government, such as the government provides guarantees for bonds issued by the SOE, then this SOE should be considered a 'public body'. In this regard, Watanabe (2020) observed the 'soft budget-constraint' on Chinese SOEs as a source of the 'level playing field' problem. If such observation indicates that the funding of Chinese SOEs is effectively backed by the Chinese government, then these SOEs should be found to be 'public bodies'. Accordingly, the proposed interpretation of the term 'public body' would address the problematic nature of certain Chinese SOEs.

This interpretation appears to be not far from the Appellate Body's interpretation of the term 'public body' as an entity vested with governmental authority. In a case, the Appellate Body recognized that such 'governmental authority' can be of de facto nature (US – Anti-Dumping and Countervailing Duties (China), 2011, Para. 318). The finding of fact that an SOE is structurally enabled to continue activities without seeking profit could be paraphrased as a finding of de facto 'governmental authority'.

Market-Distorting Subsidy

The second issue concerns the 'serious prejudice' claim under Article 6 of the ASCM. Article 6.3 requires proof of the trade impact of subsidies, but the exclusive focus on 'trade impact' might be biased toward non-market economies. Non-market economies often fail to make reliable market data and analyses publicly available, and without such data and analyses, it is practically difficult to establish 'serious prejudice' of subsidies. A focus should be on the objective structure of subsidy measures.

For markets to operate properly, no subsidy should be allowed that has the effect of distorting market conditions. Any such distortion prevents trade liberalization from optimizing the production and allocation of goods and services. This does not mean that no subsidy is permissible. In practice, any product market is, more or less, imperfect and often needs governmental intervention to internalize some 'externality' or to correct any other 'market failure' within the meaning of standard economic theory; for example, research and development (R&D) subsidies are granted to internalize an 'externality', which is a malfunctioning of the market mechanism such that the level of R&D activities tend to be suboptimal since such activities generate a positive 'external effect', that is, a spill-over of technological information to other entities without adequate return. If a subsidy is optimally designed to correct a 'market failure' in the relevant market, then such a subsidy should be permitted, even if it causes significant trade impact. Conversely, any subsidy that is not so designed should be prohibited, because such subsidy, by nature, impedes the proper functioning of the market.

Indeed, Article 6.3 of the ASCM does not refer to the policy objective of subsidies. However, its text evidently hints at the previous interpretation in providing that serious prejudice 'may' arise when a subsidy generates trade impact. In addition, the proposed shift of focus towards the objective structure of subsidies will also be beneficial to subsidizing Members by improving the governance on their subsidizing practices.

Market Benchmark

The third topic is the benchmark for 'benefit' calculation of any financial contribution by the government. In a case, the Appellate Body required a comparison with a market benchmark (Canada – Renewable Energy, 2013, Para. 5.164), thereby effectively giving preference to non-market economies given the lack of reliable market benchmarks in non-market economies.

The aforesaid discussion on the trade impact of subsidies argues that any subsidization should be challengeable by a 'serious prejudice' claim unless the subsidizing Member reasonably explains that it is optimally designed to correct a specific 'market failure'. This will significantly reduce difficulties arising from the required comparison with a relevant market benchmark for 'benefit' quantification, including the US out-of-country benchmark concern. The quantification of a benefit will still be necessary to determine the rate of applicable countervailing duties but unnecessary to seek Part III remedies, for which the existence of a 'benefit' is sufficient. The proposed requirements for reasonable explanation will induce a subsidizing Member to quantify the benefit of each subsidy as part of this explanation. Transparency can be further enhanced by requiring the publication of the benefit amount of each subsidy and the basis for quantification (e.g., clarifying this item to be included in the notification required under Art. 25 of the ASCM).

Notably, the required structure of a 'public body' provides a *prima facie* case that any financial contribution by such an entity generates a 'benefit' to its recipient. As discussed previously, a 'public body' and a 'government' are structurally enabled to continue activities without seeking profit. It is thus reasonable to infer that the conditions of financial contribution by such entities are different from those of comparable action, if any, by private enterprises (e.g., loans) and that they accordingly deviate from the relevant market benchmark. Obviously, no private entity voluntarily receives any loss-bearing financial contribution (e.g., loans with an interest rate higher than that available in the market). Thus, any financial contribution by a 'public body' is presumably accompanied by a 'benefit'.

The consequent allocation of the burden of proof to the respondent Member is reasonable and rather required to ensure the proper functioning of the domestic markets of WTO Members. If a Member allows any 'public body' to participate in the market, for example, for the procurement of goods and services that it needs to carry out its assigned tasks, then this Member should ensure that such 'public body' follows prevailing market practices, for example, by requiring that it use open bidding. By explaining what it did, the Member can rebut the presumption of 'benefit'. This is consistent with Article XVII:1 of the GATT 1994. Subparagraph (b) obligates Members to 'require that [state] enterprises shall . . . make any such purchases or sales solely in accordance with commercial considerations'.

In my view, the previous three changes in the interpretations of the WTO Agreement will take place if judicial overreach is guided to ensure the proper functioning of markets, thereby treating more appropriately both non-market and market economies. As explained previously, these changes squarely respond to US concerns on judicial overreach in relation to Chinese SOEs, together with possible changes in the interpretations of national treatment obligation that I have proposed elsewhere (Kometani, 2009).

Closing Remarks

The working hypothesis of this article is that the Appellate Body crisis is caused by perceptions as to its exercise of judicial discretion resulting in its perceived inability to discipline non-market economies. Assessing the legitimacy of judicial discretion requires, on the basis of Dworkin's 'unity of value', that interpretative exercises by WTO adjudicators be guided to attain 'sustainable development' as the common goal of the WTO Agreement rather than basing decisions on the premise of conflicting interests that may result in judicial discretion being deprived from WTO adjudicators. The consequent re-examination of the jurisprudence on subsidization, particularly in relation to SOEs, reveals that such guided interpretative exercises could ensure more appropriate treatment of non-market economies.

The proposal further aims to upgrade the WTO framework. In order to ensure the proper functioning of the Members' domestic markets, WTO adjudicators may legitimately 'interpret' indeterminate textual aspects of the WTO Agreements, thus prompting WTO Members' rule-making. Concurrently, all Members would be required to cooperate with one another in improving their code of conduct and, if necessary, guarding against judicial deviations.

Given the absence of a hegemonic superpower in international trade relations, Members may consider rebuilding the dispute settlement mechanism on the 'unity of value' premise, with a view to upgrading the 'rule of law' in the WTO framework. If the WTO remains based on conflicting interests, then it will remain legitimate to criticize exercises of judicial discretion, particularly those perceived as treating non-market economies favorably, as unjustifiable judicial overreach, and consequently, the security and stability of the WTO dispute settlement mechanism and even of the WTO itself will be seriously questioned.

Note: The author is Of Counsel at Nishimura & Asahi and Visiting Professor at the Graduate School of Public Policy, The University of Tokyo. He previously worked as General Counsel for International Legal Affairs, Trade Policy Bureau,

Ministry of Economy, Trade and Industry of Japan. The author submits this chapter in his personal capacity, and, thus, the views expressed here are attributable solely to the author, not to any organization to which the author is or was associated.

References

All subsequent websites were last visited on 20 June 2023.

Berlin, I. (1969). *Four Essays on Liberty*. London: Oxford University Press.

Canada – Certain Measures Affecting the Renewable Energy Generation Sector (Canada – Renewable Energy) (2013). *WTO Appellate Body Report, WT/DS412/AB/R*. Available at: https://www.wto.org/english/tratop_e/dispu_e/cases_e/ds412_e.htm

Dworkin, R. (1986). *Law's Empire*. Cambridge: Harvard University Press.

Dworkin, R. (2008). *Justice in Robes*. London: Harvard University Press.

Dworkin, R. (2013). *Justice for Hedgehogs*. London: Harvard University Press.

European Communities – Measures Prohibiting the Importation and Marketing of Seal Products (EU – Seal Products) (2014). *WTO Appellate Body Report, WT/DS400&401/AB/R*. Available at: https://www.wto.org/english/tratop_e/dispu_e/cases_e/ds400_e.htm

Hart, H. L. A. (2012). *The Concept of Law*. Oxford: Oxford University Press.

Hirsh, B. (2019). *Resolving the WTO Appellate Body Crisis: Proposals on Overreach*. Paper Commissioned by the National Foreign Trade Council, December. Available at: https://www.nftc.org/default/trade/WTO/Resolving%20the%20WTO%20Appellate%20Body%20Crisis_Proposals%20on%20Overreach.pdf

Kometani, K. (2009). Current Application of the WTO Rules to Domestic Policy Measures: An Effective Promotion of Trade, or an Unnecessary Distortion of Markets? In: Kotera, A., Araki, I. and Kawase, T. eds., *The Future of the Multilateral Trading System: East Asian Perspectives*, Ch. 5. London: Cameron May.

Lo, C. F., Nakagawa, J. and Chen, T. F. (2020). *The Appellate Body of the WTO and Its Reform*. Heidelberg: Springer.

Payosova, T., Hufbauer, G. C. and Schott, J. J. (2018). *The Dispute Settlement Crisis in the World Trade Organization: Causes and Cures* (No. PB18-5). Available at: https://www.piie.com/sites/default/files/documents/pb18-5.pdf

United States – Definitive Anti-Dumping and Countervailing Duties on Certain Products from China (US – Anti-Dumping and Countervailing Duties (China)) (2011). *WTO Appellate Body Report, WT/DS379/AB/R*. Available at: https://www.wto.org/english/tratop_e/dispu_e/cases_e/ds379_e.htm

United States Trade Representative (2018). *The 2018 National Trade Estimate Report on Foreign Trade Barriers*. Available at: https://ustr.gov/sites/default/files/files/Press/Reports/2018%20National%20Trade%20Estimate%20Report.pdf

United States Trade Representative (2020). *Report on the Appellate Body of the World Trade Organization*. Available at: https://ustr.gov/sites/default/files/Report_on_the_Appellate_Body_of_the_World_Trade_Organization.pdf

United States Trade Representative (2021). *The 2021 National Trade Estimate Report on Foreign Trade Barriers*. Available at: https://ustr.gov/sites/default/files/files/reports/2021/2021NTE.pdf

US, EU, Japan (2019). *Joint Statement of the Trilateral Meeting of the Trade Ministers of the United States, European Union, and Japan*, 23 May. Available at: https://ustr.gov/about-us/policy-offices/press-office/press-releases/2019/may/joint-statement-trilateral-meeting

Watanabe, M. (2020). *Competitive Neutrality of State-owned Enterprises in China's Steel Industry: A Causal Inference on the Impacts of Subsidies*. Available at: www.rieti.go.jp/en/publications/summary/20020019.html?ref=rss

World Commission on Environment and Development (1987). *Report of the World Commission on Environment and Development: Our Common Future*. London: Oxford University Press, pp. 1–300.

World Trade Organization (2019). *Informal Process on Matters Related to the Functioning of the Appellate Body – Report by the Facilitator, H.E. Dr. David Walker (New Zealand), JOB/GC/222*. Available at: https://docs.wto.org/dol2fe/Pages/SS/directdoc.aspx?filename=q:/Jobs/GC/222.pdf

8 International Law Matters

The Legality of Unilateral Embargoes, Suspensions of Air Transport, and Restrictions on Investment by Reason of Pandemic or National Security Considerations, or in Response to Serious Breaches of International Law

Kazuhiro NAKATANI

Preface

Are unilateral restrictions on international economic transactions in response to a pandemic permissible under international law? Can a State prohibit trade with another State by citing national security concerns? Is it possible for a State, as a matter of diplomatic necessity, to suspend air transport with another State that commits genocide against some minority group in the territory or control of the latter?

The practical importance of such questions is obvious in view of the current situation concerning the worldwide spread of COVID-19 and US-China antagonism. In this chapter, among various transactions, the author focuses on three distinct ones for the sake of contrast: (1) the export/import of goods, which is regulated by the General Agreement on Tariffs and Trade (GATT), (2) international air transport, which, although a mode of trade in services, is not fundamentally regulated by the General Agreement on Trade in Services (GATS) but by bilateral air agreements (BAAs), and (3) investment that is mainly regulated by bilateral investment treaties (BITs).

These problems are analyzed in accordance with the following steps. Firstly, relevant treaty provisions that refer to pandemic or national security situations are identified. Secondly, the author considers the legality of prohibitions on trade, suspensions of air transport, and restrictions on investment by reason of pandemic, national security, or diplomatic necessity.

The author would like to emphasize the following three points. Firstly, where it is controversial whether a treaty provision concerning a security exception is self-judging (i.e., a matter at the discretion of the invoking State), the modern trend is to deny such self-judging character unless it is clearly provided in the text or customarily established. Secondly, the author supports the interpretation of security exception clauses so long as this is in good faith. At the same time, general principles of law, a source of international law, such as the principle that *nullus commodum capare de sua injuria propria* or that of *ex delicto non oritur actio*, should also be taken into consideration in order to ascertain the legality of restrictions. Thirdly,

DOI: 10.4324/9781003193098-8

even if there is no provision in relevant treaties, such as GATT or BAAs, that justifies measures taken for the sake of diplomatic necessity in particular, this does not mean that all such measures are illegal under international law. Some measures in response to serious breaches of international law such as aggression or genocide may be justified as appropriate countermeasures.

Relevant Treaty Provisions that Refer to Pandemic or National Security Situations

Relevant GATT provisions that refer or relate to health crises are Article 11 paragraph 2 and Article 20. Article 11 paragraph 2 provides as follows:

> The provisions of paragraph 1 of this Article [General Elimination of Quantitative Restrictions] shall not extend to the following: (a) Export prohibitions or restrictions temporarily applied to prevent or relieve critical shortages of foodstuffs or other products essential to the exporting contracting party.

Article 20 provides that

> nothing in this Agreement shall be construed to prevent the adoption or enforcement by any contracting party of measures: (b) necessary to protect human, animal or plant life or health; (j) essential to the acquisition or distribution of products in general or local short supply.
>
> As to national security, Article 21 provides the following:
>
> Nothing in this Agreement shall be construed (a) to require any contracting party to furnish any information the disclosure of which it considers contrary to its essential security interests; or (b) to prevent any contracting party from taking any action which *it considers* necessary for the protection of its essential security interests (i) relating to fissionable materials or the materials from which they are derived; (ii) relating to the traffic in arms, ammunition and implements of war and to such traffic in other goods and materials as is carried on directly or indirectly for the purpose of supplying a military establishment; (iii) taken in time of war or other emergency in international relations (emphasis added).

Measures taken unilaterally for the sake of diplomatic necessity are not mentioned in GATT. Article 21 (c) provides that nothing in this Agreement shall be construed to prevent any contracting party from taking any action in pursuance of its obligations under the United Nations (UN) Charter for the maintenance of international peace and security. Only non-military enforcement measures under Article 41 of the Charter in pursuance of a Security Council Resolution come under this category.

No provisions in BAAs justify the suspension of air transport with a State on pandemic, national security, or diplomatic necessity grounds.

The Chicago Convention on International Civil Aviation has some relevant provisions. For instance, Article 9 provides that each contracting State may, for reasons of military necessity or public safety, restrict or uniformly prohibit the aircraft of other States from flying over certain areas of its territory under certain conditions. Article 14 refers to a pandemic situation and provides that

> Each contracting State agrees to take effective measures to prevent the spread by means of air navigation of cholera, typhus (epidemic), smallpox, yellow fever, plague, and such other communicable diseases as the contracting States shall from time to time decide to designate, and to that end contracting States will keep in close consultation with the agencies concerned with international regulations relating to sanitary measures applicable to aircraft. Such consultation shall be without prejudice to the application of any existing international convention on this subject to which the contracting States may be parties.

Furthermore, Article 89 provides for war and other emergency conditions:

> In case of war, the provisions of this Convention shall not affect the freedom of action of any of the contracting States affected, whether as belligerents or as neutrals. The same principle shall apply in the case of any contracting State which declares a state of national emergency and notifies the fact to the Council.

Legality of Unilateral Restrictions on International Economic Transactions by Reason of a Pandemic

Unilateral restrictions on the export of goods including medical equipment and vaccines used against COVID-19 may be justified by GATT Article 20(b) when it is proved that measures to prevent the spread of a pandemic are 'necessary to protect human life or health'. The restriction can also be justified by GATT Article 20(j) when it is 'essential to the acquisition or distribution of products in general or local short supply'. Such restrictions may also arguably be justified by Article 11 paragraph 2 when the goods are seen as 'products essential to the exporting contracting party'.

The Trans-Pacific Partnership Agreement (TPP) also has a clause for measures necessary to protect health. Article 29.1 paragraph 1 provides that

> For the purposes of Chapter 2 (National Treatment and Market Access for Goods), Chapter 3 (Rules of Origin and Origin Procedures), Chapter 4 (Textile and Apparel Goods), Chapter 5 (Customs Administration and Trade Facilitation), Chapter 7 (Sanitary and Phytosanitary Measures), Chapter 8 (Technical Barriers to Trade) and Chapter 17 (State-Owned Enterprises and Designated Monopolies), Article XX of GATT 1994 and its interpretative notes are incorporated into and made part of this Agreement, *mutatis mutandis* (emphasis in the original).

and Article 29.1 paragraph 2 provides the following: 'The Parties understand that the measures referred to in Article XX(b) of GATT 1994 include environmental measures necessary to protect human, animal or plant life or health'.

Regarding the suspension of air transport taken by a State in relation to another State greatly suffering by a pandemic in order to prevent the spread of the pandemic to the former, Article 14 of the Chicago Convention may provide the legal basis to argue that the suspension is among the 'effective measures to prevent the spread'. In the case of COVID-19, Kuwait and Oman have restricted their air traffic due to the pandemic by explicitly basing their arguments on Article 14 (Huremagić and Kainz, 2020).

But the rules are more complex. Chapter 2 of Annex 9 of the Chicago Convention provides that: '2.4 Contracting States shall not prevent an aircraft from calling at any international airport for public health reasons unless such action is taken in accordance with the International Health Regulations of the World Health Organization'.

The most relevant provisions of the IHR are Articles 28 and 43. Article 28 provides that 'subject to Article 43 or as provided in applicable international agreements', 'a ship or an aircraft shall not be prevented for public health reasons from calling at any point of entry' (Para. 1) and 'ships or aircraft shall not be refused free pratique by States Parties for public health reasons (Para. 2)'. Article 43 paragraph 1 provides that

> These Regulations shall not preclude States Parties from implementing health measures, in accordance with their relevant national law and obligations under international law, in response to specific public health risks or public health emergencies of international concern, which: (a) achieve the same or greater level of health protection than WHO recommendations; or (b) are otherwise prohibited under Article 25, Article 26, paragraphs 1 and 2 of Article 28, Article 30, paragraph 1(c) of Article 31 and Article 33, provided such measures are otherwise consistent with these Regulations.

As the worldwide widespread of COVID-19 was partly due to the international movement of people by air, the author considers that these articles should be modified by applying a precautionary approach to prevent the future spread of infectious deceases.

In April 2020, Argentina banned all flights until 1 September 2020, and the International Air Transport Association (IATA) suggested that the decision conflicted with existing aviation agreements (Macilree and Duval, 2020, pp. 1–2). In August 2020, Italy threatened the airline Ryanair with the suspension of flights to and from Italy for repeated violations of measures to prevent the spread of COVID-19 (Joll, 2020). Whether these measures are justified under the Chicago Convention, BAAs, and the IHR remains unclear.

Even if such measures are not justified under these rules, there may be another legal basis for them, for instance, a 'state of necessity' as one of the circumstances precluding wrongfulness under general international law. Article 25 paragraph 1 of the Articles on Responsibility of States for Internationally Wrongful Acts (A/56/83, of which the UN General Assembly took note in 2001), which codifies customary international rules of State responsibility, states that necessity may be invoked by a State as a ground for precluding wrongfulness. It provides that

> Necessity may not be invoked by a State as a ground for precluding the wrongfulness of an act not in conformity with an international obligation of that State unless the act: (a) is the only way for the State to safeguard an essential interest against a grave and imminent peril; and (b) does not seriously impair an essential interest of the State or States towards which the obligation exists, or of the international community as a whole.

Legality of Unilateral Embargoes and Suspensions of Air Transport by Reason of National Security

As to unilateral embargoes by reason of national security, Article 21 of GATT is a key provision, as mentioned previously. However, this is not without legal problems.

Firstly, on 30 November 1982, the Contacting Parties adopted the Decision concerning Article 21 (L/5426). It provides that

> The CONTRACTING PARTIES decide that:
>
> 1. Subject to the exception in Article XXI:a, contracting parties should be informed to the fullest extent possible of trade measures taken under Article XXI.
> 2. When action is taken under Article XXI, all contracting parties affected by such action retain their full rights under the General Agreement.
> 3. The Council may be requested to give further consideration to this matter in due course.

It is natural to interpret the term ‘full rights under the General Agreement’ (Para. 2) to include recourse to the dispute settlement procedures under GATT.

Secondly, when the International Court of Justice (ICJ) in its judgment in 1986 concerning the Nicaragua Case interpreted the text of Article 21 of the US-Nicaragua 1956 Treaty of Friendship, Commerce and Navigation (FCN), it took into consideration the difference with the text of GATT. Article 21 paragraph 1 of the FCN provides that ‘The present Treaty shall not preclude the application of measures: (d) necessary to fulfill the obligation of a Party for the maintenance or restoration of international peace and security, or necessary to protect its essential security interests’.

The ICJ emphasized the distinction between the FCN term (measures *necessary* to protect its essential security interests) and that of GATT (action that *it considers necessary* for the protection of its essential security interests).

According to the ICJ Judgment,

> Article XXI defines the instances in which the Treaty itself provides for exceptions to the generality of its other provisions, but it by no means removes the interpretation and application of that article from the Jurisdiction of the Court as contemplated in Article XXIV. That the Court has jurisdiction to determine whether measures taken by one of the Parties fall within such an exception, is also clear *a contrario* from the fact that the text of Article XXI of the Treaty does not employ the wording which was already to be found in Article XXI of the General Agreement on Tariffs and Trade. This provision of GATT, contemplating exceptions to the normal implementation of the General Agreement, stipulates that the Agreement is not to be construed to prevent any contracting party from taking any action which it 'considers necessary for the protection of its essential security interests', in such fields as nuclear fission, arms, etc. The 1956 Treaty, on the contrary, speaks simply of 'necessary' measures, not of those considered by a party to be such (p. 116).

The ICJ suggested that, *a contrario*, a panel and the Appellate Body of the WTO have no jurisdiction to determine action taken under GATT Article 21. This seems to be in harmony with *ut res magis valeat quam pereat*, that is, the principle of effective treaty interpretation.

Thirdly, however, the WTO Panel in the Russia Transit Case in 2019 negated such an interpretation. It denied the self-judging character of GATT Article 21 and stated that it had jurisdiction to determine whether an action that a State considers necessary for the protection of its essential security interest is justified.

It is noteworthy that the Panel emphasized the need for good faith in the interpretation of obligations as follows:

- 7.132 . . . the discretion of a Member to designate particular concerns as 'essential security interest' is limited by its obligation to interpret and apply Article XXI (b)(iii) of the GATT 1994 in good faith. The Panel recalls that the obligation of good faith is a general principle of law and a principle of general international law which underlies all treaties, as codified in Article 31 (1) . . . and Article 26 . . . of the Vienna Convention.
- 7.133 The obligation of good faith requires that Members not use the exceptions in Article XXI as a means to circumvent their obligations under GATT 1994.
- 7.134 It is therefore incumbent on the invoking Member to articulate the essential security interests said to arise from the emergency in international relations sufficiently enough to demonstrate their validity.
- 7.138 The obligation of good faith, referred to in paragraphs 7.132 and 7.133 above, applies not only to the Member's definition of the essential security interests said to arise from the particular emergency in international relations, but also, and most importantly, to their connection with the measures at issue. Thus, as concerns the application of Article XXI(b)(iii), this obligation is crystallized in demanding that the measures at issue meet a minimum requirement of

plausibility in relation to the proffered essential security interests, i.e. that they are not implausible as measures protective of these interests.

- 7.139 The Panel must therefore review whether the measures are remote from, or unrelated to, the 2014 emergency that it is implausible that Russia implemented the measures for the protection of its essential security interests arising out of the emergency.

The Panel concluded that Russia had satisfied the conditions of the chapeau of Article XXI(b) of the GATT 1994 and that it had met the requirement for invoking Article XXI(b) (iii) of the GATT 1994 in relation to the measures at issue; therefore, the measures were covered by Article XXI(b) (iii) of the GATT 1994 (7.148 and 7.149).

The author supports the fact that the Panel introduced the need for good faith in the interpretation of Article 21. However, the author does not support its conclusions. The Panel paid little attention to a crucial fact: Russia's illegal annexation of Crimea. The UN General Assembly adopted Resolution 68/262 on 27 March 2014 and called upon all States to desist and refrain from actions aimed at the partial or total disruption of the national unity and territorial integrity of Ukraine, including any attempts to modify Ukraine's borders through the threat or use of force or other unlawful means (Para. 2). Once the Panel applied good faith in its report, it also should have applied, as corollaries of good faith, the notions of *nullus commodum capare de sua injuria propria* (no one can be allowed to take advantage of their own wrong), *ex delicto non oritur actio* (an unlawful act cannot serve as the basis of an action in law), and of *ex injuria non oritur jus* (illegal acts cannot create law) (Cheng, 1953, pp. 149–158, 187). Russia's invocation of Article 21 clearly runs against these general principles and, therefore, should have been dismissed. The Panel report has deplorably allowed the unjustified enrichment of Russia. This is against the principle of clean hands.

This Panel's report is not universally respected. The TPP has its own security exception clause in Article 29.2, which provides as follows:

> Nothing in this Agreement shall be construed to: (a) require a Party to furnish or allow access to any information the disclosure of which it determines to be contrary to its essential security interests; or (b) preclude a Party from applying measures that it considers necessary for the fulfillment of its obligations with respect to the maintenance or restoration of international peace or security, or the protection of its own essential security interests.

But it does not refer to GATT Article 21. It contrasts with TPP Article 29.1 on general exceptions, which refers to GATT Article 20. This might suggest that the TPP contracting parties did not intend to follow the WTO jurisprudence on the security exception (Zhou, 2020).

As to the suspension of air transport by reason of national security, the measure is clearly justified when it comes under Article 9 or 89 of the Chicago Convention. Also, when the measure is justified by necessity, the wrongfulness that might arise from the conflict with the Chicago Convention and/or some BAA can be precluded.

Legality of Restrictions on Foreign Investment by Reason of National Security

A remarkable distinction between restrictions on investment when compared to embargoes and suspensions of air transport is that restrictions on investment are twofold. Firstly, investment in some strategic industries is restricted *in limine*. Secondly, specific investments are restricted based on a security exception clause.

As to the first category of restrictions *in limine*, the Organisation for Economic Co-operation and Development (OECD) Code of Liberalisation of Capital Movements, which is binding on OECD Member States, clearly permits restrictions on capital movements based on public order or national security. Article 3 of the Code provides that

> The provisions of this Code shall not prevent a Member from taking action which it considers necessary for: (1) the maintenance of public order or the protection of public health, morals and safety; (2) the protection of its essential security interests; (3) the fulfillment of its obligations relating international peace and security.

Remarkably, this Article has been interpreted and implemented as self-judging among OECD Member States, and each Member State has imposed restrictions on investment in some 'strategic' industries at its own discretion.[1] However, this does not mean that such discretion is unlimited. In recent G7 Summit meetings, some relevant soft law guidelines have been developed such as (1) Paragraph 11 of the Heiligendamm Summit Declaration on Growth and Responsibility in the World Economy (2007), which provides that 'We remain committed to minimizing any national restrictions on foreign investment. Such restriction should apply to very limited cases which primarily concern national security. The general principles to be followed in each case are non-discrimination, transparency and predictability'. (2) Paragraph 6 of the Hakkaido Toyako Summit Leaders Declaration on World Economy (2008) provides that 'Any foreign investment restrictions should be very limited, focusing primarily on national security concerns, and should adhere to the principles of transparency, predictability, proportionality, and accountability'. In 2009, the OECD Council adopted Guidelines for Recipient Country Investment Policies relating to National Security. In these Guidelines, the Council recommends that a restriction of investment designed to safeguard national security should be guided by the principles of non-discrimination, transparency of policies, predictability of outcomes, proportionality of measures, and accountability of implementing authorities. These guidelines are particularly important to the restriction on investment by Sovereign Wealth Funds (SWFs). It is also remarkable that in 2008, the US Department of the Treasury concluded a trilateral agreement with Singapore (Singapore Investment Corporation) and Abu Dhabi (Abu Dhabi Investment Authority), which provides that 'Any restrictions imposed on investments for national security reasons should be proportional to genuine national security risks raised by transactions'.[2]

As to the second category of restrictions on foreign investment based on security exception clauses, an excellent comprehensive study by Blanco and Pehl (2020) is most instructive. The interpretation of GATT Article 21 by the WTO Panel in the Russia Transit Case will certainly affect the future interpretation of national security exception clauses contained in investment agreements. However, not only the text of the clause as such but also the *travaux préparatoires* should be considered in the interpretation. Whether the security exception clause contains a self-judging term (e.g., '*it considers*') can serve in principle as a litmus test of deciding its self-judging character, but this presumption may also be reversed by resorting to contradictory *travaux préparatoires*. It is remarkable that the US Department of State considers that, even in the absence of the term '*it considers*' in the security exception clauses of the US's BITs with Georgia, Bolivia, and Honduras, the clauses are self-judging (Blanco and Pehl, 2020, p. 48). Some recent investment agreements clearly mention self-judging. Article 8 of the Protocol to the Russia-US BIT (1992, not in force) states that it is self-judging whether a measure taken by a Party is to protect its essential security interest. This is the first agreement in which the US considers the application of essential security measures to be self-judging (Blanco and Pehl, 2020, pp. 47–49).

It is also remarkable that some recent BITs clearly state that security measures are not subject to investor-State dispute settlement (ISDS). The Buenos Aires Protocol for Intra-Mercosur Investment (2017) and Cooperation and Facilitation Agreement between Brazil and UAE (2019) are such examples (Blanco and Pehl, pp. 66–67). The interpretative difficulty as to the self-judging character of a provision might arise when the security exception clause is ambiguous. The dissenting opinion by Judge Anzilotti and Judge Huber in the PCIJ Judgment of the Wimbledon (1923) states that the right of a State to adopt the course that it considers best suited to the exigencies of its security is so essential a right that, in case of doubt, treaty stipulations cannot be interpreted as limiting it (p. 37). Although this is an interpretation of a treaty provision in favor of state sovereignty, it is very doubtful whether it would still be sustained nowadays. Blanco and Pehl (2020, pp. 42–43) point out that recent investment tribunals have consistently held that, as a rule, security clauses are self-judging only if the parties expressly ascribe such character to them.

Legality of Unilateral Restrictions on International Economic Transactions in Response to Serious Breaches of International Law

Economic sanctions are measures calculated to cause damage to a State that commits an internationally wrongful act for the purpose of stopping such an act. Distinct from the national security exceptions mentioned previously, there are typically no exception clauses in economic agreements, such as GATT, GATS, and many Economic Partnership Agreements (EPAs), FTAs, and BITs, that expressly justify restrictions as sanctions against internationally wrongful acts. Therefore, economic sanctions on their face conflict with key provisions of economic agreements, such as that of most favored nation (MFN) or the prohibition of quantitative restrictions.

Nevertheless, such sanctions may be justified countermeasures when they meet certain requirements, such as those of prior demand of redress and proportionality.

Article 22 of the Articles on Responsibility of States for Internationally Wrongful Acts provides that

> The wrongfulness of an act of a State not in conformity with an international obligation towards another State is precluded if and to the extent that the act constitutes a countermeasure taken against the latter State in accordance with chapter II of part three.

In 1978, the arbitral award of the Case Concerning the Air Service Agreement between the United States and France clearly justified countermeasures as follows:

> If a situation arises which, in one State's view, results in the violation of an international obligation by another State, the first State is entitled, within the limits set by the general rules of international law pertaining to the use of armed force, to affirm its rights through countermeasures (p. 443).

As the author has already analyzed in detail this subject in two earlier articles (Nakatani, 1996, 1998), it is best to avoid repetition here. The essence of these articles is that in cases of a serious breach of international law against the international community as a whole, namely, a breach of *erga omnes* obligations[3] or an international crime,[4] such as aggression and genocide, not only the direct victim State but also States not directly affected by such acts can take countermeasures, including embargoes, suspensions of air transport, and restrictions on investment, as these countermeasures meet the requirements of, for example, prior demand of redress and proportionality.[5]

Unilateral economic sanctions may target not only States that commit internationally wrongful acts but also individuals who are directly responsible for such acts. The US, in accordance with the Global Magnitsky Human Rights Accountability Act, has imposed measures of inadmissibility into the US (i.e., denying entry to the US) and blocking accessibility to the property of persons who are responsible for extrajudicial killings, torture, or other gross violations of internationally recognized human rights. Denial of entry to and freezing the financial assets of responsible persons are also key measures of smart sanctions within the framework of non-military enforcement measures decided by the UN Security Council. Under general international law, denial of entry is a measure of retorsion, which is unfriendly but discretionary and lawful as such. Freezing financial assets is a temporary suspension of the owner's right to dispose of their financial property but can be a lawful countermeasure against an internationally wrongful act if the need for proportionality and other conditions are satisfied. No conflict with the Articles of Agreement of the International Monetary Fund (IMF; including Art. 8, Para. 2) arises if the State imposing the freezing of financial assets notifies the IMF Executive Board in advance or within 30 days after imposing such a restriction and the Executive Board does not object to such a restriction. This is provided by the

IMF Executive Board Decision No.144-(52/51) of 14 August 1952. There is no precedent where the Executive Board has objected to such a restriction (Ruys and Ryngaert, 2020, pp. 35–37).

Final Remarks

It is sometimes stated that the WTO system constitutes a self-contained regime. The precise meaning of this is that reactions against a breach of GATT, for example, are limited to those provided by GATT. We must note that the idea of self-containment does not provide for trade measures against serious breaches of non-WTO norms and serious breaches of customary international law, in particular those concerning aggression or genocide.

The remarks in this chapter might not be favorable to those who believe in or promote unbridled free trade and investment. However, justifications for restrictions of international transactions certainly exist and serve as safeguards or relate to sovereign prerogatives reserved by States. We must remain aware of these realities. International economic law experts must be mindful of the fundamental importance and role of general international law in the international legal system.

Notes

1 In addition to Article 3, Article 2 of the Code allows Member States to restrict foreign investment by lodging reservations. On the Code and the Japanese laws concerning restrictions on foreign investment, see Nakatani, 2010.

2 Principle 4 of the Policy Principles for Countries Receiving SWF Investment. On restrictions on investment by SWFs, see Nakatani, 2015.

3 In the Judgment of the Barcelona Traction Case in 1970, the ICJ stated that

> In view of the Importance of the rights involved, all States can be held to have a legal interest in their protection: they are obligations *erga omnes*. Such obligations derive, for example, in contemporary international law, from the outlawing of acts of aggression, and of genocide, as also from the principles and rules concerning the basic rights of human person, including protection from slavery and racial discrimination (p. 32).

4 Article 19 of the Draft Articles on State Responsibility provisionally adopted by the International Law Commission on first reading in 1996 (*UN Doc*. A/51/10, p. 60) provides that

> 2. An internationally wrongful act which results from the breach by a State of an international obligation so essential for the protection of fundamental interests of the international community that the breach is recognized as a crime by that community as a whole constitutes an international crime.
>
> Paragraph 3 cites aggression, colonial domination, slavery, genocide, apartheid, massive pollution of the atmosphere or of the sea as examples of international crime.

5 Among the requirements for countermeasures, the requirement of proportionality, in practice, is the most important. Article 51 provides that 'Countermeasures must be commensurate with the injury suffered, taking into account the gravity of the internationally wrongful act and the rights in question'.

References

All subsequent websites were last visited on 18 September 2022.

Belguim v. Spain (Barcelona Traction) (1970). I.C.J. 3, Judgment. I.C.J. Reports, 1970, p. 3.

Blanco, S. M. and Pehl, A. (2020). *National Security Exceptions in International Trade and Investment Agreements: Justiciability and Standard of Review*. Berlin: Springer.

Cheng, B. (1953). *General Principles of Law as Applied by International Courts and Tribunals*. London: Stevens.

Huremagić, H. and Kainz, F. (2020). *COVID-19, China and International Aviation Law: A Ticket to The Hague?* Available at: www.ejiltalk.org/covid-19-china-and-international-aviation-law-a-ticket-to-the-hague/

Joll, J. (2020). *Italy Threatens to Ban Ryanair Over Alleged Covid-19 Violations*. Available at: www.theguardian.com/business/2020/aug/06/italy-threatens-to-ban-ryanair-alleging-covid-19-guideline-violations

Macilree, J. and Duval, D. T. (2020). Aeropolitics in a Post-COVID-19 World. *Journal of Air Transport Management*, 88, pp. 1–4.

Nakatani, K. (1996). Sanctions Related to International Air Transport and International Law. *Korean Journal of Air and Space Law*, 8, pp. 97–131.

Nakatani, K. (1998). Economic Sanctions and Compliance. In: Schoenbaum, T. J., Nakagawa, J. and Reif, L. C. eds., *Trilateral Perspectives on International Legal Issues: From Theory into Practice*. Ardsley: Transnational Publishers, pp. 347–364.

Nakatani, K. (2010). Restrictions on Foreign Investment in the Energy Sector for National Security Reasons: The Case of Japan. In: MacHarg, A. *et al.* eds., *Property and the Law in Energy and National Resources*. Oxford: Oxford University Press, pp. 311–325.

Nakatani, K. (2015). Sovereign Wealth Funds: Problems of International Law between Possessing and Recipient States. *International Review of Law*, 2015(2). Available at: www.qscience.com/content/journals/10.5339/irl.2015.swf.7

Nicaragua v. United States of America (1986). I.C.J. Judgment. I.C.J. Reports, p. 14.

Russia – Measures Concerning Traffic in Transit (Russia – Traffic in Transit) (2019). *WTO Panel Report, WT/DS512/R*. Available at: https://www.wto.org/english/tratop_e/dispu_e/512r_e.pdf

Ruys, T. and Ryngaert, C. (2020). Secondary Sanctions: A Weapon out of Control? The International Legality of, and European Responses to, US Secondary Sanctions. *British Yearbook of International Law*, pp. 35–37. Available at: https://doi.org/10.1093/bybil/braa007

UK v. Japan (S.S. Wimbledon) (1923). P.C.I.J. Judgment. PCIJ Series, A (1), p. 15.

United Nations (1978). Air Service Agreement of 27 March 1946 Between the United States of America and France. *Reports of International Arbitral Awards*, XVIII, pp. 417–493. Available at: https://legal.un.org/riaa/cases/vol_XVIII/417-493.pdf

US. Department of the Treasury (2008). *Policy Principles for Countries Receiving SWF Investment*. Available at: https://home.treasury.gov/system/files/206/052008_appendix.pdf

Zhou, J. (2020). New WTO Ruling on National Security in Qatar-Saudi Arabia Case and Its Impact on South Korea-Japan Dispute. *ASIL Insights*, 24(22). Available at: www.asil.org/insights/volume/24/issue/22/new-wto-ruling-national-security-qatar-saudi-arabia-case-and-its-impact

9 Security Clauses and Evolving Notions of National Security in the WTO in the Age of 'Securitization of Everything'[1]

Tsuyoshi KAWASE

Introduction: Emerging Conflict between Trade and Security

Formerly, trade and security seldom encountered one another, as if they dwelled in parallel universes. For the past 70 years at least, the security clauses of the General Agreement on Tariffs and Trade (GATT)/World Trade Organization (WTO) Agreement (namely, GATT, Art. XXI, the General Agreement on Trade in Services (GATS), Art. IVX *bis*, and the Agreement on Trade-Related Aspects of Intellectual Property Rights (TRIPS Agreement), Art. 73)[2] were very seldom officially invoked, and the number of disputes regarding trade and security was very small. In fact, only in a handful of controversial GATT 1947 cases, including *US – Export Restrictions (Czechoslovakia)* (1949) and *US – Nicaragua Trade* (1986), had parties referred to GATT Article XXI, while the adjudicators in those cases neither actually interpreted nor applied this provision.

Under the WTO, *US – Helms-Burton* (1998) and *Nicaragua – Imports* from Honduras and Colombia (2000) are cases where the parties could have potentially discussed the applicability of security clauses. Again, the panels in those cases never reached any legal conclusions on these provisions. It was not until 2019 that the WTO witnessed its very first panel decision involving a security clause (*Russia – Traffic in Transit*, 2019). Up to that point for the previous 70 years, trade-restrictive measures purportedly necessary on security grounds had only been subject to political and diplomatic controls under national security exceptionalism (Heath, 2020, pp. 1050–1059).

In fact, WTO members were prudent enough to exercise self-restraint in the invocation of security clauses (*Russia – Traffic in Transit*, 2019, Para. 7.81). Members also cautiously applied trade-restrictive measures argued necessary for security within internationally agreed frameworks of non-proliferation export control or in accordance with relevant UN Security Council decisions on sanctions, so as not to abuse such measures. Moreover, members realized that WTO disputes were likely to undermine the legitimacy of the WTO if panels and the Appellate Body were to condemn measures purportedly taken for security purposes, or impair WTO rules if they were too deferential to member discretion to take such measures. Therefore, members have been sensible enough to avoid such disputes over trade and security (Bown, 2020, p. 305; Kazeki, 2016, pp. 41–42). Furthermore, prior to

DOI: 10.4324/9781003193098-9

the early 2000s, China and the former USSR, along with most of its satellite states, had not acceded to the GATT/WTO regime. Accordingly, security measures against such communist/socialist states had seldom been legally challenged in GATT/the WTO (Kawase, 2022, pp. 112–113).

In March 2018, the landscape concerning trade and security dramatically changed. United States (US) President Trump broke the state of equilibrium between trade and security by exercising powers under Section 232 of the 1962 Trade Expansion Act to impose additional duties on steel and aluminum products on 'national security' grounds. This move was followed by the US imposing retaliatory tariffs on a broad range of Chinese products under Section 301 of the Trade Act of 1974 (1975), thus sparking US-China trade hostilities. The underlying cause of Section 301 tariffs was also US security concerns regarding the rivalry between the two superpowers for hegemony. Both the Trump and Biden administrations successively imposed bans and restrictions on transactions with China under the US's national security regime, including the Export Administration Regulation (ERA) (2021), the National Defense Authorization Act (NDAA) (2018), and the International Emergency Economic Authorization Act (IEEPA) (1977).

In July 2019, Japan also suddenly announced its review of export controls over chemical products, including hydrogen fluoride destined for South Korea. Referring to vulnerabilities in South Korea's export control administration and to undisclosed cases of 'improper management' of these substances, Japan claimed that the measure in question amounted to a legitimate implementation of non-proliferation export control (METI, 2019). This measure has been perceived as 'weaponizing trade' rather than a genuine domestic implementation export control based on the control lists of the Wassenaar Arrangement and the Australia Group (Kawase, 2021; Mulgan, 2019).

Around this period, the WTO dispute settlement system coincidentally started experiencing a surge of security-related cases. In addition to the previously mentioned Russian case, the panel in *Saudi Arabia – IPRs* (2020) discussed the applicability of TRIPS Agreement Article 73 in the context of the Qatar Diplomatic Crisis. The US steel and aluminum tariffs and Japan's export control review resulted in two further WTO disputes (*US – Steel and Aluminium Products* (2019), *Japan – Products and Technology* (2020)), where the responding countries will inevitably invoke GATT Article XXI. In March 2022, the European Union (EU), Japan, the US, and other western democratic allies declared to revoke Russia's most favored nation (MFN) status and imposed bans on their trade with Russia due to its aggression against Ukraine. Again, the allies invoked GATT Article XXI to justify such measures (WTO General Council, 2022).

Expansion and Evolution of the Notion of National Security: 'Securitization of Everything'

What underlies the increase in the use of trade-restrictive measures on security grounds seems to be the evolution and expansion of the notion of 'security'. After World War II ended, at the dawn of the United Nations (UN), the primary security concern lied in preventing 'succeeding generations from [experiencing] the scourge of war, which twice in our lifetime has brought untold sorrow to mankind', as enshrined in the preamble of the UN Charter. Subsequently, security concerns regarding a potential nuclear war dominated in the UN for the duration of the Cold War (Nasu, 2021, p. 27). During these periods, the understanding of 'national security' was confined to 'defense against conflicts and territorial infringement' (Slawotsky, 2021, p. 16) and 'tended to be filtered through an adversarial lens' of interstate rivalries (Heath, 2020, p. 1033).

After the Cold War, we witness an expansion of national security agendas and the evolution in the conceptualization of national security. National security becomes amorphous and extensive. As one can see in a couple of handbooks recently published by Oxford University Press, namely, *The Oxford Handbook of International Security* (2018) and *The Oxford Handbook of the International Law of Global Security* (2021), a catalogue of security agendas covers a great variety of non-military and non-interstate-rivalry issues including global warming, pandemics, energy security, human security, terrorism, cybersecurity, and even, more broadly, the economy. As Nasu (2021) describes, our world has been experiencing the 'securitization of everything'.

The most eminent reflection of securitization of everything is observable in National Security Law of the People's Republic of China (2015). This law encompasses eleven considerations pertaining to national security, each of which independently constitutes a security ground: politics, territory, the military, the economy, culture, society, science and technology, information, ecology, resources, and nuclear competence. China has been making an effort to propagate such conception to international law through the conclusion of various economic agreements and enforcement of its 2015 National Security Law (Cai, 2017, pp. 84–87).

Furthermore, these newly securitized considerations are differentiated from military and state-centric national security with respect to threats, and they also differ in other aspects including actors (not only states but also individuals and groups), vulnerabilities (e.g., sectors and products), temporalities (not only emergency but also long-term), and politics surrounding trade and security (Heath, 2020, pp. 1034–1050).

It is worth noting that some of the recent trade and security disputes in the WTO involve very hard-core, traditional national security considerations. The Russia-Ukraine and the Saudi Arabia-Qatar cases are of this type. However, in the remaining cases, the measures in question appear to be motivated by non-military concerns. So, what are the 'security' concerns in these latter cases? Are they justifiably labelled 'security' or are they protectionism under the guise of 'security' concerns? Although I do not provide an extensive account of new security issues in this chapter, I touch upon some of the issues that seem focal to trade and security debates.

Economy

Securitization of economic issues was already observed in the UN General Assembly Resolution 38/188 in the mid 80s, which includes political and economic power, trade deficits, and financial debt (Nasu, 2021, p. 42). In the context of international investment law, several arbitrations in the International Center for Settlement of

Investment Disputes (ICSID) opined that an economic crisis could fall within the ambit of essential security interests, as is discussed later in this chapter.

Recent US-China bilateral trade conflicts arose from fierce competition for global economic hegemony between these parties. Under the existing geo-economic order, which involves competition and rivalry among states aimed at their individual economic gain, inescapably involve zero-sum dynamics. In particular, when the relative size of the economy of a strategic rival grows comparable to that of a dominant power, the latter becomes less supportive of free trade. This is because economic power reinforces military power. This is the very development that we have observed between the US and China for the past couple of decades (Roberts, Moraes and Ferguson, 2019).

This struggle for hegemony drove President Trump to state that 'Economic security is national security'. His National Security Strategy states that a '[s]trong economy protects the American people and sustains American power' and 'a growing and innovative economy allows the United States to maintain the world's most powerful military and protect our homeland' (The White House, 2017, p. 17). For the Trump administration, the promotion of free, fair, and reciprocal economic relationships was one of the policy goals under the 'Promote American Prosperity' pillar, and combating unfair trade practices was among that administration's policy actions towards that end (The White House, 2017, pp. 18–20). This led to the imposition of a series of retaliatory tariffs on imports from China.

Economic dominance is also essential for US national security for several other reasons. For example, so far, the US has successfully taken advantage of the US dollar's status as a key currency in imposing sanctions that prevent a foreign entity from making US dollar-denominated international settlements. If China successfully achieves the digital yuan or de-dollarizes through newly established financial institutions such as the Asian Infrastructure Investment Bank (AIIB) and the New Development Bank (NDB), composed mainly of Brazil, Russia, India, China, and South Africa (BRICS), and its yuan is deemed a replacement of the US dollar, then the US's sanction power would be attenuated, and consequently, its ability to safeguard what it defines as its national interests may be substantially hindered. For the US, sanctions are 'a replacement of war' (Slawotsky, 2021, pp. 22–23, 26–27). In fact, the effectiveness of US dollar sanctions is, to an extent, evident by the measures imposed by the US and its allies on Russia in March 2022 due to Russia's aggression against Ukraine (Meyers, 2022).

The resilience of global supply chains is another example of recent key US security concerns. In accordance with Executive Order 14017 issued by US President Biden (Executive Office of the President, 2021a), the White House issued a report in June 2021 to assess vulnerabilities and consider potential improvements to US global supply chains in four critical and strategic industries, namely, semiconductors, high-capacity batteries, rare-earth elements, and pharmaceuticals. The report regards reliance on specific foreign sources – China, in particular – as risk-heavy for such materials. It recommends that the Biden administration reduces dependence on and diversifies foreign sources, and it incentivizes its own domestic industries to expand their production capacity (The White House, 2021).

The Biden administration also negotiated the Indo-Pacific Economic Framework (IPEF) – specifically, a new regional framework of economic cooperation with US allies – which also reportedly covers supply chain issues (Halpert, 2022).

Regarding semiconductors in particular, in order to strengthen the research and development (R&D) and production capacity of its own domestic industries, the US enacted the CHIPS for America Act (2020) and is currently striving to secure funding for incentive programs under this legislation by introducing two bills, namely, the US-Innovation and Competition Act in the Senate (US. 117th Congress (Senate), 2021), and the America COMPETES Act of 2022 in the House of Representatives (US. 117th Congress (House of Representatives), 2022), which the Congressional conference committee is expected to reconcile. The US has also embarked on international cooperation in this area. It has already concluded bilateral frameworks to this effect with Japan, South Korea, and Taiwan. The EU-US Trade and Technology Council (TTC) also annexes the Statement on Semiconductor Supply Chains to their joint statement of September 2021, where both parties agreed to cooperate in various aspects of semiconductor supply chains (EU-US TTC, 2021).

Japan is also fully aware of the importance of its economic security. The Kishida administration has attempted to enact legislation aimed at Japan's economic security. For this purpose, the administration has established an expert consulting body, which submitted its report to the minister in charge in February 2022. In line with the recommendation in the experts' report, the administration has submitted the Economic Security Promotion Bill (Japan. 208th National Diet, 2022) to the National Diet. This proposed legislation comprises four pillars, namely, security of key infrastructure, supply chain stability, public-private cooperation on cutting-edge technology, and an undisclosed patents system for critical technologies (Nagata, 2022).

Emerging Technologies

The US's Section 301 report and subsequent negotiations with China revealed that US imposition of Section 301 tariffs was originally motivated by concerns regarding fierce rivalry between the two countries for hegemony in emerging and advanced technologies (Chen, Chen and Dondeti, 2020; Kim, 2019). In fact, the 301 report denounces China's state-driven 'theft' and infringement of US intellectual property (USTR, 2018, pp. 10–18). The draft deal presented by the US during the May 2018 bilateral talks also explicitly required China to cease policy intervention aimed at promoting its 'Made in China 2025' industrial policy, which covers extensive sectors including robotics, aerospace, information, and new materials (Caporal, 2018). Concerns regarding R&D and highly advanced technologies in such sectors that have significant and cutting-edge military applications are also shared in the US automobile 232 reports (USDOC, 2019a. p. 8). China's impressive achievements in advanced technologies have caused the US to perceive itself as weaker than China, and, by now, this perception may be borne out in reality (Slawotsky, 2021, p. 25).

Recent US-led international security initiatives have also focused on the importance of such technologies. In September 2021, QUAD, consisting of Australia, Japan, the UK and the US, recognized that '[t]echnology should not be misused or abused for malicious activities such as authoritarian surveillance and oppression, for terrorist purposes, or to disseminate disinformation' (QUAD, 2021). In the same month, AUKUS, comprising Australia, the UK, and the US, also urged member countries to enhance their joint capabilities and interoperability in cyber capabilities, artificial intelligence (AI), and quantum technologies (AUKUS, 2021). The EU-US TTC also agreed to foster stewardship of trustworthy AI and provide scalable, research-based methods to advance trustworthy approaches to AI (discussed previously).

Among such technologies, 5G is of extraordinary concern to the US. The US singled out Huawei – the global leader in successfully providing the most advanced and cost-effective 5G networks – as posing a serious security risk to the US, given Huawei's proximity to the Chinese state including the People's Liberation Army (Slawotsky, 2021, pp. 25–26). 5G technology has been securitized in the US because of its potential for 5G infrastructures to take on an importance that far surpasses that of any other digital infrastructure previously relied upon. The implications of the risk of espionage increase significantly with 5G. The consequences of potential sabotage also increase as 5G becomes the backbone for new functions, including remote control, Internet of Things (IoT), and automated systems (Friis and Lysne, 2021, pp. 1177–1181). The US has now decided to deny equipment authorizations by the US Federal Communications Commission (FCC) for products from its 'Covered List' entities, including Huawei, ZTE, and Dahua, under the Secure Equipment Act of 2021.

AI is another next-generation threat to national security. There is no doubt that applications of AI to the physical realm, such as AI software identifying attack targets by drones, can result in lethal consequences. However, even AI applications associated with genuinely virtual realms can more indirectly produce such consequences. For example, AI-controlled web-based bots could incite acts of terrorism, or even ethnic cleansing or genocide, by spreading fabricated news, hate speech and other instances of agitation on social media. AI-based cyberattacks could paralyze computer networks critical to the provision of vital services including energy, healthcare, telecommunications, etc. (Kunz and Héigeartaigh, 2021, pp. 632–634).

In the Xinjiang Uyghur Autonomous Region, China, AI-based facial recognition systems contribute to the oppression of Uyghurs, which are mostly Muslim communities. The Trump administration regarded the provision of such technologies for the crackdown on dissent in the region as 'contrary to the national security or foreign policy interests of the United States' (USDOC, 2019b, pp. 54002–54003). As we saw in suspected Russian interference in the 2016 US presidential election, AI could influence the selection of a national leader of other sovereign states and even disrupt their democratic processes (Kamarck, 2018). Amid the Russian invasion of Ukraine, President Zelensky's fake video announcing surrender was also enabled by AI. This could be 'the first weaponized use of deepfakes during an armed conflict' (Simonite, 2022), which could affect fundamental decisions of a sovereign state.

Climate Change

Climate change is a further example of what the notion of 'security' may encompass. Global warming jeopardizes human security because it can pose threats to human existence, such as premature death and negative impacts on agricultural productivity, water and food security, and livelihoods. Sea-level rise poses threats to the physical survival of small-island nations such as Tuvalu and the Maldives. Impacts on human security may cause internal and external migration and violent conflicts over fertile land, food, water, and other natural resources, which lead to the sociopolitical instability of nations (Gupta and Bosch, 2021, pp. 551–555). A UN Environment Programme (UNEP) study, focusing on the state of play in the Sahel region countries, describes in detail threats posed by potential impacts of climate change on livelihoods dependent on natural resources such as farming, fishing, and herding and increases in the pressure of environmentally-induced migration due to disasters (e.g., flood, drought, etc.) and the associated loss of livelihoods. The UNEP study also raises concerns about the escalation of tension and potential conflicts over increasingly scarce natural resources, coupled with the availability of small arms and light weapons (UNEP, 2011).

Currently, a global consensus is emerging that climate change will stress the economic, social, and political systems underpinning each state. These risks were recognized as threats to national security by the UN General Assembly in a resolution of 2009 (UNGA, 2009b) that led to a milestone report in that year (UNGA, 2009a). As late as 2017, the UN Security Council finally adopted a resolution, recognizing 'the adverse effects of climate change . . . on the stability . . . including through water scarcity, drought, desertification, land degradation, and food insecurity' (UNSC, 2017).

Previously, the US, under the Obama administration, also cited climate change as a major security issue, as it contributes to increased natural disasters, refugee flows, and conflicts over basic resources such as food and water (The White House, 2015, p. 12). This approach was also taken by the Biden administration. In January 2021, right after taking office, President Biden declared that his administration would put 'the climate crisis at the center of United States foreign policy and *national security*' (emphasis added) (Executive Office of the President, 2021b, p. 7619).

Public Health/Pandemics

From the 1990s to the early 2000s, the HIV/AIDS epidemic broke out in Sub-Saharan Africa. This crisis forced the US to commence 'securitizing' global health issues in its own policy documents and initiate debate in the UN Security Council (Heath, 2021, pp. 589–590; Peterson, 2018, pp. 625–626). The efforts of the US and other western countries successfully legalized global health security in the 2005 revision of the International Health Regulations (IHR) under the World Health Organization (WHO; Heath, 2021, pp. 590–596). Indeed, transboundary public health events, including epidemics and pandemics, can be a threat to national security in its traditional sense. Such events can menace domestic and international stability by weakening military forces, causing significant increases in population mortality, affecting governance, and devastating the economy. Securitization of public health has also been widely observable in the discourse of relevant actors including academics and practitioners (Peterson, 2018, p. 625).

That said, securitization of public health has not enjoyed broad support by international relations scholars because the empirical link between security and public health has been far from evident. For example, the HIV/AIDS epidemic has, in fact, never seriously affected military forces and state survival despite the fear initially shared at the outset of the debate on the securitizing public health (Peterson, 2018, pp. 627–629).

However, the ongoing global pandemic must change skepticism towards the securitization of public health. COVID-19 has been spreading across the globe since late 2019, resulting in the death of at least 6.12 million people globally at the time of this writing (March 29, 2022), according to the WHO. In the US, the number of COVID-19 deaths (namely, 405,399 by January 2021) had already exceeded the country's toll of military fatalities in World War II, according to a tracker maintained by Johns Hopkins University (The Economic Times, 2021), and has now more than doubled to over 970,000 a year after, according to the Centers for Disease Control and Prevention (CDC; March 29, 2022). For the US, COVID-19 amounts to a major catastrophe comparable to a large-scale war as far as mortality is concerned.

The nationwide spread of the virus and consequent lockdown in a national capital and major cities could paralyze the normal function of a government and other public services in a country. Even the national leaders of leading countries including President Trump of the US and Prime Minister Johnson of the UK were infected and forced to temporarily leave office, which are circumstances capable of causing temporary power vacuums and vulnerabilities in national security.

Pandemics and the consequent decline in human activity may also result in stagnant economic activity across production, distribution, or consumption. Lockdowns and other restrictions on outdoor activities have resulted in plant shutdowns in major manufacturing countries such as China and the US and in logistics setbacks (e.g., flight cancellations, railway shutdowns) at logistics hubs such as Egypt and Latvia. All of these have had fragmentary effects on global supply chains (Cai and Luo, 2020, pp. 410–413). Such fragmentation contributed in particular to serious global shortages of essential medical products including medicines, surgical masks and gowns, ventilators, alcohol, hand-wash liquid, etc. in Spring 2020, shortly after the outbreak of COVID-19 (The White House, 2021, pp. 229–230). Such shortages hinder the prevention of COVID-19 infections and the hospitalization of those infected, and they could have lethal consequences as they may result in higher mortality rates.

The COVID-19 pandemic also has more traditional security implications in that it occasionally mobilizes the military. In several countries including Italy, Japan,

South Korea, and the US, military forces have been engaged in various COVID-19 related operations. These include quarantines, nursing of those infected, lockdowns of cities, border control, vaccinations, burial and cremation of infected corpses, etc.

Energy

Energy is also a modern security concern. Energy products such as coal, petroleum, and natural gas exist unevenly across a limited number of resource-rich regions (e.g., petroleum in Gulf countries). For this reason, net importers of energy resources such as Japan must heavily rely on foreign imports, and this reliance exposes such states to geopolitical instability for several reasons. Firstly, such importers might experience coercive pressure from resource-rich/exporting countries that place restrictions on them, including bans on their natural resource exports as a means of economic statecraft. Secondly, energy importers are particularly vulnerable to deterioration in the relationship between resource exporters and transit countries. Lastly, exogenous factors uncontrollable even for exporters (e.g., oil price crashes, domestic instability in an exporting country, etc.) could affect stable energy supplies to importing countries (Morgandi and Viñuales, 2021, pp. 453–454).

The natural gas disputes among Russia, Ukraine and the EU are good examples of the first two previous reasons. Both Ukraine and EU countries heavily depend on Russia for natural gas. Therefore, when Russia imposed an embargo on natural gas to Ukraine on three occasions (namely, in 2006, 2009, and 2014), not only Ukraine but also the EU, which imports gas via pipelines running through Ukraine, was exposed to serious gas shortages. In severe winter conditions in these regions, gas shortages have mortality implications for human populations. Following the 2014 Crimea crisis, even the US began to view Russia's control over the gas trade as the 'weaponization' of natural gas and to perceive EU energy security as an extension of its own national security (Bocse, 2020, pp. 3–4).

In contrast, Russian gas supply and the EU market are interdependent. Due to product characteristics and the pipeline networks extending from Russia to the whole of Europe, Russian natural gas is largely locked in the EU market, and profitable market alternatives to the EU are hardly available for Russia, at least in the short term. Russia is also dependent on the EU for a large portion of its total gas revenue. For these reasons, historically, Russia has not had strong incentives to weaponize its natural gas (Siddi, 2018).

In light of the particularities of natural gas and gas markets, expert views on whether Russia would impose gas export bans diverged before the 2022 Russian invasion of Ukraine. Some experts were of the view that Russia would not be imposing such bans for the time being (e.g., Bradshaw, 2022), while others suggested that Russia might opt for tit-for-tat retaliation if the EU imposed economic sanctions on Russia (e.g., Tocci, 2022). In reality, Russia has not turned its gas tap off yet despite severe economic sanctions imposed by EU countries. Instead, Russia promulgated a presidential decree to demand importing countries to pay for Russian gas supplies in rubles, and it threatened to halt gas flows if buyers did not meet this condition (Rashad, 2022).

The EU, for its part, began to seriously consider the need to mitigate its disproportionate dependence on Russian energy supplies. Shortly after the Russian invasion, the European Commission officially proposed to diversify its sources of natural gas including liquified natural gas (LNG), reduce gas imports from Russia by two-thirds by the end of 2022, and reduce overall natural resource deliveries from Russia to zero by 2030 (European Commission, 2022).

Essential Security Interests under International Economic Law – *Flexible Enough to Address New Security Concerns?*

WTO Security Clauses

The previous section addressed the *status quo* of securitization in the world such that a variety of non-traditional issues are now perceived to be encompassed by security concerns. In this age of securitization of everything, we now encounter a fundamental question: Can current WTO rules adequately accommodate the expanded and evolving notion of security? Put differently, is the term 'essential security interests'[3] under the security clauses including GATT Article XXI broad and flexible enough to cover such issues?

Trade-restrictive measures argued along non-traditional security grounds are not necessarily 'alleged abuses' but may be taken in 'good-faith but novel' (Heath, 2020, p. 1024). That being so, failure to adequately address such concerns could undermine the legitimacy of the WTO. Several authors often qualify the WTO as a 'constitutional' regime and argue that it is expected to be equipped with a mechanism to vertically allocate competence between the WTO and each member and to reconcile free and non-discriminatory trade with other legitimate interests and values, among other things, enshrined within this legal order (Dunoff, 2006). This logic applies to the relationship between trade and security (Kawase, 2022).

The chapeau of Article XXI(b) of GATT contains self-judging language, which reads:

> Nothing in this Agreement shall be construed
>
> ...
>
> (b) to prevent any contracting party from taking any action which *it considers* necessary for the protection of its essential security interests (emphasis added).

For this chapeau, the panel in *Russia – Traffic in Transit* left it to each member to designate certain matters as 'essential security interests' (*Russia – Traffic in Transit*, 2019, Para. 7.131). At the same time, however, the panel imposed some limitation on such discretion (Crivelli and Pinchis-Paulsen, 2021, pp. 590–592), as discussed in the following.

As to the determination of 'essential security interests', first, the panel required that the party invoking this clause to articulate what are its own 'essential security interests' (*Russia – Traffic in Transit*, 2019, Para. 7.131). Second, more importantly, the panel defined the concept of 'essential security interests' under GATT XXI as 'those interests relating to the quintessential functions of the state, namely, the protection of its territory and its population from external threats, and the maintenance of law and public order internally' (*Russia – Traffic in Transit*, 2019, Para. 7.130). Put differently, the panel limited the sphere of interests to 'core State interests – the protection of physical territory, defense of its citizens, and preserving law and order' (Slawotsky, 2021, p. 21), which approximate the traditional understanding of national security in a military and defense sense. Another panel also subsequently agreed with this interpretation (*Saudi Arabia – IPRs*, 2020, Paras. 7.249–7.250).

This narrow reading of security clauses seems contextually proper. Paragraph (b) of each of the security clauses in GATT, GATS, and the TRIPS Agreement consists of a chapeau and three subparagraphs, namely, (i) through (iii). As the panel in *Russia – Traffic in Transit* explained, the interests enumerated in these subparagraphs are 'all defence and military interests, as well as maintenance of law and public order interests' (*Russia – Traffic in Transit*, 2019, Para. 7.76). WTO adjudicators cannot ignore these subparagraphs as providing immediate context in their interpretation of 'essential security interests' in accordance with customary norms concerning treaty interpretation (as reflected in the provisions of the Vienna Convention on the Law of Treaties (VCLA) Art.31). If they refer to these subparagraphs as a relevant context in examining the meaning of 'essential security interest', then it would be natural for adjudicators to consider the interest to be one of a military and defense nature.

This interpretation is also supported by the normative structure of the security clauses, one of which is GATT Article XXI. Judicial review of trade-restrictive measures taken on security grounds enforces a two-step analysis. Primary limitations label 'certain types of purported "security interests", or certain declared "emergencies", as out-of-bounds and thus outside the treaty's security exception'. After this gatekeeping phase, secondary limitations 'investigate the nexus between the security interest and the particular measure adopted' (Heath, 2020, pp. 1064–1065).

This approach was actually taken in *Russia – Traffic in Transit* (Heath, 2020, p. 1064). The primary limitation in GATT Article XXI(b) is to examine whether a measure before a panel comes under any one of the subparagraphs. The subparagraphs 'qualify and limit the exercise of the discretion accorded to members under the chapeau to these circumstances' (*Russia – Traffic in Transit*, 2019, Para. 7.65). Accordingly, a measure must pass the primary limitation before being examined under the second limitation, i.e., the chapeau, and, as a result, be related to 'all defence and military interests, as well as maintenance of law and public order interests'. As far as this measure relates to interests of such nature, the 'essential security interests' in the chapeau, that is, 'interests relating to the quintessential functions of the state', would logically be of a similar nature.

The interpretative approach indicates that WTO security clauses may only in a limited way cover non-traditional security matters discussed in this chapter. Even though a panel's good faith review leaves members ample discretion to determine their own essential security interests under the chapeau, any new security concern must fit into the parameters of one of the subparagraphs.

For example, certain authors are of the view that, so long as the US president perceives climate change as a security issue, his authority under Section 262 could be invoked to impose carbon tariffs at the US border (Meyer and Tucker, 2020). It seems, however, that this measure hardly meets the conditions of the subparagraphs in GATT Article XXI(b). Climate change as an ongoing concern would not necessarily suffice to be an 'emergency' under subparagraph (iii), without concrete international consequences arising from it coupled with a sudden cross-border conflict to be qualified as an 'emergency in international relations' (Van Vaerenbergh and Hazarika, 2020, pp. 423–424). Subparagraphs (i) and (ii) would also be inapplicable, as products and transactions covered by them are too limited to justify the imposition of a carbon tax on a broad range of imports. Thus, since the subparagraphs are closely tied to traditional military/defense and public order interests, the primary limitation considerably impedes GATT Article XXI(b) from addressing new security concerns.

Another commentator pays attention to the panel's interpretation in *Russia – Traffic in Transit* to equate 'emergency' in subparagraph (iii) with a 'crisis', which could 'give future panels broad flexibility to deal with new kinds of threats', including global warming (Heath, 2019). However, we must not disregard the panel's delineation of the interests under the subparagraphs in (b) as 'all defence and military interests, as well as maintenance of law and public order interests'.

Implication of Security Clauses in Investment Treaties: More Simplified, More Flexible?

When looking at other international economic orders, one often encounters security clauses drafted in simpler terms. A good example is Article XI of the 1991 US-Argentina Investment Treaty, which reads as follows:

> This Treaty shall not preclude the application by either Party of measures necessary for the maintenance of public order, the fulfillment of its obligations with respect to the maintenance or restoration of international peace or security, or the protection of its own essential security interests.

There is a striking contrast between this provision and GATT Article XXI(b) in that it lacks the subparagraphs constituting the primary limitation. Although this provision is not drafted in self-judging language (in contrast to the formulation 'which it considers' that appears in GATT Art. XXI(b)), there is no contextual restraint on situations where it is applicable.

Due to this flexibility, several arbitration tribunals having regard to Argentina's economic and financial crisis in 2001 have accepted Argentina's claim that essential security interests under the previous provision encompass those relating to its 2001 crisis. At the same time, these tribunals focused on the gravity of the crisis in question (*CMS Gas Transmission Co. v. Argentina*, 2003, Paras. 359–365;

Continental Casualty Company v. Argentina, 2006, Paras. 175–181; *LG and E Energy Co. et al. v. Argentina*, 2006, Para. 238). One of the tribunals equated the severity of the economic crisis with that of a military invasion (*LG and E Energy Co. et al. v. Argentina*, 2006, Para. 238).

The essence of this opinion is that 'the security exception might be justified in the context of a financial crisis that weakens the State to such an extent that territorial integrity is imperiled' (Slawotsky, 2021, p. 19). That being so, a security clause without a counterpart to the GATT Article XXI(b) subparagraphs would not necessarily mean that their scope is broad enough to cover new security issues.

A further example of a simplified security clause is India-Mauritius BIT Article 11(3), which reads

> The provisions of this Agreement shall not in any way limit the right of either Contracting Party to apply prohibitions or restrictions of any kind or take any other action which is directed to the protection of its essential security interests, or to the protection of public health or the prevention of diseases in pests and animals or plants.

One tribunal under the Permanent Court of Arbitration (PCA), which examined this provision, concluded that the term 'essential security interests' covers only the needs of defense and para-military forces. According to the tribunal, India's public utility services, social needs, and needs for strategic requirements are all beyond the scope of such interests (*CC/Devas Ltd. v. India*, 2016, Paras. 354–356).

Another PCA tribunal interpreted Article 12 of the Germany-India BIT, which is similar to the security clause of the India-Mauritius BIT, and rejected India's essential security interest claim because of India's failure to specify its 'military needs' (*Deutsche Telekom v. India*, 2017, Paras. 243–245). Contrasting security with other public or societal interests, the tribunal emphasized that 'the limits of essential security interests contemplated in Article 12 cannot be stretched beyond their natural meaning'. Furthermore, the tribunal opined that, without distorting the natural meaning of 'essential security interests', a reasonable reading of the security clause would not allow it to extend over other 'societal needs' such as train-tracking, disaster management, tele-education, tele-health, and rural communication (*Deutsche Telekom v. India*, 2017, Paras. 236, 281).

The previous two awards regarding India's BITs clearly exclude non-military or non-defense concerns from essential security interests (Heath, 2020, p. 1044). In particular, the *Deutsche Telekom* tribunal understood the choice of the term 'essential security interests' to be an indication of military or defense concerns. These rulings confirm that exclusion of non-military or non-defense concerns from 'essential security interests' is inherent in the very terms cited, with or without any other contextual limitation imposed by the subparagraphs.

General Exceptions as Interpretative Context of Security Clauses

Moreover, it is notable that both PCA tribunals concerning India's BITs pointed out that non-military public policy concerns are to be addressed by other provisions in those agreements. This reasoning implies that some other relevant provision on public policy exceptions can amount to relevant context for the purposes of treaty interpretation to prevent adjudicators from imparting too broad a meaning to the term 'essential security interests'.

This has significant implications for interpretation of security exceptions in trade and investment agreements given that such agreements are normally equipped with provisions for general exceptions and economic safeguards. According to the interpretative approach mentioned in the previous paragraph, given that GATT, for example, has specific provisions – namely, Articles XIX and XX – Article XXI would not extend to non-military concerns. Indeed, GATT Article XX has always been available to address what are nowadays perceived as new security concerns. For this reason, members have seldom had recourse to Article XXI (Kazeki, 2016, pp. 49–53).

An excellent example is *EU – Energy Sector* (2018), where the panel found energy security to fall within the ambit of the public order exception under GATS Article XIV(a). The panel found, in accordance with the definition of the term 'public order' in footnote 5 of GATS, that energy security belongs to a fundamental interest of society, and foreign control over EU energy supplies could pose a genuine and serious threat to such an interest (*EU – Energy Sector*, 2018, Paras. 7.1142–7.1202). Two WTO cases from the 2010s regarding China's export restrictions also illustrate that GATT Article XX(g) could potentially address scarcity of natural resources including energy products and strategic minerals; however, China's measures in question were found to be disguised protectionism (*China – Raw Materials*, 2011, Paras. 7.418–7.435; *China – Rare Earths*, 2014, Paras. 5.108–5.175). In one of the cases, the measures halting exportation of rare earth minerals were partly motivated by its territorial disputes with Japan (Blaster, 2010).

An excessively broad interpretation of the term 'essential security interests' could potentially nullify GATT Article XX and similar general exception clauses in other trade and investment agreements. Such interpretative approach is inconsistent with the notion of *effet utile* in treaty interpretation. As far as other general exceptions explicitly refer to non-military security concerns, such exceptions should be invoked to justify measures taken for public policy purposes.

That said, GATT Article XXI and similar security clauses are appealing to WTO members and to parties to regional trade agreements (RTAs) and BITs. They may enjoy more leeway under these clauses to justify measures purportedly taken for their own essential security interests. In particular, the necessity test in the chapeau of security clauses is far more relaxed than those in GATT Article XX(a), (b) and (d) (Crivelli and Pinchis-Paulsen, 2021, p. 592; Kawase, 2022, pp. 98–99; *Russia – Traffic in Transit*, 2019, Paras. 7.138–7.145) and even a reasonableness review (Lapa, 2020, p. 25). The panel even opined, 'it is for Russia to determine the 'necessity' of the measures for the protection of its essential security interests' (*Russia – Traffic in Transit*, 2019, Para. 7.146). Thus, the panel avoided providing ammunition to its critics to the effect that it usurped the role of governments in choosing their best tool to protect their own security interests (Voon, 2020, pp. 101–102).

For this reason, pressure exerted by countries to expand the scope of the term 'essential security interests' to cover modern security concerns is likely to persist.

Some Final Thoughts: What Goes Around Comes Around

As we have seen so far, tribunals are cautious about broadening the scope of the term 'essential security interests', while security concepts are expanding in the real world. The negotiating history of GATT Article XXI reveals that the US, a leading drafter of the Havana Charter, then GATT, originally opposed the lax interpretation of the security exception to develop the never-to-be forerunner to the WTO – namely, the International Trade Organization (ITO) – as an institution of trade liberalization and non-discriminatory trade (Pinchis-Paulsen, 2020). The panel in *Russia – Traffic in Transit* (2019, Paras. 7.83–7.99) seems to share this view.

As we have seen so far here, the classic conception of 'essential security interests' is challenged nowadays. It is imperative for the WTO and other international trade and investment forums to update their security concepts and strike a proper balance between 'new' quintessential functions of the state and free and non-discriminatory trade and investment. Otherwise, they could see their constitutional legitimacy waning.

That said, WTO members and parties to other international economic agreements may face dilemmas as to ensuring flexibility in the invocation of security clauses. Even though some of these new security concerns are broadly shared among communities internationally, the line between legitimate and illegitimate remains hard to draw. For instance, as discussed early on, China has developed a broad notion of national security in its 2015 National Security Law. Relinquishing the traditional abuse-averse interpretation of security clauses could endow China with nearly unfettered discretion to invoke security clauses in accordance with its own notions of national security.

This concern is serious and imminent in the context of China's accession to the Comprehensive and Progressive Agreement for Trans-Pacific Partnership (CPTPP). China officially applied for accession to CPTPP in September 2021. Although China is likely to face difficulties in adjusting its authoritarian state-capitalist regime to CPTPP rules (Schott, 2021), it seems to be under the impression that it can overcome such discrepancies between CPTPP rules and its state-centric system with the lax application of CPTPP Article 29.2 (Gao and Zhou, 2021). Indeed, China's participation in the CPTPP is indispensable for the future development of the Free Trade Area of the Asia-Pacific (FTAAP). If China does not hesitate to arbitrarily invoke the security clause, then it will seriously undermine any meaningful economic integration in the Asia-Pacific region.

Notes

1 The facts and cases presented in this chapter are as of April 22, 2022.

2 The author is fully aware that while Article XXI of the GATT and its counterparts in GATS and TRIPS Agreement are all officially titled and also described in some academic writings as security exceptions (e.g., Heath, 2020; Lapa, 2020, p. 11; Voon, 2020, p. 100), *Russia – Traffic in Transit* (2019) deliberately blurred the legal nature of these clauses (*exemption* or *exception*, in particular) (Kawase, 2022, pp. 103–105). This chapter refers to these provisions, for the most part, as 'the security clause(s)' to avoid prejudging the question as to their exact nature.

3 Paragraphs (a) and (c) in each of the security clauses are beyond the scope of the present analysis. Paragraph (a) only covers disclosure of information. Paragraph (c) is applicable only to measures in pursuance of a WTO member's obligation under Chapter VII of the UN Charter, where national security in a traditional sense is at stake. These paragraphs, therefore, neither involve the recent increase of security measures with trade impacts nor the expansion of the notion of 'security'.

References

All subsequent websites were last visited on 22 April 2022.

AUKUS (2021). *Joint Leaders Statement on AUKUS*. Available at: www.whitehouse.gov/briefing-room/statements-releases/2021/09/15/joint-leaders-statement-on-aukus/

Blaster, K. (2010). Amid Tension, China Blocks Vital Exports to Japan. *New York Times*, 22 September. Available at: www.nytimes.com/2010/09/23/business/global/23rare.html

Bocse, A. M. (2020). From the United States with Shale Gas: Ukraine, Energy Securitization, and the Reshaping of Transatlantic Energy Relations. *Energy Research & Social Science*, 69, Art. 101553.

Bown, C. P. (2020). Export Controls: America's Other National Security Threat. *Duke Journal of Comparative and International Law*, 30(2), pp. 283–308.

Bradshaw, M. (2022). *Ukraine: Russia Probably Won't Turn off the Gas, but the Problem Won't Go Away Any Time Soon*. Available at: https://theconversation.com/ukraine-russia-probably-wont-turn-off-the-gas-but-the-problem-wont-go-away-any-time-soon-176817

Cai, C. (2017). Enforcing a New National Security: China's National Security Law and International Law. *Journal of East Asia and International Law*, 10(1), pp. 65–89.

Cai, M. and Luo, J. (2020). Influence of COVID-19 on Manufacturing Industry and Corresponding Countermeasures from Supply Chain Perspective. *Journal of Shanghai Jiao Tong University (Science)*, 25(4), pp. 409–416.

Caporal, J. (2018). China Rejects New Slate of U.S. Trade Demands as Tariffs Loom. *Inside US Trade*, p. 15.

CC/Devas Ltd. v. India (2016). PCA Case No. 2013–09, Jurisdiction and Merits.

Chen, A. W., Chen, J. and Dondeti, V. R. (2020). The US-China Trade War: Dominance of Trade or Technology? *Applied Economics Letters*, 27(11), pp. 904–909.

China – Measures Related to the Exportation of Rare Earths, Tungsten, and Molybdenum (China – Rare Earths) (2014). WTO Appellate Body Report, WT/DS431/AB/R, WT/DS432/AB/R, WT/DS433/AB/R.

China – Measures Related to the Exportation of Various Raw Materials (China – Raw Materials) (2011). WTO Panel Report, WT/DS394/R, WT/DS395/R, WT/DS398/R.

CMS Gas Transmission Co. v. Argentina (2003). ICSID Case No. ARB/01/8, Decision on Jurisdiction.

Continental Casualty Company v. Argentina (2006). ICSID Case No. ARB/03/9, Decision on Jurisdiction.

Creating Helpful Incentives to Produce Semiconductors (CHIPS) for America Act (2020) (US). Available at: www.congress.gov/116/plaws/publ283/PLAW-116publ283.pdf

Crivelli, P. and Pinchis-Paulsen, M. (2021). Separating the Political from the Economic: The Russia – Traffic in Transit Panel Report. *World Trade Review*, 20(4), pp. 582–605.

Deutsche Telekom v. India (2017). PCA Case No. 2014–10, Interim.

Dunoff, J. L. (2006). Constitutional Conceits: The WTO's 'Constitution' and the Discipline of International Law. *European Journal of International Law*, 17(3), pp. 647–675.

The Economic Times (2021). US Covid-19 Deaths Exceed WWII Military Toll: Tracker. *The Economic Times*, 21 January. Available at: https://economictimes.indiatimes.com/news/international/world-news/us-covid-19-deaths-exceed-wwii-military-toll-tracker/articleshow/80380461.cms?utm_source=contentofinterest&utm_medium=text&utm_campaign=cppst

EU-US Trade and Technology Council (TTC) (2021). *Inaugural Joint Statement The EU-US TTC the Joint Statement adopted at Pittsburgh in September 2021*. Available at: https://ec.europa.eu/commission/presscorner/detail/en/STATEMENT_21_4951

European Commission (2022). *REPowerEU: Joint European Action for More Affordable, Secure and Sustainable Energy*. Available at: https://eur-lex.europa.eu/legal-content/EN/TXT/?uri=COM%3A2022%3A108%3AFIN

European Union and Its Member States – Certain Measures Relating to the Energy Sector (EU – Energy Sector) (2018). WTO Panel Report, WT/DS476/R.

Executive Office of the President (2021a). America's Supply Chains, Executive Order 14017 of February 24, 2021. *Federal Register*, 86(38), pp. 11849–11854.

Executive Office of the President (2021b). Tackling the Climate Crisis at Home and Abroad, Executive Order 14008 of January 27, 2021. *Federal Register*, 86(19), pp. 7619–7633.

Export Administration Regulation (ERA) (2021) (US). Available at: www.govinfo.gov/content/pkg/CFR-2021-title15-vol2/xml/CFR-2021-title15-vol2-subtitleB-chapVII-subchapC.xml

Friis, K. and Lysne, O. (2021). Huawei, 5G and Security: Technological Limitations and Political Responses. *Development and Change*, 52(5), pp. 1174–1195.

Gao, H. and Zhou, W. (2021). China's Entry to CPTPP Trade Pact Is Closer than You Think. *Nikkei Asia*. Available at: https://asia.nikkei.com/Opinion/China-s-entry-to-CPTPP-trade-pact-is-closer-than-you-think

Gupta, J. and Bosch, H. (2021). Climate Change and Security. In: Geiß, R. and Melzer, N. eds., *The Oxford Handbook of the International Law of Global Security*. New York: Cambridge University Press, pp. 548–565.

Halpert, M. (2022). Bianchi: IPEF to Include 'High-Ambition', Binding Trade Commitments. *Inside US Trade*, pp. 1, 4–5.

Heath, J. B. (2019). *Trade, Security and Stewardship (Part IV): A Variable Framework for Security Governance*. Available at: https://ielp.worldtradelaw.net/2019/05/guest-post-trade-security-and-stewardship-part-iv-a-variable-framework-for-security-governance.html

Heath, J. B. (2020). The New National Security Challenge to the Economic Order. *Yale Law Journal*, 129(4), pp. 1020–1098.

Heath, J. B. (2021). Pandemics and Other Health Emergencies. In: Geiß, R. and Melzer, N. eds., *The Oxford Handbook of the International Law of Global Security*. New York: Cambridge University Press, pp. 585–605.

The International Emergency Economic Authorization Act (IEEPA) (1977) (US). Available at: https://uscode.house.gov/view.xhtml?path=/prelim@title50/chapter35&edition=prelim

Japan. 208th National Diet (2022). *Keizai Anzenhosho Suishin Hoan* [Economic Security Promotion Bill]. Available at: www.sangiin.go.jp/japanese/joho1/kousei/gian/208/pdf/t0802080372080.pdf

Japan – Measures Related to the Exportation of Products and Technology to Korea (Japan – Products and Technology (Korea)) (2020). WT/DS590 (WTO panel proceeding continuing). Available at: www.wto.org/english/tratop_e/dispu_e/cases_e/ds590_e.htm

Japan. Ministry of Economy. Trade and Industry (METI) (2019). *Update of METI's Licensing Policies and Procedures on Exports of Controlled Items to the Republic of Korea*. Available at: www.meti.go.jp/english/press/2019/0701_001.html

The John S. McCain National Defense Authorization Act (NDAA) for Fiscal Year 2019 (2018) (US). Available at: www.congress.gov/115/plaws/publ232/PLAW-115publ232.pdf

Kamarck, E. (2018). *Malevolent Soft Power, AI, and the Threat to Democracy*. Available at: www.brookings.edu/research/malevolent-soft-power-ai-and-the-threat-to-democracy/

Kawase, T. (2021). *Potential Conflict Between the WTO System and the Security Trade Control System in the Japan-South Korea Dispute*. Available at: www.jiia.or.jp/en/column/2021/04/13-research-reports-potential-conflict-between-the-wto-system-and-the-security-trade-control-system-in.html

Kawase, T. (2022). Trade, Security, and Constitutionalism at Crossroads: Achieving the Right Balance Between the Regulatory Power of WTO and National Sovereignty. *Japanese Yearbook of International Law*, 64, pp. 76–116.

Kazeki, J. (2016). Bōeki to Anzen-hoshō: Jitsumuka kara Mita Hō no Shihai [Trade and Security: Rule of Law from a Perspective of a Practitioner]. *Kokusai-hō Kenkyū [Tokyo Review of International Law]*, 4, pp. 39–62.

Kim, M. H. (2019). A Real Driver of US – China Trade Conflict: The Sino – US Competition for Global Hegemony and Its Implications for the Future. *International Trade, Politics and Development*, 3(1), pp. 30–40.

Kunz, M. and Héigeartaigh, S. Ó. (2021). Artificial Intelligence and Robotization. In: Geiß, R. and Melzer, N. eds., *The Oxford Handbook of the International Law of Global Security*. New York: Oxford University Press, pp. 624–640.

Lapa, V. (2020). The WTO Panel Report in Russia – Traffic in Transit: Cutting the Gordian Knot of the GATT Security Exception? *QIL, Zoom-in*, 69, pp. 5–27.

LG and E Energy Co. et al. v. Argentina (2006). ICSID Case No. ARB/02/1, Decision on liability.

Meyer, T. and Tucker, T. N. (2020). *Trump's Trade Strategy Points the Way to a US Carbon Tariff*. Available at: www.lawfareblog.com/trumps-trade-strategy-points-way-us-carbon-tariff

Meyers, Z. (2022). *Russia May Ditch the Dollar – But It Needs the Euro*. Centre for European Reform. Available at: www.cer.eu/sites/default/files/insight_ZM_russia_dollar_euro_29.3.22.pdf

Morgandi, T. and Viñuales, J. E. (2021). Energy Security in International Law. In: Geiß, R. and Melzer, N. eds., *The Oxford Handbook of the International Law of Global Security*. New York: Oxford University Press, pp. 450–467.

Mulgan, A. G. (2019). *Is Japan Weaponising Trade Against South Korea?* Available at: www.eastasiaforum.org/2019/11/22/is-japan-weaponising-trade-against-south-korea/print/

Nagata, K. (2022). New Bill Looks to Beef up Japan's Economic Security, But Firms Are Wary. *The Japan Times*. Available at: https://advance.lexis.com/api/document?collection=news&id=urn:contentItem:64SJ-KCY1-JB8B-S044-00000-00&context=1516831

Nasu, H. (2021). The Global Security Agenda: Securitization of Everything? In: Geiß, R. and Melzer, N. eds., *The Oxford Handbook of the International Law of Global Security*. New York: Oxford University Press, pp. 37–53.

National Security Law of the People's Republic of China (2015) (CN). Available at: http://lawinfochina.com/display.aspx?id=19663&lib=law&EncodingName=big5

Nicaragua – Measures Affecting Imports from Honduras and Colombia (Nicaragua – Imports from Honduras and Colombia) (2000). WT/DS188 (No WTO panel composed); WT/DS201 (No WTO panel established). Available at: www.wto.org/english/tratop_e/dispu_e/cases_e/ds188_e.htm, and https://www.wto.org/english/tratop_e/dispu_e/cases_e/ds201_e.htm

Office of the United States Trade Representative (USTR) (2018). *Findings of the Investigation into China's Acts, Policies, and Practices Related to Technology Transfer, Intellectual Property, and Innovation Under Section 301 of the Trade Act of 1974*. Available at: https://ustr.gov/sites/default/files/Section%20301%20FINAL.PDF

Peterson, S. (2018). Global Health and Security: Reassessing the Links. In: Gheciu, A. and Wohlforth, W. C. eds., *The Oxford Handbook of International Security*. New York: Oxford University Press, pp. 624–627.
Pinchis-Paulsen, M. (2020). Trade Multilateralism and US National Security: The Making of the GATT Security Exceptions. *Michigan Journal of International Law*, 41(1), pp. 109–193.
QUAD (2021). *QUAD Principles on Technology Design, Development, Governance, and Use*. Available at: www.whitehouse.gov/briefing-room/statements-releases/2021/09/24/quad-principles-on-technology-design-development-governance-and-use/
Rashad, M. (2022). *Europe Signals Unity Against Russian Gas Payment Demands*. Available at: www.reuters.com/business/energy/gas-still-flows-russia-europe-buyers-navigate-putins-rouble-order-2022–04–01/
Roberts, A., Moraes, H. C. and Ferguson, V. (2019). Toward a Geoeconomic Order in International Trade and Investment. *Journal of International Economic Law*, 22(4), pp. 655–676.
Russia – Measures Concerning Traffic in Transit (Russia – Traffic in Transit) (2019). WTO Panel Report, WT/DS512/R.
Saudi Arabia – Measures Concerning the Protection of Intellectual Property Rights (Saudi Arabia – IPRs) (2020). WTO Panel Report, WT/DS567/R.
Schott, J. J. (2021). *China's CPTPP Bid Puts Biden on the Spot*. Available at: www.piie.com/blogs/trade-and-investment-policy-watch/chinas-cptpp-bid-puts-biden-spot
The Secure Equipment Act of 2021 (2021) (US). Available at: www.congress.gov/117/plaws/publ55/PLAW-117publ55.pdf
Siddi, M. (2018). *Identities and Vulnerabilities: The Ukraine Crisis and the Securitisation of the EU-Russia Gas Trade*. In: Szulecki, K. ed., *Energy Security in Europe: Divergent Perceptions and Policy Challenges*. Cham: Palgrave Macmillan, pp. 251–273.
Simonite, T. (2022). *A Zelensky Deepfake Was Quickly Defeated. The Next One Might Not Be*. Available at: www.wired.com/story/zelensky-deepfake-facebook-twitter-playbook/
Slawotsky, J. (2021). The Fusion of Ideology, Technology and Economic Power: Implications of the Emerging New United States National Security Conceptualization. *Chinese Journal of International Law*, 20(1), pp. 3–62.
Tocci, N. (2022). *Europe Is Ready to Pay the Cost of Russia Sanctions*. Available at: www.politico.eu/article/europe-energy-russia-ukraine-crisis-eu-gas-prices/#
Trade Act of 1974 (1975) (US). Available at: https://uscode.house.gov/view.xhtml?path=/prelim@title19/chapter12&edition=prelim
Trade Expansion Act 1962 (1962) (US). Available at: https://uscode.house.gov/view.xhtml?path=/prelim@title19/chapter7&edition=prelim
United Nations Environment Programme (UNEP) (2011). *Livelihood Security Climate Change, Migration and Conflict in the Sahel*. Available at: https://wedocs.unep.org/20.500.11822/8032
United Nations General Assembly (UNGA) (2009a). *Climate Change and Its Possible Security Implications: Report of the Secretary-Genera*. A/64/350. Available at: www.securitycouncilreport.org/atf/cf/%7B65BFCF9B-6D27-4E9C-8CD3-CF6E4FF96FF9%7D/sg%20report%202009.pdf
United Nations General Assembly (UNGA) (2009b). *Resolution 63/281: Climate Change and Its Possible Security Implications*. A/RES/63/281. Available at: www.securitycouncilreport.org/atf/cf/%7B65BFCF9B-6D27-4E9C-8CD3-CF6E4FF96FF9%7D/res%2063%20281.pdf

United Nations Security Council (UNSC) (2017). *Resolution 2349 (2017) Adopted by the Security Council at Its 7911th Meeting, on 31 March 2017*. S/RES/2349. Available at: www.securitycouncilreport.org/atf/cf/%7B65BFCF9B-6D27-4E9C-8CD3-CF6E4FF96FF9%7D/S_RES_2349.pdf

United States – Certain Measures on Steel and Aluminium Products (US – Steel and Aluminium Products) (2019). DS544, DS547, DS552, DS554, DS556 and DS564 (WTO panel proceeding), DS548, DS550, DS551 (WTO case withdrawn). Available at: www.wto.org/english/tratop_e/dispu_e/dispu_status_e.htm

United States Department of Commerce (USDOC) (2019a). *The Effect of Imports of Automobiles and Automobile Parts on the National Security: An Investigation Conducted Under Section 232 of the Trade Expansion Act of 1962, As Amended*. Available at: www.bis.doc.gov/index.php/documents/section-232-investigations/2774-redacted-autos-232-final-and-appendix-a-july-2021/file

United States Department of Commerce (USDOC) (2019b). Addition of Certain Entities to the Entity List. *Federal Register*, 84(196), pp. 54002–54009.

United States Export Restrictions (US – Export Restrictions (Czechoslovakia)) (1949). GATT Contracting Parties Decision, Article XXI of GATT, GATT/CP.3/SR22.

United States – The Cuban Liberty and Democratic Solidarity Act (US – Helms Burton) (1998). WT/DS38 (Authority of panel lapsed). Available at: www.wto.org/english/tratop_e/dispu_e/cases_e/ds38_e.htm

United States – Trade Measures Affecting Nicaragua (US – Nicaragua Trade) (1986). GATT Panel Report, L/6053.

US. 117th Congress (House of Representatives) (2022). *United States Innovation and Competition (America COMPETES) Act of 2021*, H.R.4521. Available at: www.congress.gov/117/bills/hr4521/BILLS-117hr4521eas.pdf

US. 117th Congress (Senate) (2021). *United States Innovation and Competition Act of 2021*, S.1260. Available at: www.congress.gov/117/bills/s1260/BILLS-117s1260es.pdf

Van Vaerenbergh, P. and Hazarika, A. (2020). Climate Change as a Security Risk: Too Hot to Handle? *Journal of World Trade*, 54(3), pp. 417–438.

Voon, T. (2020). Russia – Measures Concerning Traffic in Transit. *American Journal of International Law*, 114(1), pp. 96–103.

White House (2015). *National Security Strategy 2015*. Available at: https://obamawhitehouse.archives.gov/sites/default/files/docs/2015_national_security_strategy_2.pdf

White House (2017). *National Security Strategy 2017*. Available at: https://trumpwhitehouse.archives.gov/wp-content/uploads/2017/12/NSS-Final-12-18-2017–0905.pdf

White House (2021). *Building Resilient Supply Chains, Revitalizing American Manufacturing, and Fostering Broad-Based Growth: 100-Day Reviews Under Executive Order 14017*. Available at: www.whitehouse.gov/wp-content/uploads/2021/06/100-day-supply-chain-review-report.pdf

WTO. General Council (2022). *Joint Statement on Aggression by the Russian Federation Against Ukraine with the Support of Belarus*. WT/GC/244. Available at: https://docs.wto.org/dol2fe/Pages/SS/directdoc.aspx?filename=q:/WT/GC/244.pdf

10 Security Exceptions in International Investment Agreements

The Case of Japan

Tomoko ISHIKAWA

Introduction

The world has seen a rising backlash against economic globalization. In the field of international investment law, this backlash has manifested primarily as a result of a global trend of tightening regulations dealing with inward flow of foreign direct investment (FDI). Although recognition of the need to restrict FDI on the ground of public order and security has a long history (OECD, 2021, Art. 3), in the last few decades, investment liberalisation and promotion was actively pursued in many countries. However, since 2016, major economies, including the United States, Germany, France, the United Kingdom, and the European Union have started to turn the tide towards stricter FDI regulations. The coronavirus disease 2019 (COVID-19) pandemic, in particular the economic situations and concerns over industries that are critical to infrastructure, technology, or input, and especially the health-related industries that it brought about, accelerated this trend (OECD, 2020a). In all cases of amendment towards stricter FDI regulations mentioned previously, the policy shift is typically justified by the need to safeguard essential security interests. For example, Regulation (EU) 2019/452 (2019) identifies the factors that may be considered when determining whether a particular investment is likely to affect security or public order, including the potential effects of proposed FDI on critical infrastructure, critical technologies and dual-use items, and the supply of critical inputs (Grieger, 2019).

Amendments of Japanese Foreign Exchange and Foreign Trade Act and the New Land-use restriction Bills

Japan is no exception to this trend. Until quite recently, the history of the Japanese FDI screening mechanism was one of gradual investment liberalisation. In particular, the Foreign Exchange and Foreign Trade Control Law (which was subsequently renamed to the Foreign Exchange and Foreign Trade Act (FEFTA, 1949)), which laid down the cross-sectoral regulations on inward FDI in Japan, was amended in 1991 to replace the principle of advance screening with the principle of post-reporting, subjecting only specific business sectors and activities (collectively 'businesses') alone to the obligation of advance notification and

DOI: 10.4324/9781003193098-10

screening by the relevant ministers (Art. 27(1)) (Watai, 2018). However, a fundamental reform towards tightening inward FDI screening regulations took place in 2017 and 2019 through the amendment of FEFTA, relevant governmental orders, and public notices. The 2019 amendment, which entered into force on 8 May 2020, introduced a system for exemption from the requirement of prior notification under certain conditions (Ministry of Finance, 2019) yet at the same time, dramatically expanded the concept of inward FDI that is subject to notification in various ways, in particular by reducing the threshold for acquiring shares of listed companies subject to prior notification from 10% to 1%. Under the 2019 amendment, foreign investments in 'designated business sectors' are subject to tightened regulations. The COVID-19 pandemic brought about the expansion of the scope of 'core designated business sectors', which are subject to the most extensive regulations under the amended FEFTA, to include manufacturing industries for pharmaceuticals and highly controlled medical devices. According to the list issued by the Japanese Ministry of Finance (last amended in November 2021), the majority of Japanese listed companies fall within the designated business sectors.

Beyond the FEFTA framework, the National Diet of Japan in June 2021 passed a bill that introduced a restriction on the use of land near defence facilities and other areas with national security implications ('the land-use restriction bill').[1] The land-use restriction bill accords to Japanese government the power to investigate and regulate the purchase and use of land and buildings that are in close proximity to these areas ('watch zones').

Tension with Investment Protection Obligations

Japan's policy shift towards tightening FDI regulations raises a question of conformity between these regulations and the international obligations undertaken by Japan in its international investment agreements (IIAs). Although the FDI screening processes primarily occur at the pre-investment stage, insofar as there is investment of the relevant foreign investor that is affected by the FDI regulations, a conflict with investment protection obligations may arise, for example, see *Deutsche Telekom v. India* (2017, Paras. 174–182). In this regard, it should be noted that the land-use restriction bill sets out restrictions on transactions of the existing lands in 'watch zones' (Art. 13) and expropriation (Arts. 19 to 28) under certain conditions.

When the relevant restrictive measures taken on the grounds of the protection of security interests are challenged as inconsistent with the investment protection obligations, the government would seek to rely on a security exception clause, when available, under the relevant IIA. The state may also invoke the customary international law defence of necessity, yet in most cases, a security exception clause would be a preferred defence. This is because the customary law defence of necessity exempts the state from responsibility only after a violation of international law is established (*CMS v. Argentina*, 2007, Para. 129), whereas a security exception clause functions to prevent the occurrence of a violation (*CC/Devas v.*

India, 2016a, Paras. 253–254), by carving out measures from the scope of the international obligation (Burke-White and Staden, 2007).

This underscores the importance of security exception clauses as a means to address the conflict between the intensifying FDI regulations for security reasons, on the one hand, and investment protection obligations under IIAs, on the other hand. As discussed later, investment arbitration case law reveals that differences in the wording of security exception clauses have played a crucial role in the tribunals' interpretation and application of these clauses. One of the most significant textual differences among the existing security exception clauses is the existence or absence of 'self-judging' wording, by which a state reserves the right to be free or derogate from obligations under the instrument where 'it considers' that certain security and public order issues exist (Briese and Schill, 2010).

Turning to Japanese IIAs, security exception clauses are available in the majority (48 out of 58) of them. Notably, most (47 out of 48) Japanese IIAs that provide security exception clauses, including the Energy Charter Treaty (ECT, 1994), adopt 'self-judging' wording. With this background, the next section discusses the security exception clause of the ECT (Art. 24(3)) because its *traveaux preparatoire* provide insights into the relevant considerations behind the drafting of security exception clauses.

Security Exception Clauses in Japanese IIAs: Article 24(3) of the ECT

Article 24(3) of the ECT reads

> (3) The provisions of this Treaty other than those referred to in paragraph (1) shall not be construed to prevent any Contracting Party from taking any measure which it considers necessary:
>
> (a) for the protection of its essential security interests including those
>
> (i) relating to the supply of Energy Materials and Products to a military establishment; or
> (ii) taken in time of war, armed conflict or other emergency in international relations;
>
> (b) relating to the implementation of national policies respecting the non-proliferation of nuclear weapons or other nuclear explosive devices or needed to fulfil its obligations under the Treaty on the Non-Proliferation of Nuclear Weapons, the Nuclear Suppliers Guidelines, and other international nuclear non-proliferation obligations or understandings; or
> (c) for the maintenance of public order. Such measure shall not constitute a disguised restriction on Transit.

The drafting history of this provision reveals that the first draft text of the security exception (then Art. 18) did not include 'self-judging' wording. The Draft

Basic Protocol (European Energy Charter Conference Secretariat, 1991a) was also limited to exceptions to 'prohibitions or restrictions on imports, exports or goods in transit'.

However, the 'self-judging' wording ('which it considers necessary') was quickly adopted by the draft presented one month after. Furthermore, the limitation on scope was abandoned ('taking any action') in this draft. The Draft Basic Agreement 4 (European Energy Charter Conference Secretariat, 1991b) was based on suggestions by the US, Canada, Austria, Greece, Australia, and Japan. In all the subsequent drafts, the concept of 'essential defence interests', which was later substituted from Draft Basic Agreement 15 (European Energy Charter Conference Secretariat, 1992b) – under suggestions from the US and European Commission – with 'essential security interests', was consistently accompanied by 'self-judging' wording (European Energy Charter Conference Secretariat, 1992a).

In the Draft Basic Agreement 15 (European Energy Charter Conference Secretariat, 1992b), the security exception clause that was modelled on GATT XXI was introduced for the first time by Canada. It then became the basis of subsequent negotiations (European Energy Charter Conference Secretariat, 1993). These textual developments might reflect the negotiating parties' recognition, which was confirmed in one of the earlier meetings, that 'there is every interest in keeping the nature and detail of the obligations created under the Charter as close as possible to those in the GATT system' (Note from the Secretariat, 'Relationship to GATT – main issues'). Nevertheless, important textual differences exist between Article 24(3) of the ECT and GATT XXI.

One of the differences is that, although GATT XXI(b) provides an exhaustive list of the circumstances that condition 'essential security interests', Article 24(3) of the ECT makes the list non-exhaustive by adding the term 'including'. A hint for the adoption of this non-exhaustive list approach was found in the negotiating history through the suggestion of the US and Japan 'to delete these subparagraphs [(i) and (ii)], since essential security interests should not be limited in this way' (European Energy Charter Conference Secretariat, 1993).

The implication of this addition is not small in the light of the approach of the WTO panel in *Russia – Traffic in Transit* (2019). In this case, the panel held that the exhaustive list in GATT XXI(b) means that the determination of the circumstances in each subparagraph is subject to objective judicial review, and this is true regardless of whether the self-judging wording of GATT XXI(b) extended to the question of whether a measure is necessary to protect essential security interests (Para. 7.101). In *Saudi Arabia – IPRs* (2020), this approach was endorsed by the disputing parties and by the panel in interpreting Article 73(b)(iii) of the TRIPS Agreement, which mirrors Article XXI(b)(iii) (Paras. 7.230–7.231). By contrast, adding the term 'including', as is the case with Article 24(3) of the ECT, would arguably subject all circumstances to 'self-judging' wording (Nolan and Sourgens, 2011). This may make the panel's 'objective judicial review' approach for the exhaustive list inapplicable.

The drafting history of Article 24(3) of the ECT therefore suggests that, despite the initial absence in the first draft text, the final draft text emphasised the 'self-judging' nature of security exception clauses by broadening the scope of essential security interests beyond that under GATT XXI(b). On this consideration, the following sections provide a brief analysis of the effects of 'self-judging' security exception clauses compared with non-self-judging security exception clauses.

Interpretation(s) of Security Exception Clauses

Non-Self-judging Security Exception Clauses

As of the date of writing, the security exception clauses of three IIAs, that is, the 1991 Argentina – United States of America BIT, the 1998 India – Mauritius BIT, and the 1995 Germany – India BIT, have been interpreted by the investment arbitration tribunals. None of these IIAs adopts 'self-judging' wording for security exception clauses. The 1998 India – Mauritius BIT and the 1995 Germany – India BIT were discussed in the recent and related *CC Devas* (2016a) case and *Deutsche Telekom* (2017) case. These cases arose out of a cancellation of an agreement for the lease of S-band electromagnetic spectrum on two satellites between a state-owned corporation, Devas Multimedia, which is Deutsche Telekom's indirect subsidiary and in which CC Devas and other claimants had shares, and India. India invoked the security exception clauses (India – Mauritius BIT 1998, Art. 11(3); India – Germany BIT 1995, Art. 12), arguing that the cancellation was based on the strategic need for spectrum capacity, including the growing demands from the military forces.

As noted, both Article 11(3) of the India – Mauritius BIT (1998) and Article 12 of the India – Germany BIT (1995) lacked 'self-judging' wording. This led both tribunals (*CC/Devas v. India*, 2016a, Para. 219) (*Deutsche Telekom v. India*, 2017, Para. 231) to the same conclusion that without clear indications in the text of IIAs, it is impossible to infer that the exception clause is 'self-judging'. They reached this conclusion by referring to the earlier International Court of Justice (ICJ) cases of *Nicaragua v. United States of America* (1984, Para. 282), *Islamic Republic of Iran v. United States of America* (2003, Para. 43), and *Hungary v. Slovakia* (1997, Para. 51). They also relied on investment arbitration cases in which tribunals discussed Article XI of the US-Argentina BIT: *CMS Gas Transmission Co. v. Argentina* (2005, Paras. 370, 373), *Enron Corp. and Ponderosa Assets, L.P. v. Argentina* (2007, Paras. 331–332), and *El Paso Energy International Co. v. Argentina* (2011, Para. 561). This reasoning of Article 12 of the India-Germany BIT (1995) by the *Deutsche Telekom* tribunal was later confirmed by the judgment of the Swiss Federal Supreme Court in *Republique de l'Inde v. AG* (2018, Para. 3.2.3.3.4). Therefore, it is concluded that under the current jurisprudence, a non 'self-judging' security exception defence in IIAs is subject to an objective review of all the elements of the clause.

Nevertheless, there was a major textual difference between Article 11(3) of the India-Mauritius BIT (1998) and Article 12 of the India – Germany BIT (1995): the former employs the expression 'any other action which is <u>directed to</u> the protection of its essential security interests' (emphasis added), whereas the latter reads 'prohibitions or restrictions to the extent necessary for the protection of its essential security interests' (emphasis added), thereby incorporating the necessity requirement as a condition to invoke security exception clauses. In the *Devas* case (2016a), the tribunal noted the absence of the word 'necessity' in Article 11(3) of the India-Mauritius BIT (1998) to reach the following conclusion:

> While, in the present case, the Respondent does not have to demonstrate necessity in the sense that the measure adopted was the only one it could resort to in the circumstances, it still has to establish that the measure related to its essential security interests (Para. 238).

The tribunal emphasised the function of the term 'essential' as a limitation (Para. 243).

The majority then recognised the 'wide measure of deference' to the determination by the Respondent state, stating that

> An arbitral tribunal may not sit in judgement on national security matters, as on any other factual dispute arising between an investor and a state. National security issues relate to the existential core of a state. An investor who wishes to challenge a state decision in that respect faces a heavy burden of proof, such as bad faith, absence of authority, or application to measures that do not relate to essential security interests (Para. 245).

Applying these considerations to the facts, the majority held that the concepts of 'strategic requirements', 'strategic needs', and 'societal needs', which were found to be the bases of the government's decision, cover a wide range of activities that go beyond the 'essential security interests'; the majority also held that the decision was 'directed to the protection of its essential security interests' only in undefined part (*CC/Devas v. India*, 2016a, Para. 371). On this basis, the tribunal concluded that

> a reasonable allocation of spectrum directed to the protection of the Respondent's essential security interests would not exceed 60% of the S-band spectrum allocated to the claimants, the remaining 40% being allocated for other public interest purposes and being subject to the expropriation conditions under Article 6 of the Treaty (Para. 373).

Arbitrator Haigh dissented on both the majority's recognition of deference to the host state's determination and the finding that 60% of the cancellation could be covered by security exception (*CC/Devas v. India*, 2016b, Dissenting Opinion of Arbitrator David R. Haigh, Paras. 3 and 82).

In the *Deutsche Telekom* case, the tribunal also accepted a degree of deference to a state's assessment with respect to the existence of essential security interests '*given the state's proximity to the situation, expertise, and competence*', while recognising that such deference cannot be unlimited (*Deutsche Telekom v. India*,

2017, Paras. 235 and 238). It therefore assessed the conditions under Article 12 of the India – Germany BIT (1995) regarding the existence of 'essential security interests' and the 'necessity' requirement. Regarding the former, the tribunal interpreted the concept of essential security interests as requiring 'the presence of interests concerned with security (as opposed to other public or societal interests) that are "essential", i.e. that go to the core (the "essence") of state security', which is of higher value than any 'public interest' (Para. 236). This understanding is in line with the majority's understanding of 'essential security interests' in the *CC Devas* case (2016a, Paras. 355–371) and arguably narrower than the earlier investment arbitration tribunals' interpretation of the same concept in Article XI of the US-Argentina BIT (1991), which consistently held that the concept encompassed severe economic crisis (UNCTAD, 2009).

Regarding the 'necessity' requirement, the tribunal adopted the 'primarily aimed at' and 'less restrictive alternatives' tests, stating that

> To assess the necessity of the measures to safeguard the state's essential security interests, the Tribunal will determine whether the measure was principally targeted at protecting the essential security interests at stake and was objectively required to achieve that protection, taking into account whether the state had reasonable alternatives that were less in conflict or more compliant with its international obligations.
>
> (*Deutsche Telekom v. India*, 2017, Para. 239)

Applying these tests to the facts of the case, the tribunal concluded that only some of the reasons for the annulment of the Agreement could be said to relate to 'essential security interests', and it noted that the government did not consider the reasonable, least restrictive, and available alternative measures; the tribunal finally concluded that the measure did not meet the necessity requirement (*Deutsche Telekom v. India*, 2017, Paras. 284, 289).

Given that the *Deutsche Telekom* tribunal also emphasised the distinction between the concepts of 'necessity' and 'related to' (*Deutsche Telekom v. India*, 2017, Para. 238), it can be safely concluded that the different conclusions reached in the *Devas* and *Deutsche Telekom* cases reflect the difference in wording between Article 11(3) of the India-Mauritius BIT (1998), which states the concept of 'directed to', and Article 12 of the India-Germany BIT (1995), which requires 'necessity'.

Self-judging Security Exception Clauses

No investment arbitration case so far has interpreted a 'self-judging' clause. Guidance for the interpretation of 'self-judging' security exception clauses has to be sought from decisions of other international courts and tribunals, in particular the WTO panels' reports in *Russia – Traffic in Transit* (2019) and *Saudi Arabia – IPRs* (2020) and the judgement of the ICJ in *Certain Questions of Mutual Assistance in Criminal Matters, Djibouti v. France* (2008), even though caution should be applied when referring to them regarding investor-state disputes.

A detailed analysis of this case law from the WTO and the ICJ on this issue is beyond the scope of this chapter. Here, it suffices to note that, in these cases (*Russia – Traffic in Transit*, 2019, Para. 7.132; *Saudi Arabia – IPRs*, 2020, Para. 7.283; *Djibouti v. France*, 2008, Para. 145), 'self-judging' security exception clauses were understood to fall under the general obligation of a state to carry out its commitments in good faith (Vienna Convention on the Law of Treaties, 1969, Art. 26), and this good faith standard is subject to judicial review. *Russia – Traffic in Transit* (2019) then requested the invoking state to 'articulate the essential security interests said to arise from the emergency in international relations sufficiently enough to demonstrate their veracity' (Para. 7.134). This approach was followed by the panel in *Saudi Arabia – IPRs* (2020, Paras. 7.230–7.231) and is generally supported by scholars, for instance, Van den Bossche and Akpofure (2020), Boklan and Bahri (2020), and Heath (2020a).

By contrast, in investment arbitration, the *Devas* (2016a) tribunal suggested, in obiter dictum, that 'self-judging' wording would preclude the justiciability of the invoking state's determination. It stated that 'in the case of self-judging clauses, it suffices for the state to declare, in its discretion, that it considers the adopted measure necessary for the protection of its security interests' (2016a, Para. 242).

The *declaration* requirement for claiming necessity and the existence of security interests, however, does not sufficiently address the concern over the abuse of security exception clauses. That is, at the centre of the current controversies over the FDI restrictions, there is the concern that the concept of national security is used as a pretext for protectionism, such as to enhance international competitiveness of strategically important domestic industries (Heath, 2020a) or to respond to populist sentiment in the political arena. The risk of 're-labelling' of economic or political interests as essential security interests (*Russia – Traffic in Transit*, 2019, Para 7.133) to escape liabilities under IIAs is acute in the growing geopolitical tension around FDI and the current backlash against globalisation. These considerations also offer support for the application of the 'good faith review' approach in the context of investment disputes.

In the application of the good faith review, particular attention should be given to the following considerations. First, the newly emerging security threats brought about by social and technological advancement such as the internet of things and advanced artificial intelligence (AI) are extremely difficult to predict, let alone scientifically proven. Moreover, Heath (2020b) suggested that identification of these threats suffers from the need to protect sensitive information on national security issues, which is normally classified and exempted from public disclosure. Second, a distinctive feature of the IIA regime is that it requires a balance between the protection of the investor's interests and the host state's regulatory power.

In light of this evidential difficulty and the need to balance public interests against private rights, a possible approach would be to focus on the assessment of the due process by which the measure was applied to the investor's investment. The Organisation for Economic Co-operation and Development (OECD, 2009) Guidelines for Recipient Country Investment Policies relating to National Security and the OECD's recent report (2020b) both emphasise the need for procedural fairness and predictability throughout the process of FDI review. Although outside the context of a security exception clause, the judgement of the US Court of Appeals for the District of Columbia in *Ralls Corporation v. Committee on Foreign Investment in the United States* (2014) is suggestive on this account. This case arose out of presidential orders to rescind, following reviews by the Committee on Foreign Investment in the United States (CFIUS), the purchase of a wind farm operation by a Chinese company through its Delaware-incorporated subsidiary, for the reasons, amongst others, of the proximity of the turbines to a US Naval weapons testing site and the possible interference with radar operations. The claimant raised a due process challenge against the prohibition of its investment by the CFIUS and presidential order, arguing that the orders breached the Due Process Clause of the Fifth Amendment to the United States Constitution. Significantly, the Court of Appeals stated that the determination of whether the transaction threatens the national security is 'in the realm of foreign policy and national security', whereas the due process claim 'is susceptible to judicially manageable standards'. On the merits of the case, the court concluded that the presidential order deprived Ralls Corporation of constitutionally protected property interests without due process of law.

Conclusion

The global trend of tightening FDI regulations magnifies the importance of security exception clauses in IIAs. In addition, the current political climate and the COVID-19 crisis will intensify rather than abate the tension between investment protection and security issues. This suggests that the role of IIAs' security exception clauses in investment disputes will increase. Future IIA-making should therefore treat security exceptions even more cautiously, based on the clear recognition that textual differences in these clauses play a crucial role in their interpretation and the outcome of the disputes, as demonstrated by the limited investment arbitration case law. Drafting a security exception clause should also reflect a cautious consideration of how to balance the need to address newly emerging security threats that are difficult to predict and the risk of its abuse for protectionist purposes; this risk is particularly severe in the current geopolitical tension and competition.

Note

1 Available at: www.sangiin.go.jp/japanese/joho1/kousei/gian/204/pdf/t1002040182040.pdf

References

All subsequent websites were last visited on 25 December 2021.

Argentina – United States of America BIT (1991) [US-Argentina BIT] in force 20 October 1994.

Boklan, D. and Bahri, A. (2020). The First WTO's Ruling on National Security Exception: Balancing Interests or Opening Pandora's Box? *World Trade Review*, 19(1), pp. 123–136.

Briese, R. and Schill, S. (2010). *Djibouti v. France*: Self-judging Clauses before the International Court of Justice. *Melbourne Journal of International Law*, 10, pp. 308–329.

Burke-White, W. W. and Staden, A. (2007). Investment Protection in Extraordinary Times: The Interpretation and Application of Non-Precluded Measures Provisions in Bilateral Investment Treaties. *Virginia Journal of International Law*, 48(2), pp. 307–410.

CMS v. Argentina (2005). ICSID Case No. ARB/01/8, Award.

CMS v. Argentina (2007). ICSID Case No. ARB/01/8, Decision of the ad hoc Committee on the Application for Annulment of the Argentine Republic.

Deutsche Telekom v. India (2017). PCA Case No. 2014–10, Interim Award.

Devas v. India (2016a). PCA Case No. 2013–09, Award on Jurisdiction and Merits.

Devas v. India (2016b). PCA Case No. 2013–09, Dissenting Opinion of Arbitrator David R. Haigh.

Djibouti v. France (Certain Questions of Mutual Assistance in Criminal Matters) (2008). Judgment, I.C.J. Reports, p. 177.

El Paso v. Argentina (2011). ICSID Case No. ARB/03/15, Award.

Enron v. Argentina (2007). ICSID Case No. ARB/01/3, Award.

European Energy Charter Conference Secretariat (1991a). *Draft Basic Protocol to the European Energy Charter*. Available at: www.energycharter.org/fileadmin/DocumentsMedia/ECT_Drafts/1_-_Basic_Protocol.pdf

European Energy Charter Conference Secretariat (1991b). *Basic Agreement 4.21/91, BA–4*. Available at: www.energycharter.org/fileadmin/DocumentsMedia/ECT_Drafts/3_-_BA_4__31.10.91_.pdf

European Energy Charter Conference Secretariat (1992a). *Basic Agreement 6. 4/92, BA–6*. Available at: www.energycharter.org/fileadmin/DocumentsMedia/ECT_Drafts/4_-_BA_6__21.01.93_.pdf

European Energy Charter Conference Secretariat (1992b). *Basic Agreement 15. 37/92, BA–15*. Available at: www.energycharter.org/fileadmin/DocumentsMedia/ECT_Drafts/8_-_BA_15__12.08.92_.pdf

European Energy Charter Conference Secretariat (1993). *Basic Agreement. 20/93, BA–37*. Available at: www.energycharter.org/fileadmin/DocumentsMedia/ECT_Drafts/14_-_BA_37__01.03.93_.pdf

European Energy Charter Conference Secretariat (1994). *Draft Energy Charter Treaty Seventh Version. 17/94, CONF 96*. Available at: www.energycharter.org/fileadmin/DocumentsMedia/ECT_Drafts/21_-_ECT_7__17.03.94_.pdf

Foreign Exchange and Foreign Trade Act (Act No. 228 of December 1, 1949), Last Version: Act No. 60 of 2019. https://www.mof.go.jp/english/policy/international_policy/fdi/FEFTA.pdf

Germany – India BIT (1995) [India-Germany BIT] in force 13 July 1998, terminated 3 July 2017.

Grieger, G. (2019). *EU Framework for FDI Screening*. Available at: www.europarl.europa.eu/thinktank/en/document.html?reference=EPRS_BRI(2018)614667

Heath, B. (2020a). Trade and Security Among the Ruins. *Duke Journal for Comparative & International Law*, 30(2), 223–266.

Heath, B. (2020b). The New National Security Challenge to the Economic Order. *Yale Law Journal*, 129(4), 1020–1098.

Hungary v. Slovakia (Gabčíkovo-Nagymaros Project) (1997). Judgment, I.C.J. Reports, p. 7.

India-Mauritius BIT (1998) in force 20 July 2000, terminated 22 March 2017.

Islamic Republic of Iran v. United States of America (Oil Platforms) (2003). Judgment, I.C.J. Reports, p. 16.

Japan. Ministry of Finance (2019). *Exemption from Prior-notification Required for Designated Business Sectors and Clarification of the Prior-notification Exemptions and Burden Mitigation Measures*. Available at: www.mof.go.jp/english/international_policy/fdi/kanrenshiryou_191021.pdf

Japan. Ministry of Finance (2021). *Update of the List of Classifications of Listed Companies Regarding the Prior-notification Requirements on Inward Direct Investment*. Available at: www.mof.go.jp/english/policy/international_policy/fdi/20211102.html

Japan. The National Diet (2021). *Kokka Anzen Hoshō jō Jūyō na Tochi tō ni Kakaru Torihiki tō no Kisei tō nikansuru Hōritsu an* [A bill on a restriction on the use of land near defence facilities and other areas with national security implications]. Available at: www.sangiin.go.jp/japanese/joho1/kousei/gian/204/pdf/t1002040182040.pdf

Nicaragua v. United States of America (Military and Paramilitary Activities in and against Nicaragua) (1984), Judgment, I.C.J. Reports, p. 431.

Nolan, M. and Sourgens, F. (2011). *The Limits of Discretion? Self-Judging Emergency Clauses in International Investment Agreements*. In: Sauvant, K. P. ed., *Yearbook of International Investment Law and Policy 2010–2011*. Oxford: Oxford University Press, pp. 362–419.

OECD (2009). *Guidelines for Recipient Country Investment Policies Relating to National Security: Recommendation Adopted by the OECD Council on 25 May 2009*. Available at: www.oecd.org/daf/inv/investment-policy/43384486.pdf

OECD (2020a). *Investment Screening in Times of COVID-19 and Beyond*. Available at: www.oecd.org/coronavirus/policy-responses/investment-screening-in-times-of-covid-19-and-beyond-aa60af47/

OECD. (2020b). *Transparency, Predictability and Accountability for Investment Screening Mechanisms*. Available at: www.oecd.org/daf/inv/investment-policy/2009-Guidelines-webinar-May-2021-background-note.pdf

OECD. (2021). *OECD Code of Liberalisation of Capital Movements 2021*. Available at: www.oecd.org/investment/investment-policy/Code-capital-movements-EN.pdf

Ralls Corporation v. Committee on Foreign Investment in the United States (2014). United States Court of Appeals, D.C. Cir., Case No. 13–5315.

Regulation (EU) 2019/452 establishing a framework for the screening of foreign direct investments into the Union (2019). Official Journal LI 79/1, p. 40.

Republique de I'lnde v. AG (2018). Bundesgericht/Tribunal federal/Tribunale federale/Tribunal federal, 4A_65/2018.

Russia – Measures Concerning Traffic in Transit (Russia – Traffic in Transit) (2019). WTO Panel Report, WT/DS512/R.

Saudi Arabia – Measures concerning the Protection of Intellectual Property Rights (Saudi Arabia – IPRs) (2020). WTO Panel Report, WT/DS567/R.

UNCTAD (2009). The Protection of National Security in IIAs. *UNCTAD Series on International Investment Policies for Development*, p. 36. Available at: https://unctad.org/system/files/official-document/diaeia20085_en.pdf

Van den Bossche, P. and Akpofure, S. (2020). The Use and Abuse of the National Security Exception Under Art. XXI(b)(iii) of the GATT 1994. *WTI Working Paper, 3*. Available at: www.wti.org/media/filer_public/50/57/5057fb22-f949-4920-8bd1-e8ad352d22b2/wti_working_paper_03_2020.pdf

Vienna Convention on the Law of Treaties (1969), in force 27 January 1980.

Watai, R. (2018). Nihon Ni Okeru Tainai Chokusetsu Toshi No Hensen [Development of Foreign Direct Investment Regulation in Japan]. *Hogaku Kenkyu [Journal of Law, Politics, and Sociology]*, 91(1), pp. 97–120.

11 Intellectual Property and National Security

Masabumi SUZUKI

Introduction

From the perspective of national security, protecting information has long been an extremely important issue. Indeed, the term 'intelligence' used in the context of national security literally refers to certain types of information. In modern times, the relationship between security and protection of information has become complicated due to the globalization of business activities, movement of people, the opaque boundary between military and civilian technology, and the increase in dual-use technology. This chapter focuses primarily on information with economic value, that is, the subject matter of intellectual property (IP), and examines the relationship between IP protection and national security measures.

The plan of the chapter is as follows. First, the international legal frameworks concerning IP protection are provided. In particular, case law relating to the national security provision entailed within Art. 73 of the Agreement on Trade-Related Aspects of Intellectual Property Rights (the TRIPS Agreement or TRIPS) is explained. Second, four types of measures that often involve issues concerning the relationship between IP and national security are presented, namely, (i) promoting IP protection to deal with security issues, (ii) weakening or limiting IP protection out of security concerns, (iii) controlling the exportation of sensitive goods and technologies, and (iv) 'forced' technology transfer. Third, each of the previous four types of measures is elaborated with analyses of actual examples. Specifically, measures such as Japan's new act for the Promotion of Economic Security, Japan's legislative system for protecting trade secrets in foreign territories, Japan's export control measures of certain products concerning the Republic of Korea, and China's measures relating to technology transfer are discussed. Fourth, this chapter concludes with an outlook on the foreseeable future developments.

Relevant International Legal Frameworks

International Law for IP Protection

Many multilateral treaties concerning IP protection have been enacted, starting with the Paris Convention for the Protection of Industrial Property and the Berne

DOI: 10.4324/9781003193098-11

Convention for the Protection of Literary and Artistic Works, both of which were signed at the end of the 19th century (Abbott, Cottier and Gurry, 2019, pp. 3–5). The most comprehensive and fundamental treaty today is the TRIPS Agreement, which was concluded as a part of the World Trade Organization (WTO) Agreement and entered into effect in 1995. Specifically, TRIPS provides minimum standards for the protection of various kinds of IP, detailed rules for the enforcement of intellectual property rights (hereinafter 'IPR'), and an effective dispute resolution system based on the WTO dispute settlement mechanism. Such characteristics, combined with a large number of Members (164 countries and regions as of March 2022), enable TRIPS to play an important role in the international harmonization of the IP system. Within the TRIPS Agreement, Art. 73 allows national security exceptions to the obligations under the agreement. This provision will be examined in detail later.

In this century, international agreements other than those specifically enacted for IP protection are also becoming increasingly relevant. First, many regional or bilateral economic agreements (e.g., free trade agreements, economic partnership agreements) have been concluded, and many of them contain provisions for IP protection. For example, Japan signed the Comprehensive and Progressive Agreement for Trans-Pacific Partnership (CPTPP) with ten other countries in 2018 and the Regional Comprehensive Economic Partnership Agreement (RCEP) with fourteen other countries in 2020. Both of these agreements have a chapter on IP that contains detailed provisions.

Second, other regulatory fields in relation to a broader range of subjects have an increasing impact on IP-related issues. For example, the provisions that originally provided for trade in goods or services, such as the provisions of the General Agreement on Tariffs and Trade 1994 (GATT) and the General Agreement on Trade in Services (GATS), are often referred to in recent WTO disputes concerning measures relating to IP. Furthermore, the impact of international investment agreements (IIAs) has been observed as being increasingly relevant for IP-related issues in recent years (Klopschinski, Gibson and Ruse-Khan, 2021; Suzuki, 2015). IP is a type of 'investment' under IIAs, which may shift the focus to considerations that are not regulated under IP or trade agreements. Moreover, the number of IIAs is increasing (economic partnership agreements such as CPTPP and RCEP also include chapters on investment), and many IIAs contain special dispute resolution systems that allow the investor, a private entity, to initiate dispute resolution measures (e.g., arbitration) against the host state (the investor-state dispute settlement (ISDS)). Due to these advantages, some parties have sought to resolve IP-related matters under IIAs by initiating ISDS arbitration cases.

The previously mentioned treaties not specifically enacted for IP protection (i.e., regional or bilateral economic agreements, GATT, GATS, IIAs, and so on) usually have a provision for security exceptions. Such provisions include, for example, CPTTP Art. 1 (incorporating Art. 29.2 of the Trans-Pacific Partnership Agreement (TPP)), RCEP Art. 17.13, GATT Art. XXI, and GATS Art. XIV *bis*; Art. 18 of the Japan-Korea-China Investment Agreement (2014) is an example in IIAs.

Security Exception in the TRIPS Agreement

Let us examine TRIPS Art. 73 as an example of security exception provisions in the international legal frameworks for IP protection. The TRIPS Agreement has provisions to allow exceptions and limitations for each kind of IP under certain conditions (generally called the 'three-step test'). Such provisions include Arts. 13 (for copyright and related rights), 17 (for trademarks), 26.2 (for industrial designs), and 30 (for patents). In contrast, Art. 73 allows for more general exceptions regarding the obligations mandated by TRIPS.

TRIPS Art. 73 provides as follows:

> Nothing in this Agreement shall be construed:
>
> (a) to require a Member to furnish any information the disclosure of which it considers contrary to its essential security interests; or
> (b) to prevent a Member from taking any action which it considers necessary for the protection of its essential security interests;
>
> (i) relating to fissionable materials or the materials from which they are derived;
> (ii) relating to the traffic in arms, ammunition, and implements of war and to such traffic in other goods and materials as is carried on directly or indirectly for the purpose of supplying a military establishment;
> (iii) taken in time of war or other emergency in international relations; or
>
> (c) to prevent a Member from taking any action in pursuance of its obligations under the United Nations Charter for the maintenance of international peace and security.

The WTO dispute panel report in the *Saudi Arabia – IPRs* case (2020) presented an interpretation of Art. 73. Qatar brought this dispute to the WTO Dispute Settlement mechanism against Saudi Arabia. According to the allegation by Qatar, Saudi Arabia failed to protect the copyrights of Qatar's broadcasting company ('beIN') by civil and criminal enforcement procedures, which would constitute violations of TRIPS. Saudi Arabia counter-argued that the measures at issue were justifiable by TRIPS Art. 73(b)(iii), as Saudi Arabia had been engaged in a diplomatic dispute with Qatar, leading to the severance of all relations with Qatar in June 2017, and the measures were taken as 'necessary for the protection of [Saudi Arabia's] essential security interests' 'in time of . . . emergency in international relations'.

The panel in *Saudi Arabia – IPRs* pointed out the following, citing the panel report in *Russia – Traffic in Transit* (2019), which interpreted the security exception in GATT Art. XXI for the first time (Nagy, 2021).

> [The panel in *Russia – Traffic in Transit*] held that a panel must determine for itself whether the invoking Member's actions were 'taken in time of war or

> other emergency in international relations' . . . It further found that a panel's review of whether the invoking Member's actions are ones 'which it considers necessary for the protection of its essential security interests' . . . requires an assessment of whether the invoking Member has articulated the 'essential security interests' that it considers the measures at issue are necessary to protect, along with a further assessment of whether the measures are so remote from, or unrelated to, the 'emergency in international relations' as to make it implausible that the invoking Member implemented the measures for the protection of its 'essential security interests' arising out of the emergency. According to the panel in *Russia – Traffic in Transit*, the obligation of a Member to interpret and apply Art. XXI(b)(iii) of the GATT 1994 in 'good faith' requires 'that the measures at issue meet a minimum requirement of plausibility in relation to the proffered essential security interests, i.e. that they are not implausible as measures protective of these interests'.
>
> (*Saudi Arabia – Protection of IPRs*, Para. 7.230)

The panel in *Saudi Arabia – IPRs* confirmed that the interpretation provided in *Russia – Traffic in Transit* 'can guide the assessment of . . . Art. 73(b)(iii) of the TRIPS Agreement' (*Saudi Arabia – Protection of IPRs*, Para. 7.248). By citing the view of the panel in *Russia – Traffic in Transit*, the panel in *Saudi Arabia – IPRs* then clarified that the assessment of whether the criteria of 'war or other emergency in international relations' are met must 'be made objectively rather than by the invoking Member itself' (*id.*, Para. 7.244). It found that the measures at issue were 'taken in time of war or other emergency in international relations' (*id.*, Paras. 7.256–270). The panel then concluded that Saudi Arabia's denial of access to civil remedies by Qatari nationals (i.e., the 'anti-sympathy measures') met 'a minimum requirement of plausibility in relation to the proffered essential security interests' and could thus be justified under Art. 73(b)(iii). The alleged inconsistency with Art. 61 TRIPS in the form of non-application of criminal procedures and penalties to the Saudi company ('beoutQ'), however, did not meet the minimum requirement and therefore could not be justified by Art. 73 (*id.*, Paras. 7.283–294).

Measures Related to IP and National Security Issues

This section discusses typical types of measures where the relationship between IP and national security can be problematic. Such measures are broadly divided into two categories: measures directly related to IP protection and measures related to technology transfer. Within the first category consisting of measures directly related to IP protection, there are (i) measures to strengthen and (ii) measures to weaken or limit IP protection, and both are taken from a security perspective. The second category can also be divided into two types of measures: (iii) measures to restrict technology transfer for security purposes and (iv) measures for technology transfer that raise concerns of other countries from a security perspective. A typical example of the former ((iii)) is export restrictions on products and technologies, and an example of the latter ((iv)) is so-called 'forced' technology transfer. In the following parts, each of these four types of measures is analyzed regarding their significance in and relationship with relevant fields of international law by discussing actual examples.

Promoting IP Protection to Address Security Issues

General Analysis

The IP system protects information with economic value. Thus, it protects only some elements of information of relevance for national security but nevertheless can play an important role in national security. This point is easily understandable since technologies that are industrially useful while having military applications or technologies that form the basis of a nation's industry (such as information and communication technologies (ICTs) and semiconductor-related technologies) can be protected by IP. As such, the IP system can prevent unauthorized use of information of importance for national security and encourage activities to create such information. Notably, international law directly regulating IP protection, such as the TRIPS Agreement, does not exclude technologies and other types of information related to national security from being protected by IP (for example, TRIPS, Art. 27.1 provides that 'patents shall be available and patent rights enjoyable without discrimination as to . . . the field of technology').

Institutional limitations of the IP system, however, limit its application for protecting information related to national security. Information has the characteristics of not being excludable, and it can freely be used. Maintaining such qualities is generally desirable from the perspective of fostering freedom of expression and freedom of business activities. Conversely, the IP system provides an artificial scarcity through an exclusive right to information provided for specific policy purposes. Therefore, the IP system's criteria for protectable subject matter and requirements for protection that impose restrictions on the use of information are justifiable to the extent that they fulfill policy objectives.

First, the protection of technical information is limited to such information with industrial applicability (for patents) or commercial value (for trade secrets). In other words, technologies used for completely non-industrial purposes are not protected by IPRs. In this sense, it is difficult for technology that has only military purposes to be subject to the IP system. In addition, an invention, once made public, cannot be protected by a patent.

Second, IPRs are territorial in principle, which means that the effect of IPRs extends only within the territory of the country in which the right is granted. Territoriality is a necessary principle in achieving the protection of non-exclusive goods (i.e., information) without the excessive restriction of their use. However, it can be a significant constraint from a national security perspective.

Third, patent applications are published and made available to the public. The patent system is based on the idea that a patent right is given to the inventor in exchange for her consent to make her invention public, thus making disclosure one of its fundamental principles.

Despite these limitations, IP protection of information provides options that will assist national security. The following examples showcase measures where IP protection contributes to national security, with a focus on the protection of technical information.

Example 1: Protection of Trade Secrets, Particularly in Foreign Territories

The protection of trade secrets is an obligation of WTO Members under TRIPS Art. 39.2. This provision defines trade secrets as information that is 'secret', 'has commercial value', and 'has been subject to reasonable steps . . . to keep it secret'. As mentioned previously, the requirement for commercial value may be a certain constraint for protecting information relevant to national security through trade secrets. Still, it is meaningful to protect technologies with military applications and strategic technologies for the country (e.g., technologies related to telecommunications, semiconductors, and nuclear power) as a trade secret.

In recent years, major countries have been strengthening their trade secret protection framework. For instance, the United States enacted the Defend Trade Secret Act of 2016 as a federal civil law measure. Before the Act, the United States only provided for federal criminal measures with the Economic Espionage Act of 1996, while civil law measures for trade secret protection were available only at the state level. In the same year, 2016, the European Union (EU) also enacted the Trade Secrets Directive (Directive (EU) 2016/943 (2016)) to harmonize the national laws of EU Member States for trade secret protection. In Japan, trade secrets are protected by the Unfair Competition Prevention Act (1993), which has been amended several times to widen the scope of protection and strengthen criminal sanctions against unlawful acts (for example, the 2015 amendment introduced a new type of unlawful act for trading of things resulting from unlawful use of technical secrets; in addition, criminal penalties were first introduced in 2003 and have been strengthened by several revisions).

As mentioned previously, territoriality is a principle applied in the IP system. However, in many countries, including Japan, it is understood that territoriality does not apply to the protection of trade secrets. For example, the Japanese Unfair Competition Prevention Act imposes heavier criminal penalties on foreign acts of misappropriation of trade secrets owned by businesses operating in Japan (Suzuki, 2020). The extraterritorial application of trade secret protection is desirable from the perspective of national security. At the same time, care must be taken not to compromise the predictability of commercial transactions, especially for protection in foreign markets since trade secrets are not disclosed. In this regard, it is necessary to give attention to, for example, general obligations concerning the enforcement of IPRs stipulated in TRIPS Art. 41.

Example 2: Protection of Secrecy within the Patent System

The patent system provides a powerful means of protecting technology while it also mandates the disclosure and publication of the invention, as described previously. In this context, TRIPS Art. 29 obliges WTO members to require appropriate disclosure of the invention by the applicant. In many countries, the patent office publishes the patent application containing the invention 18 months after the filing date (e.g., for Japanese patents, Japanese Patent Act 1959, Art. 64; for US patents, 35 U.S.C. §122; for European patents, European Patent Convention (EPC, 2000), Art. 93(1)(a); for PCT applications, the Patent Cooperation Treaty, Art. 21). Furthermore, information relating to a patent application and its prosecution is published after the grant of a patent (e.g., Paris Convention, Art. 12; Japanese Patent Act, Arts. 66(3) and 193).

From the national security viewpoint, however, it is not desirable for sensitive technologies to be disclosed. Therefore, many countries possess a secret patent system that grants patents while maintaining secrecy over security-related technologies. In addition, several countries provide for a system that allows only national patent applications for inventions of security-related technologies generated in that country. For example, the US Invention Secrecy Act of 1951, codified in 35 USC §§ 181–1881, § 50 of the German Patent Act (1980), and § 4(2) of the German Law on International Patent Conventions (1976) are examples of such special mechanisms. Japan provided for a secret patent system in the past, but this was abolished due to the revision of the Patent Act that came into effect in July 1948 (Sakurai, 2020). Recently, however, the need for economic security has been strongly recognized by the Japanese government, and the Diet passed the Economic Security Promotion Act, which contains provisions for a secret patent system (Arts. 65–84), in May 2022.

Do secret patent systems constitute a problem from the viewpoint of relevant treaties? At the very least, the Paris Convention and the TRIPS Agreement, the two most important multilateral treaties concerning the patent system, do not oblige their members to publish all patent applications and patents. Specifically, Art. 12 of the Paris Convention only stipulates the requirement to establish a special IP service and the obligation for the service to publish an official journal. TRIPS Art. 29 obliges member states to require patent applicants to provide a sufficient description of the filed invention. Thus, secret patent systems do not appear to be inconsistent with these treaties. As for a system that allows only patent applications in the home country for inventions of security-related technologies generated within that country, this imposes certain restrictions on the inventor and patent applicant in the home country. Since the restriction is not discriminatory in terms of the nationality of the inventor and applicant, it does not impair the National Treatment (NT) principle (TRIPS, Art. 3) and the Most-Favoured Nation (MFN) principle (TRIPS, Art. 4). In addition, it does not discriminate against a particular field of technology safeguarded by TRIPS Art. 27.1 since it does not disadvantage the grant of patents.

Example 3: Enforcement of IPRs

Strong IP protection and enforcement within other countries are generally beneficial from the viewpoint of a country's national security. Misappropriation of advanced technology in a strategic field invented by a local company abroad would not only be commercially detrimental to the company but also may, more broadly, be harmful to the national security of the home country. For example, the United States and Japan have a great deal of interest in IP protection in China and other countries and have been pointing at the deficiencies in IP protection abroad in government reports (see, e.g., USTR, 2021; METI, 2020) and at meetings of the WTO and World Intellectual Property Organization (WIPO). National security considerations may be behind such activities.

In this context, the debate over standard-essential patents (SEPs) is an interesting recent development. Patents that cover technologies that are essential for a standard are referred to as SEPs. Currently, standards related to information and telecommunication technologies, such as 5G and 6G, have significance in terms of national security, since these technologies will be the basis of interconnected industries and societies. Numerous disputes between SEP holders and users (implementers) worldwide reflect the value and importance of SEPs. In some cases, competition authorities have found certain actions of SEP holders as being anti-competitive. In recent years, SEPs have led to some tensions between countries, specifically in relation to jurisdictional questions in litigating SEPs. Some countries are issuing anti-suit injunctions that direct parties (either SEP holders or implementers) not to initiate or proceed with court proceedings in other countries, while others are issuing anti-anti-suit injunctions prohibiting parties from abiding by anti-suit injunctions by foreign courts (Cotter, 2021). In February 2022, the EU initiated a WTO dispute against China, claiming that the operation of anti-suit injunctions in China had not been transparent (*China – Enforcement of IPRs*, 2022). Furthermore, several US Senators submitted a bipartisan bill entitled ‘The Defending American Courts Act’ to Congress in the United States (Contreras, 2022; Tillis, 2022). It should, however, be noted that anti-suit injunctions are originally a feature within common law countries, such as the United States, which makes the real problem their implementation rather than anti-suit injunctions as such.

Weakening or Limiting IP Protection Out of Security Concerns

The next type relates to measures that weaken or limit IP protection due to national security interests. Examples of such measures are compulsory licenses that permit a third party to use a patented invention granted to a foreign entity without its consent. Similar mechanisms can be applied in relation to works protected by copyright, whereby a third party may be allowed to use or modify a copyrighted work of a foreign entity without its permission.

Such measures are likely to violate international law for IP protection and provisions in IIAs (e.g., prohibition of expropriation). This is where the previously mentioned security exceptions in the TRIPS Agreement, IIAs, and other treaties could be used to justify such measures. In this context, the WTO case of *Saudi Arabia – IPRs* provides a good example of this issue.

Control of Exportation of Sensitive Goods and Technologies

General Analysis

The following two types concern measures related to technology transfer. The first is export controls. Export restraints other than duties, taxes, or charges are prohibited by WTO law unless they fall under the exceptions provided by Art. XI, Paragraph 2, and Art. XX of GATT (e.g., temporal restrictions to relieve the critical shortage of essential products; measures necessary to protect human, animal, or plant life or health). However, export controls for national security purposes are permissible to a certain extent by GATT Art. XXI (Wu, 2021). In addition, voluntary associations have been formed to coordinate export controls internationally. Examples of such associations are the Wassenaar Arrangement on Export Controls for Conventional Arms and Dual-Use Goods and Technologies, the Missile Technology Control Regime (MTCR), the Australia Group (a voluntary arrangement to coordinate export controls on technologies and materials used to manufacture chemicals and biological weapons), and the Nuclear Suppliers Group.

It is customary in export controls to also control the cross-border transfer of technologies. Since some of the technologies may be protected by IPRs, export controls and the IP system are interrelated. For instance, regarding the relationship between the provisions on patents in the TRIPS Agreement and export controls, the following can be observed.

First, an export controls' restriction on a patentee regarding the exportation of patented products would not violate the TRIPS Agreement because the rights of the patentee guaranteed by TRIPS Art. 28(1) are negative rights; i.e., they aim at preventing third parties from working the patented invention. Thus, they are not positive rights to work the invention by the patentee herself. Second, a restriction on the patentee to assign the patent or license the patented invention to a third party would be inconsistent with Art. 28(2), which obliges WTO members to give rights holders 'the rights to assign, or transfer by succession, the patent and to conclude licensing contracts'. In addition, it would also violate the MFN principle under TRIPS Art. 4, where the restriction subjects the assignment or licensing to nationals of a particular foreign country. Third, the possible inconsistencies of export controls with obligations under the TRIPS Agreement could be justified where the requirements of TRIPS Art. 73 are satisfied. Specifically, Art. 73(b)(ii) and (iii) would mainly apply to export controls of weapons-related technology, and export controls for the purpose of sanctions or retaliation against countries at war or in a tense relationship with the country implementing the export control measures, respectively. As explained previously, Art. 73(b)(iii) was interpreted by the panel report of *Saudi Arabia – IPRs*.

Example: Japan – Products and Technology (Korea)

Japan – Products and Technology (Korea) is a recent case brought to the WTO Dispute Settlement system by the Republic of Korea over Japan's export control measures. Korea submitted that the Ministry of Economy, Trade and Industry (METI) of Japan started to apply more stringent licensing requirements and procedures to the export or transfer of the designated products and technologies when destined for Korea in July 2019, based on Arts. 25(1) and 48(1) of the Foreign Exchange and Foreign Trade Act of Japan. The products in question (fluorinated polyimide, resist polymers, and hydrogen fluoride, as specified under Japanese export control regulations) were primarily used in the production of semiconductors and displays for smartphones and TVs. The technologies in question included technologies related to the subject products. Japan argued that the shift in the regulations was because certain sensitive items had been exported from Japan to Korea with inadequate management by companies. Korea, however, claimed that the new measures constituted a politically motivated, disguised restriction on trade in violation of WTO provisions, including Arts. I:1, VIII, XI:1, XIII:1, and XIII:5 of GATT, Arts. 2.1, 7.7, 8.1, and 10.1 of the Agreement of Trade Facilitation (FTA), Art. 2 of the Agreement on Trade-Related Investment Measures (TRIMs Agreement), Arts. 3.1 and 4 of the TRIPS Agreement, and Arts. VI:1 and VI:5 of GATS. Regarding TRIPS, Korea also mentioned Art. 28.2 in its request for consultations (WT/DS590/1 (2019)) but somehow did not explicitly refer to this article in the request for the establishment of a panel (WT/DS590/4 (2020)).

At the Dispute Settlement Body (DSB) meeting on July 29, 2020, where the establishment of a panel was agreed on, the representative of Japan said that dialogue, not the initiation of WTO Dispute Settlement proceedings, was the best and only way to resolve this matter and expressed regret that Korea had not resumed the dialogue between their respective export control authorities (WTO DSB, 2020). The representative of the United States also emphasized that 'as it had consistently maintained in more than 70 years', national security matters were not to be judged under the WTO dispute settlement system, despite the 'erroneous panel findings' in *Russia – Traffic in Transit* (*id.*). These statements show the concerns of these two countries as to the WTO's handling of issues concerning national security. However, giving full discretion to each WTO Member concerning the security nature of its measures remains questionable when seeking to sustain and develop an international legal framework on economic matters. In fact, Japan itself has been expressing concerns about export controls by China (METI, 2020, pp. 6–7). As to the dispute between Japan and Korea, after the 'Export Policy Dialogue' held between the two countries in March 2023, Korea withdrew its complaint on March 23, 2023.

Forced Technology Transfer

General Analysis

The term 'forced technology transfer' (FTT) refers to measures that substantially obligate foreign entities to transfer technology to domestic entities as a condition for approving an investment or international licenses. Where such measures affect technology relating to national security, FTT becomes an issue of national security and not only of economic policy (Abbott, 2020).

From the perspective of international economic law, FTT leads to the following problems. Measures requiring the patent owner to license its patent could constitute a violation of TRIPS Arts. 28(1) (regarding exclusive rights conferred by patents), 28(2) (regarding patentees' rights to license), and 31 (providing requirements for the issuance of compulsory licenses). In addition, they may be inconsistent with the principle of national treatment (NT) under TRIPS Art. 3, where they impose heavier obligations on foreign entities compared to those for nationals of the country taking the measures. Second, an obligation to transfer technology as a pre-condition for approving an investment would violate the prohibition of performance requirements in IIAs. Indeed, some IIAs explicitly mention technology transfer as a type of prohibited performance (e.g., Art. 9.10(1)(f) of the TPP Agreement, incorporated into the CPTPP Agreement by its Art. 1(1)). The NT principle in IIAs is also violated where the measure discriminates between nationals of the country implementing the measure and foreign entities.

Example: FTT by China

Concerns in relation to FTT have been raised regarding measures of China. The Chinese government requires foreign entities to conduct business activities within China only through a joint venture formed with local entities. Moreover, various conditions have been imposed on foreign entities that license their patents to joint ventures (Lee, 2020; Sykes, 2021). Specifically, Art. 27 of the Regulation on the Administration of the Import and Export of Technologies (TIER) provides that an improvement resulting from a technology licensed under cross-border licensing agreements shall belong to the party making the improvement. TIER Art. 29(3) prohibits the original technology licensor from restricting a licensee's right to improve the licensed technology. TIER Art. 24 mandates that the licensor shall assume liability for an infringement of a third party's lawful rights and interests because of the licensee's use of the licensed technology. Many such restrictions are not imposed on licensing agreements between Chinese nationals.

Regarding China's FTT-related measures, the United States requested consultations under the WTO Agreement in March 2018, and a WTO Dispute Settlement Panel was established for the dispute in November 2018 (*China – IPRs II*). The EU also requested consultations under the WTO Agreement in June 2018 (*China – Transfer of Technology*). Additionally, Japan has been pointing out the seeming inconsistencies of China's measures relating to FTT with the WTO Agreement in METI's annual 'Reports on Compliance by Major Trading Partners with Trade Agreements – WTO, EPA/FTA and IIA' (e.g., METI, 2020, pp. 36–37). The specific WTO-related provisions mentioned by the United States, EU, and Japan as being violated by China's measures include Arts. 3.1, 28.1, 28.2, 33, 39.1, and 39.2 of the TRIPS Agreement, Paragraphs 1.2 and 7.3 of Part I of the Protocol on the Accession of the People's Republic of China to the WTO, and Paragraphs 49 and 203 of the Report of the Working Party on the Accession of the People's Republic of China to the WTO.

In 2019, China revised the TIER, removing some of the provisions criticized by other countries. In January 2019, the United States and China signed an Economic and Trade Agreement (the 'Phase One Agreement'). Chapter 2 of the agreement is titled 'Technology Transfer'. In relation to national security, Art. 2.3(5) and (6) state that the parties shall not pressure foreign persons to disclose 'sensitive technical information' and shall protect its confidentiality. As for the WTO dispute between the United States and China, the authority for the establishment of the

Panel lapsed in June 2021. The EU also concluded in principle the negotiations for a Comprehensive Agreement on Investment (CAI) in December 2020 with China. However, the EU imposed sanctions on multiple individuals and entities in China due to concerns about the situation of human rights violations in China in March 2021. In response, China reciprocated and sanctioned EU individuals and entities. In May 2021, the European Parliament adopted a resolution to freeze the ratification of the CAI, condemning the sanctions imposed by China. Meanwhile, the WTO consultations initiated by the EU at the WTO are not proceeding.

Closing Remarks

This chapter presented the types of measures that may affect the relationship between IP and national security and provided specific examples. It has become clear that there are, on the one hand, types of measures about which stricter compliance with international economic law, such as the WTO Agreement, is demanded from the viewpoint of national security, and on the other hand, types of measures about which security exceptions can justify deviations from specific disciplines under international law.

In recent years, economic and national security issues are becoming more intertwined. Countries are promoting the development and application of advanced technologies, such as those related to semiconductors and information and communications, as industrial policies. At the same time, countries are trying to protect technologies to safeguard their economy. This trend implies a growing tendency for countries to adopt the latter type of the previously mentioned dichotomy, that is, measures that deviate from the specific rules of international economic law justified by national security concerns. This, however, may weaken the effectiveness of international economic law and may have the ironic consequence that the former type of the previous dichotomy, specifically, measures that should strictly comply with international economic law for national security, will become more likely to deviate from the norms of international economic law.

References

All subsequent websites were last visited on 15 September 2022.

Abbott, F. M. (2020). Under the Radar: Reflections on 'Forced' Technology Transfer and the Erosion of Developmental Sovereignty. *GRUR International*, 69(3), pp. 260–263.

Abbott, F. M., Cottier, T. and Gurry, F. (2019). *International Intellectual Property in an Integrated World Economy*, 4th ed. New York: Wolters Kluwer.

China – Certain Measures Concerning the Protection of Intellectual Property Rights (China – IPRs II (US)) (2018). Request for the Establishment of a Panel by the US, WT/DS542/8.

China – Certain Measures on the Transfer of Technology (China – Transfer of Technology (EU)) (2018). Request for Consultations by the EU WT/DS549/1, G/L/1244, IP/D/39.

China – Enforcement of Intellectual Property Rights (China – IPRs Enforcement (EU)) (2022). Request for Consultations by the EU, WT/DS611/1, IP/D/43, G/L/1427.

Contreras, J. (2022). A Statutory Anti-Anti-Suit Injunction for US Patent Cases? *Patently-O Blog*, 18 March. Available at: https://patentlyo.com/patent/2022/03/contreras-statutory-injunction.html

Cotter, T. F. (2021). Is Global FRAND Litigation Spinning Out of Control? *Patently-O Law Journal*, 2021(1). Available at: https://patentlyo.com/media/2021/01/Cotter-Global-FRAND-Litigation-2021.pdf

Defend Trade Secret Act 2016 (US).

Directive (EU) 2016/943 the Protection of Undisclosed Know-How and Business Information (Trade Secrets) Against Their Unlawful Acquisition, Use and Disclosure (2016). Official Journal L 157, pp. 1–18.

Economic Espionage Act 1996 (US).

Economic Security Promotion Act 2022 (JP).

European Patent Convention 2000.

Foreign Exchange and Foreign Trade Act 1949 (JP).

Invention Secrecy Act 1951 (US).

Japan-Korea-China Investment Agreement 2014.

Japan – Measures Related to the Exportation of Products and Technology to Korea (Japan – Products and Technology (Korea)) (2019). Request for Consultations by the Republic of Korea, WT/DS590/1, G/L/1325, G/TFA/D3/1, G/TRIMS/D/45, S/L/431, IP/D/42.

Japan – Measures Related to the Exportation of Products and Technology to Korea (Japan – Products and Technology (Korea)) (2020). Request for the Establishment of a Panel by the Republic of Korea, WT/DS590/4.

Klopschinski, S., Gibson, C. S. and Ruse-Khan, H. G. (2021). *The Protection of Intellectual Property Rights Under International Investment Law*. Oxford: Oxford University Press.

Law on International Patent Conventions 1976 (DE).

Lee, J. (2020). Forced Technology Transfer in the Case of China. *Boston University Journal of Science and Technology Law*, 26(2), pp. 324–352.

Ministry of Economy, Trade and Industry (2020) (JP). *Report on Compliance by Major Trading Partners with Trade Agreements – WTO, EPA/FTA and IIA*. Available at: www.meti.go.jp/english/report/data/2020WTO/gct20_1coe.html

Nagy, C. I. (2021). A Re-conceptualization of WTO Law's Security Exceptions: Squaring the Circle and Judicializing National Security. *Currents: Journal of International Economic Law*, 24(2), pp. 49–59.

Patent Act 1959 (JP).

Patent Act 1980 (DE).

Russia – Measures Concerning Traffic in Transit (Russia – Traffic in Transit) (2019). WTO Panel Report, WT/DS512/R.

Sakurai, T. (2020). *Bōei gijutsu no mamori-kata* [The Secret Patent System in Japan]. Tokyo: Hatsumei Suishin Kyōkai.

Saudi Arabia – Measures Concerning the Protection of Intellectual Property Rights (Saudi Arabia – IPRs) (2020). WTO Panel Report, WT/DS567/R.

Suzuki, M. (2015). International Investment Agreements, Intellectual Property Rights and Public Health. *Nagoya University Journal of Law and Politics*, 261, pp. 1–16.

Suzuki, M. (2020). Reflections on International Aspects of the Protection of Trade Secrets. *Patents & Licensing*, 49(6), pp. 8–17. Available at: https://papers.ssrn.com/sol3/papers.cfm?abstract_id=3812080

Sykes, A. O. (2021). The Law and Economics of 'Forced' Technology Transfer and Its Implications for Trade and Investment Policy (and the US – China Trade War). *Journal of Legal Analysis*, 13(1), pp. 127–171.

Tillis, T. (2022). *Tillis, Coons, Cotton, Hirono, and Scott Introduce Bipartisan Bill to Prevent the Chinese Communist Party from Stealing American Intellectual Property*. Available at: www.tillis.senate.gov/2022/3/tillis-coons-cotton-hirono-and-scott-introduce-bipartisan-bill-to-prevent-the-chinese-communist-party-from-stealing-american-intellectual-property

Unfair Competition Prevention Act 1993 (JP).

United States Trade Representative (2021). *2021 Special 301 Report*. Available at: https://ustr.gov/sites/default/files/files/reports/2021/2021%20Special%20301%20Report%20(final).pdf

WTO. Dispute Settlement Body (2020). *Minutes of Meeting, Held in the Centre William Rappard on 29 July 2020*, WT/DSB/M/443. Available at: https://docs.wto.org/dol2fe/Pages/SS/directdoc.aspx?filename=q:/WT/DSB/M443.pdf&Open=True

Wu, C. H. (2021). *Law and Politics on Export Restrictions: WTO and Beyond*. Cambridge: Cambridge University Press.

12 Revisiting Subsidy Rules, after the Global Financial Crisis and COVID-19

Suggestion to Utilize Article VI:6(c) of the GATT

Osamu UMEJIMA

Introduction

The *Agreement on Subsidies and Countervailing Measures* (the *SCM Agreement*) classifies subsidies into three categories: prohibited subsidies, such as export subsidies and import-substitution subsidies, which any World Trade Organization (WTO) Members may not grant; actionable subsidies, which a WTO Member may ask a subsidy-granting Member to remove adverse effects from the subsidy; and non-actionable subsidies, which rules expired in 2000. In addition to this discipline, the *SCM Agreement* provides detailed rules on countervailing duties (CVDs), which an importing Member may apply to subsidized imports up to a per-unit amount of subsidies.

Since China's utilization of subsidies to help recovery of the economy from the Global Financial Crisis, its infusion of subsidies to state-owned enterprises (SOEs) in the forms of low-interest rate loans, energy, below-cost inputs, and lease of the land has become one of the largest concerns of other WTO Members. Reportedly, Chinese industrial subsidies to listed companies increased from less than 50 billion yuan in 2010 to more than 200 billion yuan in 2020 (Cho, 2021). The EU claims that these subsidies have led to 'an increase in unfairly traded exports from China, driving down prices globally and causing injury to many industries in importing countries' (European Commission, 2021).

This chapter analyses WTO dispute settlement ('DS') cases involving subsidies and CVDs to find practical countermeasures against these problems.

WTO Disputes on Subsidies

WTO Dispute Settlement Cases on Prohibited and Actionable Subsidies

Overview

When a WTO Member wants a subsidy-granting Member to withdraw prohibited subsidies or to remove adverse effects from actionable subsidies, the *SCM Agreement* requires the Member to bring the issue to the WTO Dispute Settlement Body (DSB). When the Member succeeds before the panel and the Appellate Body, the DSB recommends that the subsidy-granting Member take appropriate actions.

DOI: 10.4324/9781003193098-12

Members initiated, that is, filed requests for consultation on, 76 dispute settlement cases alleging Article 3 (provisions on prohibited subsidies) and 27 cases alleging Article 6 (provisions on actionable subsidies).[1] Among these, panel reports were circulated in bolded DS cases in the note.

Separating these disputes into two periods, namely, before and after the Global Financial Crisis in 2008, cases on both prohibited and actionable subsidies significantly declined from 2009–2020 to nearly one-half of the first-half period. Fifty Article 3 cases were filed from 1995–2008, and 26 were filed thereafter. Seventeen Article 6 allegations were filed in the period, and ten were filed thereafter.

Many of the initiated WTO disputes did not reach the panel report stage. Only 33 panel reports involving subsidies were circulated in total. Panel reports involving prohibited subsidies materially reduced more than half, from 23 from 1995–2008 to ten from 2009–2020. Panel reports on actionable subsidies also reduced from ten to two in the same periods.

Analysis

PROHIBITED SUBSIDIES

A review of WTO subsidy DS cases reveals that major ambiguities on export subsidies have been clarified in the first-half period. WTO Members would no longer need to bring such subsidies to the DS to ask granting Members to withdraw them.

For example, the panel in *Brazil – Aircraft* (*Art. 21.5 – Canada II*) (2001) clarified that 'the *SCM Agreement* only regulates subsidies in the goods sector'. The Appellate Body clarified in *US – Upland Cotton* (2005a) that 'not all government measures capable of conferring benefits would necessarily fall within Article 1.1(a)'. In *Canada – Aircraft* (1999), the Appellate Body stated that the benefit would be found when the recipient of the financial contribution is better off in light of what it would receive from the marketplace. In *Canada – Aircraft* (*Art. 21.5 – Brazil*) (2000), it clarified that subsidies to an industry of high export-orientation in itself are not export subsidies. Only a few Appellate Body reports were issued to clarify major issues on import-substitution subsides after 2009. The Appellate Body clarified in *Canada – Renewable Energy* (2013) that the government-created market of renewable energy would be the relevant market to determine the benefits. In *Brazil – Taxation* (2019), the Appellate Body clarified the rule to identify 'revenue foregone' under Article 1.1(a)(1)(ii) of the *SCM Agreement.*

Because of these clarifications, both subsidy-granting Members and injured Members can identify prohibited export subsides, and, thus, no dispute proceedings are required. In fact, no real issues on the nature of export subsidies were disputed in the DS after 2009. In *US – Renewable Energy* (2019), the panel found that the US measures were inconsistent with Article III.4 of the GATT 1994, and it refrained from making any findings on subsides. In *India – Export Related Measures* (2019), India did not seriously argue the nature of subsidies as prohibited but rigorously rebutted special and differential treatment thereon under Article 27 of the *SCM Agreement*.

Accordingly, discipline on prohibited subsidies under the *SCM Agreement* is effective so far as a subsidy falls into a type of prohibited subsidy.

ACTIONABLE SUBSIDIES

WTO Members also substantially reduced their reliance on DS to discipline actionable subsidies but for different reasons.

As shown previously, Members initiated 17 DS cases alleging actionable subsidies from 1995–2008 and ten in the subsequent period, which is approximately only one-third of the prohibited subsidy cases in each period. Only two cases alleging Article 6 from 2009–2020 reached the panel report stage.

These panel reports indicate that the heavy burden of proof on complaining parties has led to a low utilization of DS, such as a 'genuine and substantial relationship of cause and effect' between the subsidy and alleged serious prejudice, as clarified by the Appellate Body Report in *EC and certain Member States – Large Civil Aircraft* (2011). In fact, successful actionable subsidy allegations were supported by unique situations. In *US – Upland Cotton* (2005b), Brazil relied on the World Cotton Statistics of the International Cotton Advisory Committee, which are readily-available world statistics. In *EC and certain member States – Large Civil Aircraft* (2011) and *US – Large Civil Aircraft (2nd complaint)* (2012), the Appellate Body found that 'each of the relevant LCA product markets operates as a duopoly'. In *Indonesia – Auto* (1998), Indonesia, the responding party, submitted self-inflicting material conceding before the panel that 'the tariff and tax subsidies under the National Car programme are responsible for the significant level of price undercutting'. Such evidence was critical to show causation.

Furthermore, the panel report in *Korea – Commercial Vessels* (2005) shows that it is much easier to prevail on prohibited subsidies than on actionable subsidies because of the causation requirement. The panel found alleged subsidies as export subsidies but rejected actionable subsidy claims because 'it is far from self-evident to us that a price reduction of [BCI] per cent on three transactions out of a much larger total would constitute, or lead to, "significant price depression" for [certain categories of ships] as a whole'.

Consequently, complaining parties did not seriously pursue actionable subsidy claims in either case from 2009–2020. The Panel exercised judicial economy on the actionable subsidy issue in *US – Renewable Energy* (2019). The United States initially made allegations on the *SCM Agreement* in *India – Solar Cells* (2016) but did not include it in its request for the establishment of the panel.

Therefore, the requirement to establish a causal link is the major obstacle for Members to use DS against actionable subsidies.

WTO Disputes on Countervailing Duties

Although WTO disputes to enforce disciplines on subsidies substantially decreased from 2009–2020, Members have dramatically increased CVDs to protect their domestic industries from harmful subsidies.

Exporting Members then challenged their consistency with the *SCM Agreement*. These disputes shed light on the deficiencies therein.

CVD Measures

WTO statistics on the number of CVDs imposed by importing Members show that Members substantially increased CVDs from 129 from 1995–2008 to 215 from 2009–2020. The United States, the largest CVD user, doubled its CVDs from 54 from 1995–2008 to 119 from 2009–2020. The EU has not changed its enforcement of CVDs significantly, 24 from 1995–2008 to 21 from 2009–2020, whereas Canada (14 to 22), Australia (two to 14), India (zero to 11) and China (zero to 10) have substantially increased their CVDs (WTO, 2021a).

WTO statistics on the number of CVDs imposed by exporting Members show that the majority of CVDs (116 out of 215 in total) were imposed on Chinese products from 2009 to 2020 (WTO, 2021a, 2021b). This trend was created by the United States Department of Commerce (USDOC), which changed its CVD enforcement policy to impose CVDs on Chinese products in 2007 (USDOC, 2007). It applied 74 CVD measures against Chinese products thereafter (WTO, 2021b). The European Union (EU)'s largest target was also China, on which the EU imposed nine CVDs (WTO, 2021b). EU CVD data on its webpage show that all of them were initiated in or after 2010 (European Commission, 2020). The EU's second largest target was India for three products, while it imposed CVDs on 21 products/countries in the same period. Australia imposed 11 CVDs against Chinese products and one CVD against Indian and Malaysian products (WTO, 2021b), counting French brandy CVDs in 2000 and in 2007 as two. India imposed CVDs on six Chinese, five Malaysian, and three Indonesian and Vietnamese products (Director General of Trade Remedy, 2021).

WTO Disputes on CVDs

In contrast, the number of panel reports on CVDs from 2009–2020 declined to 13[2] from 19 from 1995–2008.[3] Three Appellate Body reports, however, raised serious problems, such as the interpretation of 'public body' and the permissive use of a third-country benchmark for the determination of the benefit and the calculation of the amount of a subsidy. The United States strongly disagreed with these reports (USTR, 2020).

PUBLIC BODY

Article 1.1(i)(a) of the *SCM Agreement* provides that a subsidy shall be deemed to exist if 'there is a financial contribution by a government or any public body'. The *SCM Agreement* provides no explicit definition for a 'public body'.

The USDOC determined that a Chinese SOE is a public body because the Chinese government owns the majority of the SOE. The Appellate Body in *US – Anti-Dumping and Countervailing Duties (China)* (2011) rejected the US criterion, stating that a public body 'must be an entity that possesses, exercises or is vested with governmental authority'.

THIRD COUNTRY BENCHMARK

Article 14 of *the SCM Agreement* provides that the method to calculate the benefit granted through the provision of goods shall be determined 'in relation to prevailing market conditions for the good . . . in question in the country of provision'.

The USDOC determined that SOEs' low-priced sales of intermediate goods granted benefit to Chinese finished goods producers, and it applied prices in third countries as the benchmark. It explained that Chinese market prices were distorted by the government intervention.

The Appellate Body in *US – Countervailing Measures (China)* (2015) rejected the USDOC's finding by stating that 'a finding of government ownership and control of certain entities alone cannot serve as the sole basis for establishing price distortion. Furthermore, government-related prices cannot be discarded in a benchmark analysis without examination of whether or not they are market determined'.

Analyses on Effectiveness of CVDs

Reasons that CVDs Are Preferable for Importing Members

A review of differences in the regimes and their legal requirements shed light on the following reasons that Members prefer CVDs to DS.

First, an importing member can impose CVDs faster than DS. The total time period from the initiation of the CVD investigation to the final determination to impose the CVD would be 'within one year, and in no case more than 18 months, after the initiation' as set forth in Article 11.11 of the *SCM Agreement*. Successful actionable subsidy DS cases, in contrast, took one year and nine months in *Indonesia – Autos* (1998) and an exceptionally long period of five years and ten months in *EC and certain member States – Large Civil Aircraft* (2011) to reach the panel report. It would take more time for the Appellate Body proceeding if appealed and for the period for the responding party to implement measures to comply.

Second, an importing Member may impose a CVD as long as it can demonstrate injurious effects of subsidized imports to the domestic industry. The Appellate Body stated in *Japan – DRAMs (Korea)* (2007) that Article 15 of the *SCM Agreement* neither envisages nor requires 'a second examination of the effects of the subsidies as distinguished from the effects of the subsidized imports on a case-by-case basis'.

Third, it not an easy task to satisfy the burden of proof to demonstrate 'genuine and substantial relationship of cause and effect' between actionable subsidies and serious prejudice, as discussed previously. For this purpose, the complaining Member would need to analyze the structure, design, and operation of subsidies (see *EC – Commercial Vessels*, 2005).

Fourth, the scope of prohibited subsidies is narrow and limited to those contingent upon export performance or import-substitution. Subsidies granted by the Chinese government or by public bodies, such as low-interest rate loans and provisions of input materials, are not export- or import-substitution subsidies. Accordingly, disciplines on prohibited subsidies do not apply to them.

Problems in Subsidies that CVDs Cannot Solve

CVDs, however, are not the perfect means to discipline for harmful subsidies.

First, CVDs cannot require subsidy-granting Members to withdraw, or to remove adverse effects of, harmful subsidies. Article 13 of the *SCM Agreement* requires the importing Members to invite the exporting Member for consultation but does not oblige either Member to conduct consultations or to reach any agreements. Accordingly, no actions may be, and in many cases were not, taken by exporting Members in response to initiation of CVD investigations.

Second, the application of CVDs is limited to subsidized imports into the CVD-enforcing Member. A CVD is not effective for the competition in third country markets. Subsidized products are still able to enjoy the effects of subsidies in third country markets, and accordingly, unfair competition continues in these markets.

Third, the Appellate Body's findings on the public body and third-country benchmarks impede the importing Members' ability to counteract low-priced imports.

Challenges that We Face

Negotiation on the Improvement of the Subsidy Regime

Facing the apparent deficiencies in the current subsidy regime under the *SCM Agreement*, WTO Members have been working on the reform of the subsidy rules.

The most significant proposals, among others from the EU (European Commission, 2018), the Ottawa group (The Ottawa Group, 2018) and Argentina, Costa Rica, the EU, Japan and the United States (WTO, 2018), would be made by trilateral trade ministers of the EU, Japan and the United States (Trade Ministers, 2020). These ministers proposed that the *SCM Agreement* should add more types of prohibited and actionable subsidies, provide explicit definition of 'public body', and clarify circumstances in which a third-country benchmark may apply. They also proposed that the subsidy reporting requirements be strengthened and that the burden of proof to show causation between actionable subsidies and serious prejudice be relaxed (Umejima, 2021). These ministers, however, have not yet published the text-based proposal because COVID-19 prevented them from discussing this in-person.

Moreover, developing countries, such as India and South Africa, strongly oppose these proposals, particularly the notification requirement (WTO, 2019a). China proposed 'during discussions on subsidy disciplines, no special or discriminatory disciplines should be instituted on SOEs in the name of WTO reform'. China also demanded that certain subsidies be excluded from actionable subsidies (WTO, 2019b).

As such, it will be a long way to reach even the text-based negotiation amongst strong opposition from major developing countries and the slow-negotiation speed due to COVID-19.

Potential Path to Advance Disciplines on Subsidies

Although no improvements to the disciplines on subsidies under the *SCM Agreement* are expected in the foreseeable future, we should consider maximizing the use of currently available tools to counteract harmful subsidies.

The largest shortcoming of CVDs are, as discussed previously, their ineffectiveness against subsidized products in third country markets. In order to remove adverse effects of subsidies in a third country market, there are three potential options. It should be noted that regular and close communications among investigating authorities of like-minded Members on harmful subsidies are critical to facilitate effective enforcement of any one of the following actions:

(a) a third country may impose a CVD against the subsidized products based on the injury to its own industry;
(b) the third country may impose a CVD on behalf of the CVD-imposed Member; and/or
(c) the injured Members jointly bring the case to DS, alleging the serious prejudice in several markets.

Concerted CVDs by Third Countries

A readily practical method to counteract the subsidized products in a third country market is that such third country Member imposes a CVD on the same subsidized product upon a finding of injury to its own industry. The other Member, which already imposed the CVD on subsidized imports, should fully cooperate with the petitioners and investigating authorities of the Member by supplying information, such as programs of harmful subsidies that the other Member found countervailing and the analysis of price and volume effects of subsidized products. The other Member should also provide information on the potential diversion of subsidized products from its domestic market to the third country market.

These supports may facilitate Members to find the subsidization of the targeted products. The information on the potential diversion may also help the Member to find the threat of material injury, even if the Member is not able to find the actual material injury.

Imposition of CVDs on Behalf of a Third Country Based on Article VI:6(c) of the GATT

As a concerted effort of like-minded Members to eliminate adverse effects of harmful subsidies, Members may consider CVDs on behalf of a third country pursuant to Article VI:6(c) of the GATT.

THE HISTORY OF ARTICLE VI:6(C)

Australia and New Zealand proposed to add subparagraph (c) to Article VI:6 of the GATT in February 1955 (GATT, 1955). The Contracting Parties accepted this as proposed with minor modifications as follows (the strikethrough shows words deleted from the original proposal, and bold was inserted into the original):

> ~~Notwithstanding the provisions of sub-paragraph (a) of this paragraph,~~ [I]n exceptional circumstances, **however**, where delay might cause damage which would be difficult to repair, a contracting party may levy a countervailing duty

> for the purpose referred to in subparagraph (*b*) of this paragraph without the prior approval of the CONTRACTING PARTIES; *Provided* that such action shall be reported immediately to the CONTRACTING PARTIES and that the countervailing duty shall be withdrawn promptly if the CONTRACTING PARTIES disapprove.

The second sentence of Article VI:6(b) obliges WTO Members to approve a request for imposition of a CVD on behalf of a third country when they find the existence of a material injury. Because the exporting Member of the subsidized products would not agree to find the injury, this provision will not work.

As such, Article VI:6(c) was added as an exception. It permits a Member to levy CVDs without the approval pursuant to Article VI:6(b) where delay 'might' cause 'damage' that would be 'difficult to repair'. The Member must withdraw the CVD only after the WTO Members 'disapprove'.

INTERPRETATION OF ARTICLE VI:6(C)

A CVD on behalf of a third country may be imposed without prior approval from WTO Members if the Member finds that delay of the CVD 'might' cause 'damage' that would be 'difficult to repair'. None of these terms are defined in the GATT, and the *SCM Agreement* does not have provisions on CVDs on behalf of a third country.

The Oxford dictionary (Joanna, 2010) states that 'might' is 'used when showing that something is or was possible'. Accordingly, the certainty to incur damage, which would be difficult to repair, may be less than probable or even likely. Australia and New Zealand explained this in their proposal:

> [T]he proposal would also allow a contracting party without prior approval to use countervailing duties to protect the industry of a third country against subsidization in exceptional circumstances and where delay might cause damage which would be difficult to repair (GATT, 1955).

The statement provides no further explanation on the meaning of terms. It does not even discuss how damage should be serious to the state of the third country industry. The only requirement is that such damage, if incurred, would be difficult to repair.

As no further rules are set forth, a Member would have substantial discretion to determine situations in which delay of imposition of a CVD will possibly cause 'damage'. For example, this requirement would be satisfied where a long-term contract is to be taken away by subsidized imports, and immediate action of the CVD would be found to be indispensable to halt such a deal.

Upon the imposition of the CVD, Article VI:6(c) requires the Member to withdraw the CVD when WTO Members 'disapprove'. This provision is unique because it requires the action by Members of 'disapproval'. No other provisions of the GATT require that WTO Members 'disapprove'. Other provisions provide that WTO Members 'do not disapprove' in Articles XVIII:21, XIX:3(a), and XX(h).

This difference is significant because the term 'disapprove' requires positive action. Members' inaction does not satisfy the requirement to 'disapprove'. The General Council, however, will not be able to reach the decision of 'disapproval' because the CVD-imposing Member and the beneficiary third country Member would not agree with the disapproval.

Accordingly, where a third country Member finds that its industry is materially injured by the subsidized imports, it may ask other like-minded Members to impose the CVD upon a finding of certain damage that would be potentially difficult to repair without the immediate imposition of CVDs.

Once such concerted actions against harmful subsidies extended to major export markets, adverse effects of these subsidies would effectively be eliminated from international trade.

Serious Prejudice of Subsidies in the Third Country

Finally, Members may consider joint DS actions alleging serious prejudice of actionable subsidies.

This option, however, faces a serious problem of the defunct Appellate Body. Even if complaining parties win the case in the panel report, the responding party incurs no obligations once the responding party appeals the case.

Definition of Public Body and Third Country Benchmark

Public Body

Although the United States complains about the Appellate Body's definition of public body, the United States found a way out of this problem, and, thus, this issue is not an immediate impediment.

The panel in *US – Countervailing Measures (China)* (*Art. 21.5 – China*) (2019b) found that the USDOC properly found that certain state-invested enterprises are public bodies because they are used 'as instrumentalities to effectuate the governmental purpose of maintaining the predominant role of the state sector of the economy and upholding the socialist market economy'. The Appellate Body confirmed this finding.

Third-Country Benchmark

In contrast, the Appellate Body found in *US – Countervailing Measures (China)* (*Art. 21.5 – China*) (2019a) that the United States has not yet offered an appropriate explanation on 'how prices have been distorted as a result of such indirect impact of the government intervention'. Accordingly, investigating authorities of like-minded Members should work together to identify situations in which a third country benchmark may be allowed.

In any event, however, this issue will not be an impediment for a while because the defunct Appellate Body would work in favor of the investigating authorities.

Conclusion

The history of the WTO DS involving subsidies and CVDs shows that CVDs would be practically more effective and efficient to counteract harmful subsidies than DS. WTO Members' efforts to improve disciplines on prohibited and actionable subsidies under the *SCM Agreement* would not be concluded in the foreseeable future.

In such situations, WTO Members should work together to take concerted actions against harmful subsidies. Among other options, like-minded Members should consider imposition of CVDs of its own or on behalf of a third country pursuant to Article VI:6(c) of the GATT.

It is hopeful that these concerted CVDs will encourage developing Members to join the negotiation to improve disciplines on subsidies under the *SCM Agreement* in the end.

Notes

1 Requests for consultation including Article 3 allegations were, by DS number, the following: **46**, 51, 52, **54, 55**, 57, **59, 64**, 65, **70**, 81, **103**, 104, 106, **108**, **113**, **126**, 127, 128, 129, 130, 131, **139**, **142**, 195, **222**, **236**, **265**, **266**, **267**, **273**, **283**, **301**, 307, **316**, 317, **339**, 340, 342, 347, **353**, 354, 357, 358, 359, 365, 380, 387, 388, 390 (i.e., 50/**23** cases from 1995–2008); **412**, 419, **426**, 451, 452, **456**, 459, **472**, **476**, **486**, **487**, 489, **497**, 507, **510**, 522, **541**, 563, 571, 580, 581, 583, 592, 593, 594, 600 (i.e., 26/**10** cases from 2009–2021). Requests including Article 6 allegations were, by DS number, as follows: **54, 55, 59, 64,** 147, 172, 173, **267**, **273**, **301**, 307, **316**, 317, 347, **353**, 357, 379 (i.e., 17/**9** cases from 1995–2008); 451, **456**, 459, 507, **510**, 519, 522, 571, 594, 598 (i.e., 10/**2** cases from 2009–2021).

2 The DS numbers are 414, 427, 436, 437, 440, 449, 464, 486, 491, 505, 523, 533, 539.

3 The DS numbers are 138, 194, 206, 212, 213, 217, 234, 221, 236, 257, 277, 295, 296, 299, 336, 341, 343, 345, 379.

References

All subsequent websites were last visited on 12 September 2022.

Brazil – Certain Measures Concerning Taxation and Charges (Brazil – Taxation) (2019). WTO Appellate Body Report, WT/DS472/AB/R, WT/DS497/AB/R.

Brazil – Export Financing Programme for Aircraft (Brazil – Aircraft) (Art. 21.5 – Canada II) (2001). WTO Panel Report, WT/DS46/RW/2.

Canada – Certain Measures Affecting the Renewable Energy Generation Sector (Canada – Renewable Energy) (2013). WTO Appellate Body Report, WT/DS412/AB/R, WT/DS426/AB/R.

Canada – Measures Affecting the Export of Civilian Aircraft (Canada – Aircraft) (1999). Appellate Body Report, WT/DS70/AB/R.

Canada – Measures Affecting the Export of Civilian Aircraft (Canada – Aircraft) (Art. 21.5 – Brazil) (2000). Appellate Body Report, WT/DS70/AB/RW.

Cho, Y. (2021). Eyeing US, China Wields $33bn Subsidies to Bolster Chips, Defense. *Nikkei Asia*. Available at: https://asia.nikkei.com/Politics/International-relations/US-China-tensions/Eyeing-US-China-wields-33bn-subsidies-to-bolster-chips-defense?n_cid=DSBNNAR

Director General of Trade Remedy (2021). *The Ministry of Commerce and Industry, the Government of India. Countervailing Duty Investigation (CVD)*. Available at: www.dgtr.gov.in/countervailing-duty-investigation

European Commission (2018). *EU Concept Paper on WTO Reform, WTO modernization Future EU Proposals on Rulemaking*. Available at: https://trade.ec.europa.eu/doclib/docs/2018/september/tradoc_157331.pdf

European Commission (2020). *Anti-Subsidy Investigation Database*. Available at: https://trade.ec.europa.eu/doclib/docs/2018/december/tradoc_157607.ods

European Commission (2021). *39th Annual Report from the Commission to the European Parliament and the Council on the EU's Anti-Dumping, Anti-Subsidy and Safeguard Activities and the Use of Trade Defence Instruments by Third Countries Targeting the EU in 2020*. Available at: https://trade.ec.europa.eu/doclib/docs/2021/august/tradoc_159782.PDF

European Communities and Certain Member States – Measures Affecting Trade in Large Civil Aircraft (EC and Certain Member States – Large Civil Aircraft) (2011). WTO Appellate Body Report, WT/DS316/AB/R.

European Communities – Measures Affecting Trade in Commercial Vessels (EC – Commercial Vessels) (2005). WTO Panel Report, WT/DS301/R.

GATT (1955). *General Agreement on Tariffs and Trade Contracting Parties – Review Working Party III on Barriers to Trade Other Than Restrictions or Tariffs – Amendment to Paragraph 6 of Article VI – Proposal by Australian and New Zealand Delegations*, W.9/214, 21 February. Available at: https://docs.wto.org/gattdocs/q/GG/W/9-214.PDF.

India – Certain Measures Relating to Solar Cells and Solar Modules (India – Solar Cells) (2016). WTO Panel Report, WT/DS456/R.

India – Export Related Measures (2019), WTO Panel Report, WT/DS541/R.

Indonesia – Certain Measures Affecting the Automobile Industry ("Indonesia – Auto") (1998). WTO Panel Report, WT/DS54/R, WT/DS55/R, WT/DS56/R and WT/DS64/R.

Japan – Countervailing Duties on Dynamic Random Access Memories from Korea (Japan – DRAMs (Korea)) (2007). WTO Appellate Body Report, WT/DS336/AB/R.

Joanna, T. (2010). *Oxford Advanced Learner's Dictionary*, 8th ed. Oxford: Oxford University Press, p. 970.

Korea – Measures Affecting Trade in Commercial Vessels (Korea – Commercial Vessels) (2005). WTO Panel Report, WT/DS273/R.

The Ottawa Group (2018). *Joint Communiqué of the Ottawa Ministerial on WTO Reform*. Available at: www.wto.org/english/news_e/news18_e/dgra_26oct18_e.pdf

Trade Ministers of Japan, the United States and the European Union (2020). *Joint Statement of the Trilateral Meeting of the Trade Ministers of Japan, the United States and the European Union*. Washington, DC. Available at: https://ustr.gov/about-us/policy-offices/press-office/press-releases/2020/january/joint-statement-trilateral-meeting-trade-ministers-japan-united-states-and-european-union

Umejima, O. (2021). *Disciplines on Industrial Subsidies: Issues and Directions for Improvements in the Changing World*. In: Drelich-Skulska, B. and Okawara, M. eds., *Current Trends in the Global Economy: From the Perspective of Japanese and Polish Economists*. Wroclaw: Publishing House of Wroclaw University of Economics and Business, pp. 29–72.

United States – Certain Measures Relating to the Renewable Energy Sector (US – Renewable Energy) (2019). WTO Panel Report, WT/DS510/R.

United States – Countervailing Duty Measures on Certain Products from China (US – Countervailing Measures (China)) (2015). WTO Appellate Body Report, WT/DS437/AB/R.

United States – Countervailing Duty Measures on Certain Products from China (US – Countervailing Measures (China) (Art. 21.5 – China)) (2019a). WTO Appellate Body Report, WT/DS437/AB/RW.

United States – Countervailing Duty Measures on Certain Products from China (US – Countervailing Measures (China) (Art. 21.5 – China)) (2019b). WTO Panel Report, WT/DS437/RW.

United States – Countervailing Measures on Certain Hot-Rolled Carbon Steel Flat Products from India (US – Carbon Steel (India)) (2014). WTO Appellate Body Report, WT/DS436/AB/R.

United States – Definitive Anti-Dumping and Countervailing Duties on Certain Products from China (US – Anti-Dumping and Countervailing Duties (China)) (2011). WTO Appellate Body Report, WT/DS379/AB/R.

United States Department of Commerce (2007). *Amended Preliminary Affirmative Countervailing Duty Determination: Coated Free Sheet Paper from the People's Republic of China*, 72 Fed. Reg. 17,484.

United States – Measures Affecting Trade in Large Civil Aircraft – Second Complaint (US – Large Civil Aircraft (2nd complaint)) (2012). WTO Appellate Body Report, WT/DS353/AB/R.

United States – Subsidies on Upland Cotton (US – Upland Cotton) (2005a). WTO Appellate Body Report, WT/DS267/AB/R.

United States – Subsidies on Upland Cotton (US – Upland Cotton) (2005b). WTO Panel Report, WT/DS267/R.

United States Trade Representative (2020). *Report on the Appellate Body of the World Trade Organization*. Available at: https://ustr.gov/sites/default/files/Report_on_the_Appellate_Body_of_the_World_Trade_Organization.pdf

World Trade Organization (2018). *Draft General Council decision on Procedures to Enhance Transparency and Strengthen Notification Requirements Under WTO Agreements*. Available at: https://docs.wto.org/dol2fe/Pages/FE_Search/FE_S_S009-DP.aspx?language=E&CatalogueIdList=249337&CurrentCatalogueIdIndex=0&FullTextHash=371857150&HasEnglishRecord=True&HasFrenchRecord=False&HasSpanishRecord=False

World Trade Organization (2019a). *An Inclusive Approach to Transparency and Notification Requirements in the WTO: Communication from African Group, Cuba, and India (Revision)*. Available at: https://docs.wto.org/dol2fe/Pages/SS/directdoc.aspx?filename=q:/Jobs/GC/218R1.pdf&Open=True

World Trade Organization (2019b). *China's Proposal on WTO Reform, WT/GC/W/773, Para. 2.16*. Available at: https://docs.wto.org/dol2fe/Pages/FE_Search/FE_S_S009-DP.aspx?CatalogueIdList=254127&CurrentCatalogueIdIndex=0

World Trade Organization (2021a). *Countervailing Measures by Reporting Member*. Available at: https://www.wto.org/english/tratop_e/adp_e/AD_MeasuresByRepMem.xlsx

World Trade Organization (2021b). *Countervailing Measures: Reporting Member vs Exporter*. Available at: www.wto.org/english/tratop_e/scm_e/CV_MeasuresRepMemVsExp.xls

13 Mainstreaming Non-trade Concerns in International Trade Law

Junji NAKAGAWA

Introduction

In the past, international trade law did not give much attention to non-trade concerns, such as environmental protection, sustainable development, and human rights. The General Agreement on Tariffs and Trade (GATT) considered non-trade concerns within the general exceptions (Art. XX) and security exception (Art. XXI). However, the margin of the exceptions was narrow, and there was little room for non-trade concerns to be allowed under the GATT. The limited space for non-trade concerns under the GATT was criticized in 1990 when *United States – Restrictions on Imports of Tuna* (the Tuna – Dolphin case, 1991) was brought to the dispute settlement panel. The panel report (*United States – Restrictions on Imports of Tuna*, 1991) outlawed the ban of US imports of tuna, which was incidentally caught with dolphins, and the decision was criticized for its lack of due respect to the environment.

In the early days of the World Trade Organization (WTO), its case law was developed to widen the permissibility of trade-restrictive measures for the sake of the environment. In the early days of the WTO, it was criticized for its lack of respect for the protection of human rights, particularly, people's right to enjoy health (International Covenant on Economic, Social and Cultural Rights, Art. 12). This criticism led to amending the Agreement on Trade-Related Aspects of Intellectual Property Rights (TRIPS Agreement). These were attempts at taking non-trade concerns into consideration in the interpretation and implementation of the WTO rules.

The treatment of non-trade concerns under the WTO entered a new stage when the United Nations (UN) announced the 2030 Agenda for Sustainable Development Goals (SDGs) in 2015 (UN General Assembly Resolution, 2015). This refers to a comprehensive set of goals and targets for the achievement of sustainable development[1] that are shared by the international community as a whole. It has impacted the status of non-trade concerns in the rules and activities of the WTO in two senses. First, trade is positioned as a means of attaining the SDGs goals and targets. The rules and activities of the WTO are also positioned to attain various goals and targets of the SDGs. Second, the SDGs encourage reforms of the rules and activities of the WTO to attain its goals and targets. These have resulted in mainstreaming non-trade issues, such as protection of human rights, environmental protection, and sustainable development, in the rules and activities of the WTO.

DOI: 10.4324/9781003193098-13

The term 'mainstreaming' is used here to refer to the situation where non-trade concerns are positioned as goals of the WTO, instead of being positioned as exceptions to the principles and rules of the WTO. This means that the rules and activities of the WTO became instrumental in achieving non-trade values, such as human rights, environmental protection, and sustainable development.

This chapter traces the changing status of non-trade concerns in international trade law since the application of the GATT to the early days of the WTO and to the era of the SDGs. Section 2 deals with the status of non-trade issues under the GATT. Section 3 addresses the status of non-trade issues in the early days of the WTO. Section 4 deals with the status of non-trade issues within the WTO rules and activities under the SDGs. Section 5 briefly describes the results of the research in this chapter, and section 6 concludes the chapter.

The GATT and Non-trade Concerns

During the GATT era, international trade law, international environmental law, and international human rights law were isolated from one another, with almost no instances of conflict (Lang, 2011, p. 40). The major goal of the GATT was the liberalization of trade in goods. It aimed at 'entering into mutually advantageous and reciprocal arrangements that substantially reduce tariffs and other trade barriers and to eliminate the discriminatory treatment in international commerce' (Preamble to the GATT, Para. 3). However, trade liberalization was not the absolute goal of the GATT. The GATT's 'embedded liberalism' allowed the parties to the agreement to implement a variety of domestic social policies through a balance of payment restrictions (Art. XII), domestic subsidies (Art. XVI), general exceptions (Art. XX), safeguards (Art. XIX), and the national security exception (Art. XXI) (Ruggie, 1982, pp. 393–398). Insofar as non-trade concerns were justified by these restrictions and exceptions, they were not in conflict with trade liberalization.

In contrast, there was a strong aversion within the GATT to any explicit link between trade and non-trade issues, such as human rights, for fear of politicizing trade relations (Alston, 1982, p. 168; Lang, 2011, p. 42).

When the linkage between trade and non-trade concerns was unavoidable, such as the case of the imposition of trade sanctions for reasons related to apartheid (Alston, 1982, pp. 161–166), the GATT could avoid politicization of the issue by allowing contracting parties to resort to trade sanctions under Article XXI, wherein the UN Security Council was allowed to impose economic sanctions on a country and/or when a contracting party felt the need to restrict trade to protect its principal security interests (Lang, 2011, p. 42). Article XXI and the self-judging character in its application made it possible for contracting parties to be practically immune from its breach at the dispute settlement procedure (Alford, 2011). The peaceful coexistence of the GATT and non-trade concerns was challenged in 1990 when Mexico challenged the US import ban of tuna caught with incidental catches of dolphins. The report of the panel dismissed the plea of the US that the ban was justified as a measure related to conserving the nonrenewable natural resources under Article XX(g) of the GATT because the ban did not aim at conserving exhaustible natural resources in the first place (GATT, 1991, Paras. 5.31–5.34). The report of the panel also dismissed the plea of the US that tuna with incidental catches of dolphins and tuna without an incidental catch were not 'like products' under the GATT Article III.4 because likeness under this article shall be decided according to the product characteristics, not the production methods thereof (GATT, 1991, Para. 5.15). The report of the panel was criticized for the lack of respect to the environment under the GATT (see, for instance, Charnovitz, 1994), and it raised inquiries about the required context where international trade law can impose constraints on states by taking actions for environmental protection and to conserve natural resources (McDorman, 1992, p. 463).

Non-trade Issues during the Early Days of the WTO

The Marrakesh Agreement Establishing the WTO referred to the protection of the environment in paragraph 1 of the Preamble; as the Parties to the agreement seek 'protection and preservation of the environment', environmental protection was positioned among the goals of the WTO. During its early days, the WTO dispute settlement mechanism developed case law that aimed at balancing free trade and environmental protection by allowing members of the WTO to justify their restrictive measures of trade for the protection of the environment under Article XX of the GATT 1994. This happened partly due to the status of the environment in the Preamble to the Marrakesh Agreement. Moreover, it was partly due to the vociferous criticism of the GATT panel report on the aforementioned Tuna – Dolphin case. The Appellate Body report on *United States – Import Prohibition of Certain Shrimp and Shrimp Products* (1998) dealt with a case that was similar to the Tuna – Dolphin case. It confirmed that the measure at issue was associated with the conservation of exhaustible natural resources (Art. XX (g)) (Paras. 141–142). Although the report concluded that the US measure violated the Article XX conditions (Para. 184), the Appellate Body report of its Article 21.5 procedure confirmed the compatibility of the implementing measures of the US with Article XX (*United States – Import Prohibition of Certain Shrimp and Shrimp Products* (US – Shrimp), 2001). The case law of the WTO clarified the conditions in which trade-restrictive measures of the members aimed at protecting the environment may be allowed under the rules of Article XX. First, the measure should be transparent and flexible, and it must be implemented through due process of law (no arbitrary discrimination). Second, measures based on a multilateral framework and negotiations among related countries should be preferred (no unjustifiable discrimination). Third, the measures must not be discriminatory among countries under similar conditions (no unjustifiable discrimination). Fourth, the measures must be published and notified before implementation, and must not be designed and structured to hide protectionist intentions (no disguised protection) (Nakagawa, 2003, pp. 188–189).

Regarding the protection of human rights, the WTO had a couple of examples of linking trade and human rights during its early days. The first was the Rough Diamonds-related Waiver Concerning Kimberley Process Certification Scheme (hereinafter 'the waiver') (WTO, 2003). The waiver enables WTO Members who are participants in the Kimberley Process to differentiate in treating rough diamonds imports and exports based on the violations of gross human rights due to its illegal trade (Schefer, 2005). Schefer criticized the waiver because it did not offer a substitute in the long term to solve the problematic relationship between the WTO trade rules and non-trade issues that the global community had to deal with. Schefer argued that the issue should have been brought to the WTO dispute settlement mechanism, where the compatibility of the discriminatory treatment might be settled according to the rules of the WTO (Schefer, 2005, p. 450), in particular Article XX (general exceptions) of the GATT 1994 (Schefer, 2005, pp. 425–437).

Another case involving waivers relating to human rights protection was the Generalized Scheme of Preferences (GSP) of the European Union (EU), which accorded additional tariff reductions (GSP plus) to developing countries with satisfied conditions including respect for fundamental labor rights. In this case, 'GSP plus' was accorded as an incentive for developing countries to improve their human rights protection. India filed a complaint against this scheme, alleging that it represented a case of waiver for GSP schemes of developed countries that violated the conditions of the Enabling Clause (GATT, 1979). The report of the Appellate Body in *European Communities – Conditions for the Granting of Tariff Preferences to Developing Countries* (2004) interpreted the 'nondiscriminatory' term in footnote 3 to paragraph 2 (a) of the Enabling Clause as the necessity of applying different treatment methods to different beneficiaries in developing countries (Para. 162). Simultaneously, the report provided that the need of the beneficiaries should be assessed based on an objective standard identified by the WTO agreement or it could be set by multilateral instruments that international organizations adopt (Para. 163). The EU reformed its GSP Scheme and set ratification of 16 international conventions dealing with human rights and fundamental labor rights and 11 international conventions relating to good governance as a condition for the eligibility of GSP plus (European Union, 2005). The linkage between trade and human rights was therefore established with reference to international human rights conventions. Ito criticized this approach as superficial, as the need of the beneficiaries should be assessed in accordance with their effective linkage with the additional tariff preferences (Ito, 2010, p. 22).

The WTO law became the target of criticism by the human rights community in its early days, namely, the criticism that the provision of the compulsory licensing TRIPS Agreement infringes the right to health of people of least developed countries (LDCs) because it obstructs the supply of affordable medicines for HIV-AIDs treatment (IISD, 2003). This criticism led to the Doha Declaration on TRIPS and Public Health on 14 November 2001 (WT/MIN (01)/DEC/2). In the sixth paragraph of the Declaration, the TRIPS Council was guided to find a quick solution. Finally, the amendment of the TRIPS Agreement (Art. 31 *bis*) entered into force in 2017 that enables the diffusion of affordable medicines in LDCs without satisfying the conditions under Article 31 (WTO TRIPS Council, 2005). This is an important step for the WTO to position human rights (namely, the right to health) to be one of its principal rules, not an exception. However, the major goal of the WTO remained trade liberalization, and there was no explicit mention of human rights in the WTO law.

There has been an instance of impositions of trade sanctions against human rights violations under the WTO. It was an act issued by the Commonwealth of Massachusetts that obligated the public authorities of the Commonwealth of Massachusetts not to purchase products or services from anyone that is a business partner with Myanmar. It was a trade sanction against violations of human rights in Myanmar. The European Communities (EC) filed a complaint against this, alleging that the act violates the Agreement on Government Procurement (GPA), specifically, Articles X, VIII (B), and XIII (WTO, 1997). The panel proceedings were suspended and later lapsed pending the issuance of a court ruling in the US, which prevented the measure at issue to be implemented. Otherwise, the panel would have produced the report in alignment with the relevant GPA rules.

WTO and Non-trade Issues under the SDGs

The status of non-trade concerns in the WTO rules and functions entered a new stage with the 2030 Agenda for Sustainable Development and the SDGs that significantly emphasize the role of trade in the promotion of sustainable development and that clearly recognize the WTO's contribution in the attainment of the various goals and targets of the SDGs, as follows (see the WTO and the SDGs) (WTO, n.d.c).

SDG 1 – No Poverty – indicates strong evidence that trade policy initiatives, which are planned in a good manner and strategically applied, can have a positive impact by reducing persistent poverty.

SDG 2 – Zero Hunger – indicates that agricultural export subsidies are eliminated by the decision made by the WTO in 2015 regarding export competition (WTO Ministerial Conference of Nairobi, 2015) that delivers on Target 2.b.[2]

SDG 3 – Good Health and Well-being – shows the aforementioned modification of the WTO's TRIPS Agreement (Art. 31 *bis*), which entered into force in 2017. It facilitates the process of accessing affordable medicines by using secure legal means for developing countries in line with Target 3.b.[3]

SDG 5 – Gender Equality – indicates that women have many opportunities for employment and economic development through trade that significantly increase their access to job opportunities.

SDG 8 – Decent Work and Economic Growth – shows that inclusive economic growth led by trade increases the capacities of countries to generate income, which represents one of the major prerequisites to achieve sustainable development.

SDG 9 – Industry, Innovation, and Infrastructure – indicates that trade increases competition between parties that, in turn, results in mutual economic gains through knowledge and technology transfer and innovation.

SDG 10 – Reduced Inequalities – shows that the WTO rules support the reduction of inequalities among Parties by applying the special and differential treatment (S&DT) principles for developing countries. Accordingly, the WTO ensures flexibility for developing countries and LDCs in managing their capacity constraints.

SDG 14 – Life Below Water – indicates that the Decision on Fisheries Subsidies adopted in December 2017 (WTO Ministerial Conference of Buenos Aires, 2017) represents a good initiative through multilateral efforts to achieve SDG Target 14.6,[4] which obligates Parties to ban subsidies for overfishing and those related to illegal, unreported, and unregulated (IUU) fishing.

Finally, SDG 17 – Partnerships for the Goals – indicates that its targets require countries to adopt a rules-based, universal, nondiscriminatory, open, and equitable multilateral system of trade (Target. 17.10); double the LDCs' share of global exports by 2020 (Target. 17.11) and implement quota-free and duty-free market access for LDCs (Target. 17.12). The WTO is the major delivery channel for these and other goals and targets.

Results

These alignments among trade, the WTO, and SDGs show that trade and the WTO rules are positioned as a means of attaining the various goals and targets of the SDGs. In this sense, non-trade concerns, such as human rights (fundamental labor rights and gender equality, among others), sustainable development, and environmental protection are placed as the major WTO goals. Moreover, promoting such mainstreaming of non-trade concerns in the rules and activities of the WTO encourages reforms of the WTO rules, such as the elimination of agricultural export subsidies, the aforementioned amendment to the TRIPS Agreement, and new discipline on fisheries subsidies. By aligning non-trade concerns with the WTO and SDGs, mainstreaming non-trade concerns in international trade law has entered into a new stage in the sense that the assessment of existing rules of the WTO and decisions on the future directions of its rule-making are guided by their conformity with non-trade issues embodied in the SDGs.

These changes of the WTO rules encouraged by the SDGs were not totally new to the WTO. First, the Marrakesh Agreement Establishing the WTO provides that sustainable development is one of the WTO goals.[5] The SDGs materialize this statement by systematically elucidating non-trade concerns and the WTO rules relationship as a 'goals and means' relationship, not vice versa, and by encouraging reforms of the WTO rules to attain the goals and targets of the SDGs. Second, reforms of the WTO had started with the built-in agenda of the Doha Development Agenda on elimination of export subsidies (see Agriculture: negotiating modalities) (WTO, n.d.a). The other reforms of the WTO rules aiming at matching the SDGs had also started before the launch of the SDGs in 2015, such as the Doha Declaration on the TRIPS Agreement and Public Health in November 2001 and fisheries subsidies negotiations that had been conducted within the Doha Development Agenda Framework of Negotiations on Rules (see Negotiations on fisheries subsidies) (WTO, 2001). The SDGs realigned these reforms with the WTO rules according to the broad goal of sustainable development.

Finally, note that the mainstreaming of non-trade issues in international trade law within the SDG framework has its own monitoring mechanism. The WTO plays an important role in accelerating the achievements of SDGs, and it closely collaborates with the UN's Department of Economic and Social Affairs to monitor the progress of achieving the SDGs. The WTO delivers annual reports to the UN's High-level Political Forum (HLPF) that review the SDGs concerning the efforts of the WTO to achieve specific trade targets (see The WTO's contribution to achieving the SDGs) (WTO, 2022). For instance, WTO's 2020 report to the HLPF (WTO, 2020) documents the recent developments in the WTO on issues related to sustainable development, such as the negotiations on fisheries subsidies (p. 2), the dialogue at the WTO's Committee on Trade and Environment concerning the trade aspects of a circular economy (pp. 4–5), the role of the WTO's Standards and Trade Development Facility in facilitating safe trade in support of the SDGs (pp. 6–7), and major activities of the WTO on trade and gender (pp. 7–9). The reports were submitted to the HLPF, and their related discussion enabled the HLPF to monitor and evaluate the rules and activities of the WTO in attaining the SDGs.

Concluding Remarks

This chapter traces the changing status of non-trade issues, such as human rights, sustainable development, and environmental protection, in international trade law since the application of the GATT to the early days of the WTO and to the SDG era. The status of non-trade concerns in international trade law shifted from their initial marginal treatment in the GATT era to a more conciliatory treatment during the early days of the WTO. Nevertheless, even the WTO during its early days treated non-trade concerns primarily in a marginal manner, namely, through the justification of restrictive measures related to trade for the sake of non-trade concerns through general exceptions in Article XX of the GATT 1994 and waivers (the Waiver Concerning Kimberley Process Certification Scheme for Rough Diamonds). The marginal status of non-trade concerns in the early days of the WTO remained unchanged in the GATT era. Free trade was the primary principle of the WTO, and non-trade concerns were positioned as exceptions to the primary principle.

In contrast, the WTO was criticized for its lack of due respect to human rights protection in the late 1990s and the beginning of the 2000s in relation to the provision of the TRIPS Agreement on compulsory licensing, as it allegedly infringes the right to health of the people in LDCs. This criticism led to the amendment in 2017 of the TRIPS Agreement (Art. 31 *bis*) that enables the diffusion of affordable medicines in LDCs without satisfying the conditions under Article 31. This was the first attempt at positioning non-trade concerns (right to health) as among the principal WTO rules, not as exceptions to them.

The status of non-trade concerns in international trade law entered a new stage by the adoption of the 2030 Agenda for Sustainable Development and the SDGs in 2015. This has two implications. First, trade and the WTO rules were positioned to become a means of attaining the various goals and targets of the SDGs. The relationship between non-trade concerns and international trade law was reversed from the earlier 'exceptions to principles' to 'goals and means'. We may call this change mainstreaming non-trade concerns in international trade law.

However, because the WTO rules remain unchanged, this development remains largely theoretical. We should note here that the SDGs encourage the reforms of the WTO rules to attain their broad-based goals and targets, such as eliminating agricultural export subsidies, the amendment to the TRIPS Agreement, and new fisheries subsidies discipline for the sake of conservation of fisheries resources. We may add negotiations on the trade liberalization of environmental goods and services as another example of WTO reforms to attain the goals and targets of the SDGs (environmental protection) (see Eliminating trade barriers on environmental goods and services) (WTO, n.d.b).

These reforms of the WTO rules encouraged by the SDGs were not totally new to the WTO, as they had been envisioned in the Preamble to the Marrakesh Agreement Establishing the WTO, which refers to sustainable development as one of the goals of the WTO. The SDGs materialize this statement by systematically elucidating non-trade concerns and the WTO relationship as a 'goals and means' relationship, not vice versa, and by encouraging reforms of the WTO rules to attain the SDGs. Moreover, reforms of the WTO rules had started before the SDGs were launched in 2015, in the form of the Doha Development Agenda on the elimination of export subsidies, the Doha Declaration on the TRIPS Agreement and Public Health in November 2001, or the fisheries subsidies negotiations that were launched within the framework of the Doha Development Agenda negotiations on Rules. The SDGs realigned these reforms of the WTO rules in accordance with the broad-based goals and targets of sustainable development.

Finally, the mainstreaming of non-trade issues in international trade law within the SDG framework has a monitoring mechanism. The WTO delivers annual reports to the UN's HLPF about the efforts of the WTO to attain SDG trade-specific targets. These reports and the ensuing discussion at the HLPF enabled it to monitor and evaluate the rules and activities of the WTO in attaining the SDGs. Therefore, the SDGs are used as yardsticks for assessing the WTO rules and activities, and they also guide their future direction toward the broad-based goal of attaining sustainable development.

Notes

1 Sustainable development has no official definition. The Brundtland report issued on 1987 and titled '*Our Common Future*' defined it to be development that 'meets the needs of the present without compromising the ability of future generations to meet their own needs'. See the World Commission on Environment and Development (1987, Para. 27). Although this definition refers to economic development that does not degrade the environment, the term 'sustainable development' may refer to a wider concept that covers not only economic development but also social development, in the sense that society sustains itself based on the principle of fairness and equity. As is shown later, the SDGs refer to the latter definition of sustainable development, covering both economic and social development. See Nakagawa (2021, n. 4).

2 Target 2.b is designed to correct and prevent trade restrictions and distortions in world agricultural markets through the parallel elimination of all forms of agricultural export subsidies and all export measures with equivalent effect according to the mandate of the Doha Development Agenda.

3 Target 3.b supports medicine and vaccine research and development (R&D) for both communicable and non-communicable diseases that mainly affect developing countries. It is also designed to provide access to affordable vaccines and medicines according to the Doha Declaration on the TRIPS Agreement and Public Health. It emphasizes that developing countries have the right to use the provisions in the TRIPS Agreement to the maximum, it ensures flexibility in public health protection, and it seeks to provide access to medicines for all.

4 Target 14.6 indicates that by 2020, specific types of subsidies to fisheries will be prohibited for contributing to overfishing and overcapacity. It is designed to suspend subsidies contributing to IUU fishing and to impede the introduction of similar new subsidies. It also recognizes that appropriate and effective special and differential treatment for developing countries and LDCs should be integrated into the WTO fisheries subsidies negotiation.

5 See Preamble to the Agreement Establishing the WTO, which provides as follows:

> with a view to raising standards of living, ensuring full employment and a large and steadily growing volume of real income and effective demand, and expanding the production of and trade in goods and services, while allowing for the optimal use of the world's resources in accordance with the objective of sustainable development, seeking both to protect and preserve the environment and to enhance the means for doing so in a manner consistent with their respective needs and concerns at different levels of economic development.

References

All subsequent websites were last visited on 19 September 2022.

Alford, R. P. (2011). The Self-judging WTO Security Exception. *Utah Law Review*, 3, pp. 697–759.

Alston, P. (1982). International Trade as an Instrument of Positive Human Rights Policy. *Human Rights Quarterly*, 4(2), pp. 155–183.

Charnovitz, S. (1994). Free Trade, Fair Trade, Green Trade: Defogging the Debate. *Cornell International Law Journal*, 27(3), pp. 459–525.

European Communities – Conditions for the Granting of Tariff Preferences to Developing Countries (EC – Tariff Preferences) (2004). WTO Appellate Body Report, WT/DS246/AB/R.

European Union. Council Regulation (EC) No 980/2005 Applying a Scheme of Generalised Tariff Preferences (2005). Official Journal L 169/1.

GATT (1979). Decision of the CONTRACTING PARTIES on 28 November 1979. L/4903.

IISD (2003). TRIPS and Public Health. *IISD Trade and Development Brief*, 9.

Ito, K. (2010). Bōeki Sochi niyoru Jinken no Hogo Sokushin no Kanō sei. [The Possibility of Promoting Human Rights Protection by Trade Measures]. *Horitsu Jiho*, 82(3), pp. 20–25.

Lang, A. (2011). *World Trade Law after Neoliberalism: Re-imagining the Global Economic Order*. Oxford: Oxford University Press.

McDorman, T. L. (1992). The 1991 US – Mexico GATT Panel Report on Tuna and Dolphin: Implications for Trade and Environmental Conflicts. *North Carolina Journal of International Law and Commercial Regulation*, 17(3), pp. 461–488.

Nakagawa, J. (2003). WTO Taisei niokeru Bōeki Jiyū ka to Kankyō Hogo no Chōsei [Accommodation of Trade Liberalization and Environmental Protection Under the WTO Regime]. In: Kotera, A. ed., *Tenkanki no WTO: Hi Bōeki teki Kanshin Jikō no Bunseki* [*WTO at the Crossroads: An Analysis of Non-trade Issue Linkages*]. Tokyo: Toyo Keizai, pp. 175–197.

Nakagawa, J. (2021). SDGs (Jizoku Kanō na Kaihatsu Mokuhyō) to Jishuteki Jizoku Kanōsei Kijun (VSS) [SDGs and VSS (Voluntary Sustainability Standards)]. In: Masaharu, Y. *et al.* eds., *Kokusai Hō Chitsujo to Gurōbaru Keizai (Mamiya Isamu Sensei Tsuitou)*

[International Iegal Order Global Economy: *Commemorating Professor Isamu Mamiya*]. Tokyo: Shinzansha.
Ruggie, J. (1982). International Regimes, Transactions, and Change: Embedded Liberalism in the Postwar Economic Order. *International Organization*, 36(2), pp. 379–415.
Schefer, K. (2005). Stopping Trade in Conflict Diamonds: Exploring the Trade and Human Rights Interface with the WTO Waiver for the Kimberley Process. In: Cottier, T. ed., *Human Rights and International Trade*. Oxford: Oxford University Press, pp. 391–450.
UN. General Assembly (2015). *Transforming Our World: The 2030 Agenda for Sustainable Development, A/RES/70/1*. Available at: https://sustainabledevelopment.un.org/content/documents/21252030%20Agenda%20for%20Sustainable%20Development%20web.pdf
United States – Import Prohibition of Certain Shrimp and Shrimp Products (US – Shrimp) (1998). WTO Appellate Body Report, WT/DS58/AB/R.
United States – Import Prohibition of Certain Shrimp and Shrimp Products (US – Shrimp) (2001). Recourse to Article 21.5 of the DSU by Malaysia, WTO Appellate Body Report, WT/DS58/AB/RW.
United States – Restrictions on Imports of Tuna (1991). Report of the Panel. DS21/R – 39S/155.
World Commission on Environment and Development (1987). *Report of the World Commission on Environment and Development: Our Common Future*. Available at: https://sustainabledevelopment.un.org/content/documents/5987our-common-future.pdf
WTO (1997). Request for Consultations by the European Communities, WT/DS88/1.
WTO (2001). *Negotiations on Fisheries Subsidies*. Available at: www.wto.org/english/tratop_e/rulesneg_e/fish_e/fish_intro_e.htm
WTO (2003). *Decision of the General Council, WT/L/518*. Available at: https://docs.wto.org/dol2fe/Pages/FE_Search/FE_S_S009-DP.aspx?language=E&CatalogueIdList=32765&CurrentCatalogueIdIndex=0&FullTextHash=371857150&HasEnglishRecord=True&HasFrenchRecord=True&HasSpanishRecord=True
WTO (2005). *Amendment of the Trips Agreement, WT/L/641*. Available at: https://docs.wto.org/dol2fe/Pages/FE_Search/FE_S_S009-DP.aspx?language=E&CatalogueIdList=225408,121046,96083,96293,69009,58276&CurrentCatalogueIdIndex=5&FullTextHash=&HasEnglishRecord=True&HasFrenchRecord=True&HasSpanishRecord=True
WTO (2015). *Ministerial Decision on Export Competition, WT/MIN (15)/45*. Available at: https://docs.wto.org/dol2fe/Pages/SS/directdoc.aspx?filename=q:/WT/MIN15/45.pdf&Open=True
WTO (2017). *Ministerial Decision on Fisheries Subsidies, WT/MIN (17)/64*. Available at: https://docs.wto.org/dol2fe/Pages/SS/directdoc.aspx?filename=q:/WT/MIN17/64.pdf&Open=True
WTO (2020). *WTO Contribution to the 2020 HLPF*. Available at: https://sustainabledevelopment.un.org/content/documents/26126WTO_HLPF_Input_2020.pdf
WTO (2022). *The WTO's Contribution to Achieving the SDGs*. Available at: www.wto.org/english/res_e/publications_e/un_hlpf_e.htm
WTO (n.d. a). *Agriculture: Negotiating Modalities*. Available at: www.wto.org/english/tratop_e/dda_e/status_e/agric_e.htm
WTO (n.d. b). *Eliminating Trade Barriers on Environmental Goods and Services*. Available at: www.wto.org/english/tratop_e/envir_e/envir_neg_serv_e.htm
WTO (n.d. c). *The WTO and the Sustainable Development Goals*. Available at: www.wto.org/english/thewto_e/coher_e/sdgs_e/sdgs_e.htm#:~:text=The%20WTO%20is%20central%20to,health%2C%20education%20and%20the%20environment

14 International Standardization in the Era of Sustainable Development Goals

Smart Cities, the Circular Economy, and Digitalization

Yoshiko NAIKI

Introduction: The WTO and International Standardization

In the World Trade Organization (WTO) era, the work of international standard-setting organizations has received a considerable amount of attention compared with the General Agreement on Tariffs and Trade (GATT) era (Scott, 2007, p. 276). This is largely because of the WTO's Agreement on the Application of Sanitary and Phytosanitary Measures (SPS Agreement) and Agreement on Technical Barriers to Trade (TBT Agreement). Both the SPS and TBT Agreements increased the role of international standards in the WTO by encouraging WTO Members to base their measures on international standards if relevant standards exist (the SPS Agreement, Art. 3(1); the TBT Agreement, Art. 2.4.).

One major difference between the SPS and TBT Agreements in terms of addressing international standards is that, although the SPS Agreement (Annex A(3)) refers to three international standard-setting bodies (the so-called 'three sister' organizations, that is, the Codex Alimentarious Commission, the International Office of Epizootics, and the International Plant Protection Convention), the TBT Agreement only provides the definition of an 'international body' and does not raise specific names of international bodies.[1] In the TBT regime, the International Organization for Standardization (ISO), the International Electrotechnical Commission (IEC), and the International Telecommunication Union (ITU) are popular standard-setting bodies. However, the TBT does not specify these bodies' names.

This was due to a disagreement between the US and the European Union (EU) during the Uruguay Round negotiations, which reflected the differences in how and the extent to which the US and the EU engage in the work of international standardization (Schepel, 2005, pp. 186–187; Naiki, 2009, p. 1272). In the TBT regimes, domestic standardization bodies in each country set national standards based on domestic firms' technical expertise – and these domestic standardization bodies participate in and set international standards in international standardization bodies, thereby ultimately exporting domestic technologies outside. Thus, international standardization is very much affected by the extent to which domestic standardization bodies engage in the processes of international standard-setting. Generally, domestic standardization bodies intend to push their national standards

DOI: 10.4324/9781003193098-14

to be accepted as international standards – otherwise, their domestic firms bear 'switching costs' to comply with new international standards and give up national standards that the firms had been in line with (Büthe and Mattli, 2011, p. 9). More precisely, it has been argued that 'domestic institutional structures of standardization' affect whether domestic bodies can 'speak with a single voice and effectively promote domestic [standards]' in international standard-setting processes (Büthe and Mattli, 2011, p. 13).

In particular, the EU has been working closely with European countries' domestic standardization bodies and strategically attempting to influence international standard-setting processes (i.e., to shape the standard contents in order to reflect European interests) in the ISO, IEC, and ITU. In contrast, in the US, the numerous domestic standardization bodies have not been well-coordinated, which prevents them from speaking with a single voice to establish US national standards as international standards. This difference in 'domestic institutional structures' has actually caused power differences within international standard-setting bodies – for example, the EU has had a greater advantage over the US in getting European standards to become international standards (Büthe and Mattli, 2011, Ch. 6). Consequently, the institutional difference between the EU and the US led to differing views between them over the specification of international standardization bodies in the TBT Agreement during the Uruguay Round. More precisely, the US did not want to specify the names of international standardization bodies.

The argument of Büthe and Mattli is called the theory of 'institutional complementarity' between the domestic and global levels (Büthe and Mattli, 2011, p. 13). Drawing upon this theory, this chapter considers that countries are basically competing for international standardization to push their own national standards up to international standards, and this international process is affected by the coordination of domestic standardization bodies. In particular, this chapter looks at the recent development of international standardizations in the context of the UN adoption of the Sustainable Development Goals (SDGs) (UN, 2015) and examines the politics among countries over international standard-setting in relation to the SDGs. Existing literature on international economic law has already noted that international standardization in the area of information and communication technologies (ICTs) has been complex (Liu, 2014). This chapter argues that the SDGs add a new area where international standard-setting activities are flourishing but are more layered and complex.

The SDGs and International Standard-Setting Bodies

One of the effects of the SDGs is to push for the accountability of business actors. Currently, corporations are asked to explain their business activities based on the SDGs – that is, which dimension of their business actions contributes to the realization of which SDG. Moreover, the demand for corporate accountability also applies to the entire value chain (i.e., from material purchases to product end life) in light of the SDGs (GRI, UNGC and WBCSD, 2015, p. 12). Investors are also accountable for taking into account corporations' SDG engagement in their investment process.

We can observe a similar accountability trend in relation to the SDGs for international standard-setting bodies. Currently, international standard-setting bodies attempt to explain in what ways their standards can contribute to the realization of the SDGs when they are used. For instance, the ISO created a table to show how many ISO standards are relevant to each SDG (ISO, n.d.). The ISO has produced international standards relevant to all SDGs. The most relevant is SDG 9 (industry, innovation, and infrastructure) – which around 14,000 standards are concerned with. This is probably not surprising as ISO standards matter for industries' manufacturing. Subsequently, around 3,000 standards are related to several other SDGs: SDG 3 (good health and well-being), 8 (decent work and economic growth), 11(sustainable cities and communities), and 12 (responsible consumption and production). This shows that the ISO is concerned not only about industries but also about citizens, workers, communities, and consumers (ISO, 2018a).

The IEC also shows how it relates to the SDGs. The IEC standards similarly contribute to all SDGs (IEC, n.d.). Among them, over 5,000 standards are concerned with SDG 9 (industry, innovation, and infrastructure). The second-highest category is SDG 7 (affordable and clean energy) to which around 3,300 standards are related. This makes sense because these two SDGs directly relate to electricity and electronics. In addition, the IEC explains that IEC standards contribute to SDG 3, 6, 11, 12, 13, and 17 (IEC, 2020, p. 8).

The SDGs have also impacted standard-setting processes. In this regard, two ISO guides are worthy of note, as they established standards for standard-setters. Firstly, the ISO published guidelines on how to take 'sustainability' into account in setting standards (ISO, 2019). This 2019 ISO guide clearly states that 'The standards development process provides standards developers with the opportunity to contribute to sustainable development, and in particular to encourage sustainable production and consumption' (ISO, 2019, p. 3). Secondly, the ISO developed a new guide that requires standard-setters to take climate change into account when developing or revising standards (ISO, 2020). This is the work of the Climate Change Coordination Task Force (CCC TF7) established in the ISO (Naden, 2020). The two ISO guides have a very similar structure, which mainly consists of three stages: (1) planning a 'business strategic plan'; (2) planning 'technical content' for a particular standard, reflecting approaches such as a life cycle or precautionary approach; and (3) identifying issues (i.e., in relation to 'sustainability' and 'climate change') to be drafted as standards (BSI, 2019, 2020).

In addition, the ISO recognizes the importance of partnerships in standard-setting processes and thus releases guidance on partnerships. It is intended to guide ISO committees on 'how to proactively look for the right partnerships (e.g., with UN and other international organizations) to enhance the value of their standards in supporting the SDGs' (ISO, 2018b). Interestingly, the guidance emphasizes that 'An excellent resource to identify relevant international and regional organizations is the UN SDG website itself' (ISO, 2018b).

Against the backdrop of the impact of the SDGs on international standardization, the next two sections turn to specific standard-setting topics, namely, smart cities and the circular economy, both of which are closely related to SDG implementation. Specifically, SDG 11 (sustainable cities and communities) is most relevant to smart cities, and SDG 12 (sustainable consumption and production) is highly concerned with the circular economy; however, both smart cities and the circular economy involve cross-sectoral topics and are thereby related to several other SDGs (Naiki, 2023).

International Standard-Setting for Smart Cities

Addressing urban issues is one of the focuses of sustainable development. The UN-Habitat (2020, p. 6) has recognized the following: The emergence of a 'global urban agenda' enshrined in multilateral accords like the 2030 Agenda for Sustainable Development, the New Urban Agenda, the Paris Agreement on Climate Change and the Sendai Framework for Disaster Risk Reduction 2015–2030 signals a formal recognition by Member States of the United Nations that urban processes hold the key to sustainable development at a worldwide scale.

One important urban agenda is related to cities' demographic growth, energy consumption, and climate change. It has been predicted that by 2035, 62% of the world's population will live in urban areas (UN-Habitat, 2020, p. 12, Table 1.1). It is also pointed out by the International Energy Agency (IEA; 2021, p. 12) that 'Cities are responsible for nearly 75% of global energy consumption and 70% of global CO2 emissions'.

Thus, cities have been responsible for tackling climate change. At the same time, cities can present solutions and opportunities for fighting climate change. On this point, for transnational cooperation between major global cities, such as C40, working to reduce CO2 emissions is a well-known case (Lin, 2018, Ch. 5). Alongside such a transnational solution for the climate change problem, cities can deal with the problem locally (Lin, 2018, p. 19). It has been pointed out that cities 'can be centres for innovation, with the capacity to test new technologies and approaches, offering a means through which novel responses to climate change could be generated' (Bulkeley, 2013, p. 9). Therefore, the smart transformation of cities can be a solution to climate change by improving infrastructure, transportation, and housing through smart technologies (World Bank, 2019).

There has been much debate over the concept of smart cities. Since numerous concepts for smart cities exist, the definition remains unclear (Ahvenniemi et al., 2017, p. 235; Albino, Berardi and Dangelico, 2015, p. 4; European Parliament, 2014, p. 17). Currently, the smart city concept entails multi-dimensions in addition to the utilization of ICTs. This is because an intense debate regarding the smart city concept arose from criticism over the primacy of technological solutions in smart-city initiatives led by global information technology (IT) companies (Hollands, 2015). Thus, there have been considerable discussions about what factors, in addition to the utilization of ICTs, should be included when measuring smart city initiatives. It has been pointed out that measuring smart-city projects using certain indicators is 'a fundamental step in setting direction; what smart cities decide to measure will impact what they invest in, how they develop solutions, and what is counted as success' (Clarke, 2017, p. 244). In other words, indicators of and standards for smart cities are important to 'establish common language and transparency in governance, to communicate benefits of investments, to manage city operations, to evaluate how well the city is performing in different areas and as support in decision-making' (Huovila, Bosch and Airaksinen, 2019, p. 142).

Currently, a large variety of smart city indicators, which are set by research institutes, universities, and national standardization bodies, exist to evaluate smart-city projects. This section focuses on standardization activities by international standard-setting bodies. The four fora that have addressed international standards for smart cities are as follows: (1) 'ISO/TC 268', dealing with sustainable cities and communities; (2) 'ISO/IEC Joint Technical Committee (JTC) 1', addressing IT; (3) 'IEC/SyC Smart Cities', concerning electrotechnical aspects of smart cities; and (4) 'ITU-T SG20', dealing with the internet of things and smart cities and communities.

Each forum has developed standards in light of its own specialty: for instance, the IEC focuses on electrotechnical aspects, and the ITU focuses on telecommunication. However, regarding the smart cities' performance measurement, we can note some overlaps in standardization, which may bring about slight confusion.

The most well-known framework in the literature is ISO 37120, titled 'Sustainable cities and communities – indicators for city services and quality of life' (ISO, 2018c). Originally, this was based on the idea of the Global City Indicators Facility developed by the University of Toronto (McCarney, 2009). Under Canada's initiative in working group 2 of the ISO/TC 268, ISO 37120 was developed and published in 2014 and then revised in 2018. ISO 37120 consists of 104 indicators and covers a wide range of aspects of smart cities, including the economy, education, energy, environment/climate change, finance, governance, health, housing, population/social conditions, recreation, safety, solid waste, sports/culture, telecommunications, transportation, agriculture/food, urban planning, wastewater, and water. ISO 37120 is currently used by the World Council on City Data for certifying and ranking cities in five levels – platinum, gold, silver, bronze, and aspirational (WCCD, n.d.).

When we look at standardization activities in the ITU, the ITU also deals with the performance measurement of smart cities. A feature of the ITU standardization activity is that it uses the concept of 'smart sustainable cities', which is defined as follows:

> [A]n innovative city that uses [ICTs] and other means to improve quality of life, efficiency of urban operation and services and competitiveness, while ensuring that it meets the needs of present and future generations with respect to economic, social, environmental, as well as cultural aspects.
>
> (ITU, 2016)

This ITU definition entails several features of smart cities: the utilization of ICTs, the improvement of quality of life, and the importance of sustainability. Based on this definition, the ITU developed a standard titled 'key performance indicators related to the use of information and communication technology in smart sustainable cities' (ITU, 2016). The key performance indicators cover six dimensions of smart sustainable cities: ICTs, environmental sustainability (e.g., air and water), productivity (e.g., investment and trade), quality of life (e.g., education and safety), equity and social inclusion (e.g., public participation and governance), and physical infrastructure.

Accordingly, measuring performance for smart cities is quite a popular activity performed by several bodies. In addition, there are numerous international standards that address specific dimensions of smart cities based on certain systems and technologies developed by firms. This aspect is more related to each country's business interests. As noted, countries are competing to be a first mover in standard-setting for smart cities, because countries intend to export their smart-city projects based on the standards initiated by themselves and adopted at international fora.

In this regard, Japan is leading two subcommittees under the ISO/TC 268. Subcommittee 1 (SC1) focuses on smart community 'infrastructures' and has already published 13 international standards related to this subject. Subcommittee 2 (SC2) is concerned with sustainable 'mobility and transportation' and has already published 16 international standards.

China has been actively participating in international standardization in the ICT sector (Liu, 2018; Peng, 2015). Recently, considerable attention has been given to China's role in international standardization since China has increasingly participated in international standard-setting. For instance, the following has been noted:

> From 2011 to 2020, the number of Chinese-occupied secretariat positions in technical committees (TCs) or subcommittees (SCs) increased by 73 percent in ISO. In IEC, they increased 67 percent from 2012 to 2020.
>
> (US-China Business Council, 2020, p. 3)

Drahos pointed out that 'China's smart-city projects are also helping Chinese companies to enter standard-setting clubs' (2021, p. 161). Such companies are Huawei and ZTE. In terms of smart cities, China is leading Working Group (WG) 11 for smart cities established in the ISO/IEC JTC 1 (ISO/IEC JTC 1 WG11, 2021). Successful international standardization will help companies to expand smart-city projects outside China: 'Huawei has been piloting smart-city initiatives in Chinese cities in cooperation with other Chinese partners, announcing plans in 2017 to export the hardware and software to cities in 20 countries' (Drahos, 2021, p. 162). Furthermore, Chinese companies' technologies and systems used in smart cities can spread along the 'Digital Silk Road' projects under China's 'Belt and Road' Initiative (Erie and Streinz, 2021, p. 71).

In October 2021, China released the 'Outline to Promote Standardized National Development' (State Council of the People's Republic of China, 2021). In the Outline, the relation between Chinese national standards and international standards is explained as follows:

> The degree of consistency between national standards and the key technical indicators of international standards will greatly improve, and the conversion rate of international standards will reach more than 85%.
>
> (CSET, 2021)[2]

This Chinese policy seems to promote increasingly more 'institutional complementarity' between the domestic and global levels, thereby increasing successful Chinese participation in international standardization.

International Standard-Setting for the Circular Economy

The standard-setting for smart cities addressed previously is not a particularly new topic – ISO/TC 268 was established in 2012, thus, standard-setting for smart cities has been active around for ten years (ISO/TC 268, n.d.). However, there are increasingly more new standard-setting topics related to the SDGs. One such relatively new topic is the circular economy. In 2018, the ISO created TC 323 to address the circular economy (ISO/TC 323, n.d.). This TC is led by French AFNOR. Currently, five working groups are set up to develop standards (however, no standard has yet been published at the time of writing).

In the international arena, the EU has been a major actor promoting the circular economy (European Commission, 2015). In 2020, the European Commission publicized 'the new action plan for circular economy' (European Commission, 2020), which is an important element of the European Green Deal set out in 2019 (European Commission, n.d.). Under a circular economy, 'the value of products, materials and resources is maintained in the economy for as long as possible, and the generation of waste minimized' (European Commission, 2015, p. 2). More specifically, actions are required 'throughout a product's life', from product design, product processes, and consumption to waste – and in this last stage of waste management, 'materials that can be recycled are injected back into the economy as new raw materials thus increasing the security of supply' (European Commission, 2015, p. 11). Thus, circular 'goals' are targeted to 'reuse, repair, and recycle' (EEA, 2019, p. 11, 2021).

There are three important features of the EU's strategy for the circular economy. Firstly, the EU has clearly stated that the EU policy for the circular economy can contribute to SDG implementation (European Commission, 2015, p. 3, European Commission, 2020, p. 3). Secondly, the EU emphasizes that the circular economy is about business: 'The circular economy will boost the EU's competitiveness by protecting businesses against scarcity of resources and volatile prices, helping to create new business opportunities and innovative, more efficient ways of producing and consuming' (European Commission, 2015, p. 2). Thirdly, digitalization is an important tool for the innovative circular economy (EEA, 2021): '[data and digitally-enabled solutions] can help enhance connectivity and information sharing; make business models, products and processes more circular; and empower citizens and consumers to contribute to the transition' (European Policy Centre, 2020, p. 2).

Against this backdrop, international standardization activity for the circular economy has been developing. Under ISO/TC 323, the development of one major standard has been conducted by Working Group 1, led by France, addressing 'terminology, principles, frameworks and management systems'. It was assumed that this standard would be based on existing national standards in the UK and France.[3]

Thus, European countries are attempting to push their national standards up to ISO standards.

Japan is also engaging in standard-setting under Working Group 2 of the ISO/TC 323. The standard under development is titled 'Practical Approaches to Develop and Implement Circular Economy', which focuses on setting business models for a circular economy. However, Groups 3, 4, and 5 are seemingly led by other European countries; therefore, the EU is taking the lead in international standardization for the circular economy.

Conclusion

Against the backdrop of the recent role of the SDGs within the international standard-setting bodies, this chapter addressed two examples of international standardization in relation to SDG implementation: smart cities and the circular economy. In both cases, countries are competing for international standardization to convert their own national standards into international standards. This is because national standards are developed on the basis of domestic firms' technologies, and international standardization means exporting domestic technologies outside. This is a common and classic strategy for international standardization, and it is the same for standards relevant to the SDGs. As the cases of smart cities and the circular economy demonstrate, increasingly more IT technologies are becoming involved in SDG implementation. In sum, SDG implementation is currently an important source of business activities and, therefore, an important topic for international standardization.

Another lesson from the two examples is that international standard-setting activity is becoming more and more complex and fragmented in the SDG era—there are too many international standard proposals for different 'green' technologies. International standardization is happening across scales—some are high-profile, but others remain small cases. Due to the complexity involved, it may be difficult to predict the real impacts of international standardization. It is necessary to discern which are the high-profile international standardization cases and give sufficient attention to the standard-setting games over such cases. On this point, it is important to note that one of the purposes of the US-EU Trade and Technology Council (TTC), launched in 2021, is to coordinate and cooperate in developing technology standards (US Department of State, 2021). This is an interesting step for the US and EU when we recall the fact that their standard-setting approaches have been very different, as stated in the beginning of this chapter.

Notes

1 The TBT Agreement, Annex 1(4), states that it is a '[b]ody or system whose membership is open to the relevant bodies of at least all Members'. Relatedly, the WTO's Appellate Body defines 'international standards' as follows: 'a recognized international standard is an approved standard by an international standardizing body, that is, a body that has recognized activities in standardization and whose membership is open to the relevant bodies of at least all Members'. Appellate Body Report, *US – Tuna II (Mexico)*, WT/DS381/AB/R (16 May 2012), para. 359.

2 Another Chinese government document explains this point in more detail: 'The degree of consistency between national standards and international standards will have increased significantly, the international standard conversion rate will have reached more than 85%, and the foreign language versions of national standards will better meet the needs of international cooperation and exchange. The degree of uniformity between the technical institutions of international standards organizations and nationwide standardization technical committees will have reached 85%' (CSET, 2021).

3 In the UK, the British Standards Institution developed a standard for the circular economy titled 'Framework for implementing the principles of the circular economy in organization' (BS 8001: 2017). In France, the Association Francaise de Normalisation developed a standard titled 'Circular economy project management system: Requirements and Guidelines' (XP X30–901 Oct. 2018). See, METI (2018) and JEMAI (2023).

References

All subsequent websites were last visited on 24 June 2023.

Ahvenniemi, H., Huovila, A., Pinto-Seppä, I. and Alraksinen, M. (2017). What Are the Differences Between Sustainable and Smart Cities? *Cities*, 60, pp. 234–245. Available at: https://doi.org/10.1016/j.cities.2016.09.009

Albino, V., Berardi, U. and Dangelico, R. M. (2015). Smart Cities: Definitions, Dimensions, Performance, and Initiatives. *Journal of Urban Technology*, 22(1), pp. 3–21. Available at: https://doi.org/10.1080/10630732.2014.942092

British Standards Institution (BSI) (2019). *Guidelines for Addressing Sustainability in Standards*. Available at: www.bsigroup.com/contentassets/fb7f1499fa6f43c6b9084be8c2378bc9/iso_guide_82_2019e – guidelines-for-addressing-sustainability-in-standards.pdf

British Standards Institution (BSI) (2020). *Guidelines for Addressing Climate Change in Standards*. Available at: www.bsigroup.com/contentassets/fb7f1499fa6f43c6b9084be8c2378bc9/iso_guide-84_2020e – guidelines-for-addressing-climate-change-in-standards.pdf

Bulkeley, H. (2013). *Cities and Climate Change*. London: Routledge.

Büthe, T. and Mattli, W. (2011). *The New Global Rulers: The Privatization of Regulation in the World Economy*. Princeton: Princeton University Press.

Center for Security and Emerging Technology (CSET) (2021). *Georgetown University, Translation: The Chinese Communist Party Central Committee and the State Council Publish the 'National Standardization Development Outline'*. Available at: https://cset.georgetown.edu/publication/the-chinese-communist-party-central-committee-and-the-state-council-publish-the-national-standardization-development-outline/

Clarke, R. Y. (2017). Measuring Success in the Development of Smart and Sustainable Cities. In: Cronin, M. J. and Dearing, T. C. eds., *Managing for Social Impact: Innovations in Responsible Enterprise*. Berlin: Springer.

Drahos, P. (2021). *Survival Governance: Energy and Climate in the Chinese Century*. Oxford: Oxford University Press.

Erie, M. S. and Streinz, T. (2021). The Beijing Effect: China's 'Digital Silk Road' as Transnational Data Governance. *New York University Journal of International Law and Politics*, 54(1), pp. 1–92. Available at: www.nyujilp.org/wp-content/uploads/2022/02/NYUJILP_Vol54.1_Erie_Streinz_1-91.pdf

European Commission (n.d.). *Circular Economy Action Plan*. Available at: https://ec.europa.eu/environment/strategy/circular-economy-action-plan_en?msclkid=10b56955aa5511eca38ee8b128ad5dad

European Commission (2015). *Communication from the Commission to the European Parliament, the Council, the European Economic and Social Committee and the Committee of the Regions, 'Closing the loop – an EU Action Plan for the Circular Economy'*, COM(2015)614 final. Available at: https://eur-lex.europa.eu/legal-content/EN/TXT/?uri=CELEX%3A52015DC0614

European Commission (2020). *Communication from the Commission to the European Parliament, the Council, the Economic and Social Committee and the Committee of the Regions 'A New Circular Economy Action Plan for a Cleaner and More Competitive Europe'*, COM (2020) 98 final of 11 March. Available at: https://eur-lex.europa.eu/legal-content/EN/TXT/?uri=COM%3A2020%3A98%3AFIN

European Environmental Agency (2019). Paving the Way for a Circular Economy: Insights on Status and Potentials. *EEA Report*, 11/2019. Available at: www.eea.europa.eu/ds_resolveuid/23d814ec83a44db7872f7a2131e2d7df

European Environmental Agency (2021). *Briefing: A Framework for Enabling Circular Business Models in Europe*. Available at: www.eea.europa.eu/publications/a-framework-for-enabling-circular?msclkid=f41847c1a9bb11ecb268ac2f05822746

European Parliament (2014). *Mapping Smart Cities in the EU*. Available at: www.europarl.europa.eu/RegData/etudes/etudes/join/2014/507480/IPOL-ITRE_ET(2014)507480_EN.pdf

European Policy Centre (2020). *The Digital Circular Economy: A Driver for the European Green Deal, Executive Summary*. Available at: www.epc.eu/content/PDF/2020/DRCE_-_Executive_summary1.pdf

Global Reporting Initiative, UN Global Compact, and World Business Council for Sustainable Development (GRI, UNGC and WBCSD) (2015). *SDGs Compass: The Guide for Business Action on the SDGs*. Available at: https://sdgcompass.org/wp-content/uploads/2015/12/019104_SDG_Compass_Guide_2015.pdf

Hollands, R. G. (2015). Critical Interventions into the Corporate Smart City. *Cambridge Journal of Regions, Economy, and Society*, 8(1), pp. 61–77. Available at: https://doi.org/10.1093/cjres/rsu011

Huovila, A., Bosch, P. and Airaksinen, M. (2019). Comparative Analysis of Standardized Indicators for Smart Sustainable Cities: What Indicators and Standards to Use and When? *Cities*, 89, pp. 141–153. Available at: https://doi.org/10.1016/j.cities.2019.01.029

International Electrotechnical Commission (IEC) (n.d.). *Where We Make a Difference, SDGs*. Available at: www.iec.ch/sdg

International Electrotechnical Commission (IEC) (2020). *IEC for SDGs: Working Towards a Sustainable Future*. Available at: https://iec.ch/system/files/2022-10/IEC_2022_for_SDGs_A4_En_LR.pdf

International Energy Agency (IEA) (2021). *Empowering Cities for a Net Zero Future: Unlocking Resilient, Smart, Sustainable Urban Energy Systems*. Available at: https://iea.blob.core.windows.net/assets/4d5c939d-9c37-490b-bb53-2c0d23f2cf3d/G20EmpoweringCitiesforaNetZeroFuture.pdf

International Organization for Standardization (ISO) (n.d.). *Sustainable Development Goals, Impact at a Glance*. Available at: www.iso.org/sdgs.html

International Organization for Standardization (ISO) (2018a). *ISO & SDGs: Contributing to the UN Sustainable Development Goals with ISO Standards*. Available at: www.iso.org/files/live/sites/isoorg/files/store/en/PUB100429.pdf

International Organization for Standardization (ISO) (2018b). *ISO Standards for the SDGs: Guidance on Partnerships for ISO Committees*. Available at: https://isotc.iso.org/livelink/livelink/fetch/%20%20%20-15620806/15620808/15623592/17856067/Guidance_to_ISO_committees_on_partnerships_for_the_SDGs.pdf?nodeid=19869731&vernum=-2

International Organization for Standardization (ISO) (2018c). *ISO37120:2018 (en) Sustainable Cities and Communities – Indicators for City Services and Quality of Life*. Available at: www.iso.org/obp/ui/#iso:std:iso:37120:ed-2:v1:en

International Organization for Standardization (ISO) (2019). *ISO Guide 82: 2019, Guidelines for Addressing Sustainability in Standards*. Available at: www.iso.org/standard/76561.html

International Organization for Standardization (ISO) (2020). *ISO Guide 84: 2020, Guidelines for Addressing Climate Change in Standards*. Available at: www.iso.org/standard/72496.html

International Telecommunication Union (ITU) (2016). *Recommendation ITU-T, Y.4901/L.1601 (06/16): Key Performance Indicators Related to the Use of Information and Communication Technology in Smart Sustainable Cities*. Available at: www.itu.int/rec/T-REC-L.1601-201606-I

ISO/IEC JTC 1, WG11 (2021). *WG 11 Smart Cities (2021)*. Available at: https://jtc1info.org/sd-2-history/jtc1-working-groups/wg-11/

ISO/TC 268 (n.d.). *Sustainable Cities and Communities*. Available at: www.iso.org/committee/656906.html

ISO/TC 323 (n.d.). *Circular Economy*. Available at: www.iso.org/committee/7203984.html?msclkid=fb377e0ca98811ec83b7e8be0d8ed09e

Japan Environmental Management Association for Industry (JEMAI) (2023). *ISO/TC 323 Circular Economy Katsudou Shoukai* [*Introduction for ISO/TC 323, Standard-setting for Circular Economy*]. Available at: https://www.jemai.or.jp/standard/d3ldbs0000000bvi-att/ISO-TC323_introduction_20230420_final_1.pdf

Lin, J. (2018). *Governing Climate Change: Global Cities and Transnational Lawmaking*. Cambridge: Cambridge University Press.

Liu, H. (2014). International Standards in Flux: A Balkanized ICT Standard-Setting Paradigm and Its Implications for the WTO. *Journal of International Economic Law*, 17(3), pp. 551–600. Available at: https://doi.org/10.1093/jiel/jgu034

Liu, H. (2018). China Standard Time: The Boundary of Techno-Nationalism in Megaregionals. In: Peng, S. *et al.* eds., *Governing Science and Technology Under the International Economic Order*. Cheltenham: Edward Elgar Publishing, pp. 114–139.

McCarney, P. L. (2009). *Global City Indicators Facility*. Available at: https://d3dqsm2futmewz.cloudfront.net/d*pp.* ocs/SCN/sept09_valleywide/globalindicators-pres.pdf

Ministry of Economy, Trade, and Industry (METI) (2018). Circular Economy ni kanrenshita kokusai hyojyunka doukou [Recent Trends of International Standard-setting for Circular Economy]. Reference for the Committee of Circular Economy Vision. Available at: www.meti.go.jp/shingikai/energy_environment/junkai_keizai/pdf/002_03_00.pdf

Naden, C. (2020). *ISO: A New ISO Guide Will Help Ensure Climate Change Issues Are Addressed in Every New Standard*. Available at: www.iso.org/news/ref2538.html

Naiki, Y. (2009). Accountability and Legitimacy in Global Health and Safety Governance: The World Trade Organization, the SPS Committee and International Standard-Setting Organizations. *Journal of World Trade*, 43(6), pp. 1255–1279.

Naiki, Y. (2023). Jizokukanouna Toshikaihatsunikansuru Kihanno Hattenkatei: SDG11, Smart City Kihan, Data Governance [Norm Pathways for Sustainable Urban Development: Assessing Complexity between the UN SDG 11, Smart City Norm, and Data Governance]. *Kokusaiseiji* [*International Politics*], 208, pp. 77–91.

Peng, S. (2015). Standards as a Means to Technological Leadership? China's ICT Standards in the Context of the International Economic Order. In: Toohey, L. *et al.* eds., *China in the New International Economic Order: New Directions and Changing Paradigms*. Cambridge: Cambridge University Press, pp. 128–147.

Schepel, H. (2005). *The Constitution of Private Governance: Product Standards in the Regulation of Integrating Markets*. Oxford: Hart Publishing.

Scott, J. (2007). *The WTO Agreement on Sanitary and Phytosanitary Measures: A Commentary*. Oxford: Oxford University Press.

State Council of the People's Republic of China (2021). *China Issues Outline to Promote Standardized National Development*. Available at: http://english.www.gov.cn/policies/latestreleases/202110/11/content_WS616370f4c6d0df57f98e1758.html

UN-Habitat (2020). *The World Cities Report: The Value of Sustainable Urbanization*. Available at: https://unhabitat.org/sites/default/files/2020/10/wcr_2020_report.pdf

United Nations. General Assembly (2015). *Transforming Our World: The 2030 Agenda for Sustainable Development*, A/70/L.1. Available at: www.un.org/en/development/desa/population/migration/generalassembly/docs/globalcompact/A_RES_70_1_E.pdf

United States Department of States (2021). US-EU Trade and Technology Council (TTC). Available at: https://www.state.gov/u-s-eu-trade-and-technology-council-ttc/

United States – Measures Concerning the Importation, Marketing and Sale of Tuna and Tuna Products (US – Tuna II (Mexico)) (2012). WTO Appellate Body Report, WT/DS381/AB/R.

US-China Business Council (2020). *China in International Standards Setting: USCBC Recommendations for Constructive Participation*. Available at: www.uschina.org/sites/default/files/china_in_international_standards_setting.pdf?msclkid=d23ac959ac9511ec93d29764111d97bc

World Bank (2019). *Feature Story: Four Things You Should Know About Climate-Smart Cities*. Available at: www.worldbank.org/en/news/feature/2019/05/31/four-things-you-should-know-about-climate-smart-cities

World Council on City Data (n.d.). *About ISO 37120-Indicators for Sustainable Cities*. Available at: www.dataforcities.org/iso-37120

15 Investment Treaties and Human Rights Violations *Outside* a Host State

Where and How Should They Be Placed *Inside* ISDS?

Azusa KIKUMA

Introduction

Investment treaties protect the rights of investors. Under their architecture is the investor on the side of those whose rights are potentially violated by a host state. The increasing number of Investor-State Dispute Settlement (ISDS) cases demonstrates that such legal instruments are founded on the reality that investors face in doing business abroad.

However, an investor can also be on the side that violates the rights of others. A typical example is forced labor, where workers' human rights are violated. An investor may conduct business using forced labor on its own or it may assist an entity conducting such business as its counterparty. It may also be a shareholder of such an entity. It can be said that the investor is *involved* with human rights in all of these cases, although the manner and extent is different in each of them. Some investors may be involved with human rights violations due to deliberate decisions. Involvement in other cases may be a result of a lack of sufficient due diligence.

There are two categories of human rights violations with which an investor may be involved. First, an investor can be involved with a violation of human rights in the territory of the host state (hereinafter human rights violations *inside*). Second, it can be involved with a violation of human rights outside the territory of the host state (hereinafter human rights violations *outside*). The former obviously impairs the interest of the host state. However, the latter can also be a matter of its concern, given the importance of the value at stake.

Thus, the government of a host state may consider taking measures against an investor as a sanction in the case of human rights violations *outside*. If the investor is engaged in a licensed business, then the revocation of the license may be one option. Another option may be discouraging (or prohibiting) its nationals to engage in business with the investor.

However, the host state's discretion is not unlimited. If the investor considers that the measure constitutes a breach of the state's obligations under investment treaties, then the investor may have recourse to ISDS. The question is whether a state can defend itself by relying on the fact that the investor is (allegedly) involved with human rights violations *outside* and how it is addressed (if at all) in ISDS.

DOI: 10.4324/9781003193098-15

This chapter outlines what legal tools may be employed in ISDS for this purpose. At the outset of the analysis, it discusses the difference between two categories of human rights violation from the viewpoint of the practical challenges that they may cause in the context of investment treaties. Then, it examines each candidate tool that may be available to a host state following the process of ISDS. The examination will reveal that some tools are not effective options in the case of human rights violations *outside*. It will also demonstrate that other tools require further development of procedural rules to ensure certainty and predictability.

Limitation on the Scope of Research

The following clarifies the scope of this chapter. First, it does not deal with the question of whether an investor (as a private entity) bears or should bear substantive human rights obligations and if so, what their content should be. Second, this article does not address the relation between human rights violations *outside* and the interpretation of substantive obligations under an investment treaty. Although the author is fully aware of the importance of the issue, the contents of the obligations are diverse from treaty to treaty.[1] The limitation of the work's length makes it impossible to conduct a comprehensive analysis on it in this short chapter.

Human Rights Violations *Inside* and *Outside*

Distinguishing between these types of human rights violations is required, because there are features that may affect the availability of legal tools. First, the ability of a host state to gather evidence is more restricted in the case of human rights violations *outside*. A host state may not be able to conduct on-site investigations and resort to compulsory measures to gather evidence, which it could perform in situations of human rights violations *inside*. It must take measures with the inherent limitation of available information and defend the measures in ISDS proceedings. On the other side of the same coin, there is the risk for an investor that a measure may be taken against it without a factual foundation, and it must be given a sufficient opportunity to defend against this. The balance of these potentially conflicting needs must be carefully struck.

Second, there is weaker connection between a host state and human rights violation *outside*. In the case of human rights violations *inside*, the territoriality is intrinsic and is the strongest connecting factor. In many cases, the victim's nationality is that of the host state. However, in the case of human rights violation *outside*, territoriality cannot, by its definition, connect them, unless the business by the investor in the host state itself is related to the violation abroad. Similarly, the nationality of victims cannot connect them in usual cases. This difference may affect the availably of tools in cases concerning each type of human rights violation.

Tools to Address Misconduct by Investors

Tribunals have employed various legal tools in cases where a host state alleged that an investor had committed misconduct and the challenged measure had been taken to address that misconduct (Kikuma, 2019; Viñuales, 2017). It is suggested that such tools are available to deal with a case where an investor is involved with human rights violation (Choudhury, 2020). This chapter examines each legal tool following the sequence of procedure in arbitration: jurisdiction/admissibility, counterclaim, and quantum.

It should be noted, however, that tribunals have used these means in cases where an investor's misconduct took place in the host state (e.g., corruption engaged in with officials of the host state, harm to the environment of the host state, and the impairment of rights held by nationals of the host state). These cases can be analogous with the cases of human rights violations *inside*. However, the characteristics of human rights violations *outside*, which is previously discussed, require further consideration about the availability of each tool.

Two questions must be answered. The first question is how each tool can effectively address the issue of human rights violations *inside*. The second is how it can be applied in the case of human rights violations *outside*.

Denial of Jurisdiction/Admissibility[2] Phase (Legality Requirement)

Many tribunals have deprived investors of all the protection under investment treaties when they were found to have committed illegal activities. They denied their jurisdiction and/or the admissibility of the claim. The tool used in these cases is the so-called 'legality requirement'. The legality requirement should be, in principle, explicitly provided in the text of a treaty (a *written legality requirement*). However, some tribunals have found that such requirement applies even when the treaty at issue does not so provide explicitly (an *unwritten legality requirement*).

Written Legality Requirement

A written legality requirement takes several forms. It can be a provision to limit the scope of treaty protection to an investment that is legally established. Another approach is to define 'investment/investor' by referring in part to its legality. The protection of investment treaties applies to 'investor' and 'investment'. If a claimant is not qualified as an 'investor', then it cannot enjoy the protection of the treaty. Article 2 (2) of Netherlands-Turkey BIT (1986) is a typical example of the former. It provides that '*[t]he present Agreement shall apply to investments . . . in the territory of the other Contracting Party which <u>are established in accordance with</u> the laws and regulations in force in the latter Contracting Party's territory*'. The example of the latter approach is Article 1(1) of Israel-Uzbekistan BIT (1994), which provides that '*[t]he term "investments" shall comprise any kind of assets, implemented in accordance with the laws and regulations of the Contracting Party*'.

While the scope and effect of a written legality requirement depend on the language of the provision, typical formulations of the legality requirement, as previously introduced, contain two restrictions. First, the illegal activity must be committed at the time when the investment is *established*. This captures only the illegality at the time of the establishment of the investment. Once the investment is lawfully established, this provision cannot deprive the investment/investor of the protection under the investment treaty (*Kim and others v. Uzbekistan*, 2017, Paras. 373–377).

Second, as a corollary of the first restriction, the relevant domestic law must exist at the time of establishment of the investment. The retrospective application of law is not permissible.

Third, it is generally understood that the illegality at issue must be beyond a certain level of seriousness (Choudhury, 2020). The effect of the legality requirement is complete deprivation of protection under the treaty. The illegality must be serious enough to deserve such a severe sanction (*Kim and others v. Uzbekistan*, 2017, Para. 396).

Written Legality Requirement and Human Rights Violations *Inside*

Theoretically, a written legality requirement can be used to deny protection under the treaty to an investor involved with human rights violations *inside*. However, the above-mentioned restrictions also apply. First, the investor's involvement with human rights violations must take place when establishing the investment. Second, the host state is required to have enacted its domestic law to prohibit such involvement *before* the establishment of investment. Third, the investor's violation of the domestic law must be a serious one in terms of the type of human rights violation and/or the manner/extent of its involvement.

The difficulty in practice, however, lies with the first restriction. Unlike corruption, involvement with human rights violations *inside* is unlikely to be committed as a means to establish an investment. On the contrary, an investor at this phase usually cannot be involved with the violation since they conduct no business activity in the host state yet. A written legality requirement is of little practical use to address an investor's involvement with human rights violations *inside*, which is usually conducted after an investment is established and its business starts operations.

Unwritten Legality Requirement and Human Rights Violations *Inside*

The practices of tribunals are divided on whether they can apply an unwritten legality requirement (Jarrett, 2019, p. 117). If it is applied, then tribunals can deprive an investor of treaty protections due to its misconduct regardless of whether the applicable treaty contains a written legality requirement. The unwritten legality requirement is more flexible. A tribunal could more freely decide the scope and the effect of the requirement since (presumably) the treaty did not contain any textual clue restricting its discretion. On the other side of the same coin, this inherently entails uncertainty and unpredictability (Kikuma, 2019, pp. 100–105).

The challenge for previous tribunals that chose to apply it was how to balance these two factors. Though there is not yet clear agreement on the scope and effect of the requirement, some tendencies can be derived from decisions by tribunals. First, except for one tribunal (*Al Warraq v. Indonesia*, 2014), tribunals applied unwritten legality requirements only to misconduct that the investor committed at the time of *establishing* its investment. The *Hulley v. Russia* tribunal (2014, Paras. 1349, 1363) clearly distinguished them and held that illegality in the making of the investment, as opposed to that in its performance, is captured by an unwritten legality requirement (see also Jarrett, 2019, pp. 157–159).[3] As its corollary, the law to be applied must exist at the time of the establishment. Second, tribunals are in agreement that the violation must be serious enough (*Cortec Mining v. Kenya*, 2018, Paras. 343–365).

As long as an unwritten legality requirement is applied with these limitations, its function is similar to a written one in relation to the involvement of the investor with human rights violation. Thus, the considerations elaborated previously in the context of the written legality requirement also apply.

Legality Requirements and Human Rights Violations *Outside* the Host State

The legality requirement may be more useful in the case of human rights violation *outside*. Often, an investor that attempts to establish its investment in a host state already has been conducting its business elsewhere. This means that an investor may have already been involved with human rights violations. If the domestic law of the host state prohibits such an investor from establishing an investment, then the legality requirement applies, and the investor loses the protection of the treaty. For example, a host state can make legislation to reject the application of investment made by such investor and, for its implementation, require an investor to submit its compliance record about human rights. If the record is not satisfactory, then the investment is not admitted at the outset. If the submitted record is satisfactory but turns out to be fraudulent later, then the host state can potentially rely on a written legality requirement and deny the protection of the treaty.

Although such domestic law would enhance the practical availability of the legality requirement, a host state should carefully consider its design. First, the domestic law must be non-discriminatory in both its text and its applications. Otherwise, it could constitute a breach of national treatment and/or most-favoured nation treatment at the establishment phase, for which recent treaties often provide.

Second, the domestic law should not impose on an investor an unrealistic requirement. Some investors deliberately submit fraudulent information. However, others submit false reports without an intention to deceive the authorities of the host state. For example, it is conceivable that the investor conducted a sufficient level of due diligence and genuinely concluded that they were not involved in human rights violation when they submitted the required record, which turned out to be inaccurate later. As for these cases, it would not be appropriate to apply a written or unwritten legality requirement. Otherwise, an investor would be permanently subject to the risk of retrospective denial of protections under treaty.[4]

It follows that the development of rules is required on two issues. The first one is the level of due diligence required of an investor. An investor wants clear guidance about the conduct that it must carry out to be *deemed* as satisfying the legality requirement. The second issue is the evidential rule to be applied in ISDS, which includes the allocation of burden of proof on the (in)sufficiency of due diligence, and the standard of proof. Without development of these rules, the application of a legality requirement to human rights violations *outside* could impair certainty and predictability.

Counterclaim

The jurisdiction of a tribunal under an investment treaty is determined by the language of the dispute settlement clause therein. Some treaties provide that only the investor can bring a dispute to arbitration. Many treaties also limit the scope of the clause to a dispute about a breach of a legal obligation by a host state. An example of a dispute settlement clause with such a narrow scope is Article 9.19 (1) of the Trans-Pacific Partnership Agreement (TPP). It provides as follows:

> *1. If an investment dispute has not been resolved . . .*
>
> *(a)* ***the claimant****, on its own behalf, may submit to arbitration under this Section a claim:*
>
> *(i) that* ***the respondent has breached****:*
>
> *(A) an obligation under Section A;*
> *(B) an investment authorisation; or*
> *(C) an investment agreement* (footnote omitted and emphasis added).

However, a state may choose to broaden the scope of the dispute settlement clause in treaties it concludes. It can provide that a host state can file a counterclaim against an investor or bring a dispute to arbitration on its own initiative. A clause with broad language can capture disputes about a breach of a legal obligation by an investor. For example, Article X of Spain-Argentine BIT (1991) provides as follows:

> *2.* ***Disputes*** *arising between a Party and an investor of the other Party in connection with investments within the meaning of this Agreement shall, as far as possible, be settled amicably between the parties to the dispute.*
>
> . . .
>
> *3. The dispute may be submitted to an international arbitral tribunal in any of the following circumstances:*
>
> *(a) At the request of* ***either party to the dispute****.*
> [English translation in the UN Treaty series (1992). The original and authentic language of the text is Spanish. Emphasis added]

Paragraph 1 does not qualify 'disputes', and a dispute about a breach of a legal obligation by an investor is within its scope as long as it is 'in connection with investments'. Furthermore, paragraph 3 provides 'either party to the dispute' can request the submission. A host state can submit to arbitration its claim about a breach of obligation by an investor. As a corollary, a last state can also file a counterclaim. This treaty is exceptional in explicitly allowing a host state to first submit a dispute to arbitration. However, dispute settlement clauses of many investment treaties do not qualify 'disputes' that can be submitted to arbitration. These treaties can be interpreted as implicitly admitting counterclaims.

Counterclaim and Human Rights Violation

Permissible causes of action for counterclaims depend on the language of the clause. They may include breach of contract and/or breach of domestic law. Breach of international law, however, will not be excluded if it is applicable to an investor. The question is whether the international law applicable to human rights can be a basis for such counterclaim.

In *Urbaser v. Argentina* (2016), the tribunal held that a counterclaim against an investor for its violation of human rights was admissible under the Spain-Argentine BIT (1991), which was previously quoted. The respondent claimed that the claimant, a water supply and sewage service supplier having operated in Argentina, violated obligations under international law based on the human right to water by failing to provide necessary investment. This was a case of (alleged) human rights violation *inside*.

The tribunal interpreted the dispute settlement clause as permitting such a counterclaim. It divided the obligation about human rights to water into two categories: obligation to perform and obligation to abstain. It found that the former obligation is imposed only on a state, but the latter is imposed on both a state and an investor (*Urbaser v. Argentina*, 2016, Para. 1210). Although the tribunal concluded that the investor was not in breach of the latter obligation and dismissed the counterclaim, the decision is generally understood to have opened the door to counterclaims against investors for potential violations of human rights.

However, it should be noted that the tribunal's analysis and elaboration on counterclaims and human rights is followed by a statement that challenges the fundamental basis of the counterclaim. It states in paragraph 1220 as follows:

> *1220. The Tribunal also notes that Respondent does not state any legal ground for any individual's right to claim damages as a consequence of an alleged violation of the human right to water. Respondent does not demonstrate either that the alleged violation of such human right entails a duty of reparation equally based on international law, with the effect that the individuals concerned by such an alleged harm obtain an appropriate compensation. Respondent failed to state such a claim.* ***This would be a reason sufficient to dismiss Respondent's Counterclaim.*** *The Tribunal adds that such failure can also be explained by the lack of any legal ground based on international law that would entitle a group of individuals to raise a claim for performance for delivery of water and sewage services directed against a company or any other private party. Accordingly, there does not exist a*

claim for compensation in case of lack of such performance not based on an obligation under international law [footnote omitted and emphasis added].

This paragraph reveals the limitations of counterclaims against human rights violation (Shao, 2021). A counterclaim is likely to be dismissed unless two additional legal grounds are established. The first one is a legal ground that entitles the affected individuals to claim reparation from it, which the *Urbaser v. Argentina* (2016) tribunal did not find. Second, even if the first legal ground can be established, the host state needs another legal ground that entitles it to claim compensation on behalf of the affected individuals. Since the *Urbaser v. Argentina* (2016) decision did not reach this point, one cannot derive many clues as to this issue.

These limitations apply to the case of human rights violation *outside*. In particular, the second limitation would be difficult to overcome. Arguably, in the case of human rights violations within the host state, the host state could be regarded as having a special link with the case because of territorial sovereignty over the place where the violation took place or the nationality of the affected individuals, which is likely to be that of the host state. But the host state cannot claim such link to human rights violations *outside*.[5]

The general conclusion is that, in cases of human rights violations *outside*, counterclaims are not an effective tool against an involved investor. If a state would like to remove the previous limitations, then possible policy options would be to include in its investment treaty an explicit provision that a host state can make such counterclaim. However, if a treaty permits a host state to file counterclaims for human rights violations *outside*, then detailed rules should also be required as to the content of the substantive obligations of the investor and as to the evidence needed to establish breach. These are analogous challenges to those that the application of the legality requirement must overcome.

Contributory Negligence and Human Rights Violation

The principle of contributory negligence has been recognized by tribunals (some tribunals refer to it as contributory fault). Article 39 of the Articles on Responsibility of States for International Wrongful Acts (ARSIWA) (2001), which is often cited by tribunals applying the principle, provides that '*[i]n the determination of reparation, account shall be taken of the contribution to the injury by wilful or negligent action or omission of the injured State or any person or entity in relation to whom reparation is sought*'. This principle consists of two elements: (i) wilful or negligent action by the injured State or any person or entity in relation to whom reparation is sought (a claimant in the context of ISDS) and (ii) contribution to injury. If this principle is applied to an investor's involvement with human rights violations, then the amount of the compensation that it can receive due to its claims will be reduced.

The first element is not a difficult condition to satisfy. Tribunals have applied the principle to a variety of investors' misconduct. For example, it was applied to a failure to obtain the necessary authorizations for the transfer of contractual rights (*Occidental v. Ecuador (II)*, 2012), the abuse of a low tax regime (*Hulley v. Russia*, 2014), and the direction of violence to a local residence (*Copper Mesa v.*

Ecuador, 2016) (Marcoux and Bjorklund, 2020). An investor's involvement with human rights violations is likely to constitute such wilful or negligent acts or omissions, whether it is *inside* or *outside*.

Difficulty exists, however, in relation to the second factor, which is an issue of causal link. Although the establishment of a causal link is often uneasy, it is more challenging in the case of human rights violation *outside*. A possible form of causal link in such a case is as follows: an allegation arises that an investor is involved in human rights violations *outside*, which impairs the support from people in the host state to the investor, and the lack of their support or the measures of the host state government to address their concerns leads to damage suffered by the investor. There are many steps, and, in each step, careful examination will be conducted on whether the chain of causation is cut.

The difficulty is illustrated by *Bear Creek v. Peru* (2017). The claimant made an investment in a silver mining project. The location of the project was an area where the Peruvian constitution prohibited foreigners from obtaining rights to natural resources unless they made a case to the Peruvian government for 'public necessity'. The claimant was successful in convincing the government that the project was for public necessity and in obtaining authorization. But it could not obtain support from the local communities due to the insufficiency of its outreach to them. Rather, their negative reaction escalated to social unrest involving violence. Finally, the Peruvian government issued a decree that substantially revoked the authorization for the project, which the respondent argued was to address the unrest. In the arbitration proceeding, the claimant argued that the measure taken by Peru constituted indirect expropriation and breach of fair and equitable treatment (FET). The respondent submitted various arguments on jurisdiction/admissibility and on the merits, which focused on the investor's failure to obtain a 'social license to operate'. On quantum, it argued that the social unrest was a direct consequence of the claimant's conduct and that the tribunal should apply the principle of contributory fault (Paras. 560–564). The decision by the arbitrators was divided. A majority of the tribunal found that the 'Respondent has the burden of proof that its breach of the [Canada-Peru] FTA . . . were to some extent caused by Claimant but [it] has not met that burden' and declined to apply contributory fault. However, Prof. Philippe Sands Q.C., the dissenting arbitrator, expressed the contrary view as follows:

> the Claimant's acts and omissions . . . contributed in material ways to the events that unfolded and then led to the Project's collapse. In particular, the Project collapsed because of the investor's inability to obtain a "social license", the necessary understanding between the Project's proponents and those living in the communities most likely to be affected by it, whether directly or indirectly. [Para. 6]

He emphasized that *the investment was made in an area in which the rights of numerous indigenous communities – under national and international law – were fully engaged* (Para. 7) and concluded that the claimant's failure in its outreach to them should lead to a reduction in damages by one half.

This award has two implications. First, it demonstrates that the establishment of a causal link is difficult regarding an investor's failure to obtain social license. Second, nevertheless, if the approach of the dissenting arbitrator were adopted, then contributory negligence could be applied more broadly. Theoretically, it could be applied to an investor who does not respect human rights.

It is beyond the scope of this chapter to examine how the issue of social license to operate should be addressed in contributory negligence. However, it should be noted that *Bear Creek v. Peru* (2017) is unique in its fact pattern. First, the investor was engaged in a mining business in which the support from landowners and the local community was essential. The dissenting arbitrator stated that '*[i]t is blindingly obvious that the viability and success of a project* ***such as this****, located in the community of the Aymara peoples, a group of interconnected communities, was necessarily dependent on local support*' (Para. 6, emphasis added). Although almost all investors who seek the success of their business need support from people in the host state, the degree of *dependence* on this will be different in each case. Second, in *Bear Creek v. Peru* (2017), the human rights that were allegedly violated were those of the same people whose support the investor's project was 'dependent on'. The direct causation between the misconduct by the investor was easier to find when compared with a case where the human rights at issue are those of individuals who are not related to the project.

These unique features require cautious consideration about whether and how the approach by the dissenting arbitrator could be generally applied to cases concerning an investor's involvement with human rights, if a tribunal in the future wished to adopt it. A convincing argument is that the case of human rights violations *outside* should be distinguished from *Bear Creek v. Peru* (2017): it is more difficult to find a causal link, which would prevent a tribunal from applying the principle of contributory negligence.

A state can potentially overcome this challenge by adding to its investment treaties a provision providing that contributory negligence is applicable to cases of human rights violations *outside*. However, the provision would need more detailed guidance about when and how a tribunal can find a causal link if states (and indeed, investors) expect it to function in a predictable manner.

Conclusion

Human rights violations *outside* should be properly placed *inside* investment treaty practice. This chapter provides an overview of the legal tools under investment treaties that can be employed in cases where an investor is allegedly involved with human rights violations *outside*. The conclusion is as follows.

First, a legality requirement could be useful with the appropriate design of applicable domestic law. However, development of rules is necessary regarding the level of due diligence required of an investor. The evidential rules to be applied in ISDS also need further elucidation.

Second, counterclaims and contributory negligence are not promising options. The former is unlikely to succeed, and the latter is likely to confront practical difficulty in establishing a causal link. These challenges could be overcome by adding new provisions to treaties. However, such provisions also need clearer rules on how they will be applied.

The development of these new rules can take various forms. Some states may prefer to include in their investment treaties provisions to deal with these issues, which will be applied and elaborated by future tribunals. Other states may attempt to legislate in their domestic law to clarify their positions on these questions, which they expect future tribunals to take into consideration when interpreting investment treaties. One could also expect an attempt at a *softer* approach such as non-binding guidelines issued by international organizations and/or stakeholders. In these cases, a state will have to consider how it relates these soft norms to its investment treaties and what instruction on this point it will give to future tribunals. Each approach is not mutually exclusive. On the contrary, the combination of these tools for rule development is required to shape legal tools that will practically work to address these challenges.

Note: The author is grateful for discussion with and comments from colleagues of the Ministry of Foreign Affairs of Japan. He is also thankful for helpful suggestions of Mr. Colin Trehearne. However, the opinions expressed in this chapter are the author's own and do not represent the view of any organization to which he belongs, and any mistake that it may contain is his own.

Notes

1 Generally, substantive obligations under investment treaties do not prevent a host state from pursuing its legitimate policy goals. They only provide that certain measures are not permissible even for achieving legitimate policy of a host state. For example, the principles of due process and proportionality apply even in the case where an investor is allegedly involved with human rights violations *outside*. However, the nature of the case may affect how these principles should be applied.

2 There seem to be no agreed criteria to practically distinguish jurisdiction and admissibility. Söderlund and Burova (2018) shows that a variety of approaches have been adopted by commentators and tribunals (see also Fontanelli and Tanzi, 2017; Gouiffes and Ordonez, 2015). Given the fact that jurisdiction and admissibility will have a similar function in relation to the topic of this chapter, the author uses them interchangeably.

3 As Dumberry (2020, p. 502) observes, commentators criticize the award in *Hulley v. Russia* that explicitly denied the 'clean hands doctrine', which has the status of a general principle of law recognized by civilized nations. However, it should be noted that when a tribunal's analysis on it was focused on denial of an investor's protection due to illegality in its performance of investments, the tribunal accepted the unwritten legality requirement to apply to illegality in the making of an investment. As Dumberry (2020, pp. 520–525) correctly points out, the *Hulley v. Russia* (2014) tribunal took into consideration as a matter of merit the illegality committed by the investor in the post-establishment phase.

4 When the investor notices its involvement with human rights violation, it must immediately stop it. If it fails to stop it, then a host state should be allowed to take regulatory measures.

However, it is a different question whether a written legality requirement can be applied in a manner to retrospectively deny the investor protection under the treaty.

5 Shao (2021) points out that a counterclaim based on domestic law can be an alternative to that grounded on general international law. It is conceivable that a host state can legislate domestic law that prohibits an investor from being involved with human rights breach *inside* and that allows the government to claim damage on behalf of the affected individuals. Arguably, such domestic law could serve as legal grounds for a counterclaim in cases like *Urbaser v. Argentina* (2016). But this alternative would not be available in the case of human rights violation *outside*, because the host state does not have authority to designate itself as the agent of individuals who are not its nationals and whose rights are violated outside its territory.

References

All subsequent websites were last visited on 25 September 2022.

Agreement between the Argentine Republic and the Kingdom of Spain on the Reciprocal Promotion and Protection of Investments (1991) [Spain-Argentine BIT], in force 28 September 1992.

Agreement between the Government of Israel and the Government of the Republic of Uzbekistan for the Promotion and Reciprocal Protection of Investors (1994) [Israel-Uzbekistan BIT], in force 18 February 1997.

Agreement on Reciprocal Encouragement and Protection of Investments between the Kingdom of the Netherlands and the Republic of Turkey (1986) [Netherlands-Turkey BIT], in force 1 November 1989.

Al Warraq v. Indonesia (2014). Final Award. Available at: www.italaw.com/sites/default/files/case-documents/italaw4164.pdf

Articles on Responsibility of States for Internationally Wrongful Acts (ARSIWA) (2001).

Bear Creek Mining Corporation v. Republic of Peru (2017). ICSID Case No. ARB/14/21, Award and Partial Dissenting Opinion by Prof. Philippe Sands Q.C.

Choudhury, B. (2020). Investor Obligations for Human Rights. *ICSID Review – Foreign Investment Law Journal*, 35(1–2), pp. 82–104. Available at: http://dx.doi.org/10.1093/icsidreview/siaa002

Copper Mesa v. Ecuador (2016). PCA No. 2012–2, Award.

Cortec Mining v. Kenya (2018). ICSID Case No. ARB/15/29, Award.

Dumberry, P. (2020). The Clean Hands Doctrine as a General Principle of International Law. *The Journal of World Investment and Trade*, 21(4), pp. 489–527. Available at: https://brill.com/view/journals/jwit/21/4/article-p489_1.xml

Fontanelli, F. and Tanzi, A. (2017). Jurisdiction and Admissibility in Investment Arbitration. A View from the Bridge at the Practice. *The Law and Practice of International Courts and Tribunals*, 16(1), pp. 3–20. Available at: http://dx.doi.org/10.1163/15718034-12341339

Gouiffes, L. and Ordonez, M. (2015). Jurisdiction and Admissibility: Are We Any Closer to a Line in the Sand? *Arbitration International*, 31(1), pp. 107–122. Available at: http://dx.doi.org/10.1093/arbint/aiv024

Hulley Enterprises v. Russia (2014). PCA Case No. 2005–03/AA226, Final Award.

Jarrett, M. (2019). *Contributory Fault and Investor Misconduct in Investment Arbitration.* Cambridge: Cambridge University Press.

Kikuma, A (2019). Tōshi kyōtei chūsai ni okeru tōshika no ihō kōi no toriatsukai [How Can an Arbitration Tribunal Address Illegal Conduct by Investors? – From the Perspective of an Investment Treaty Negotiator]. *Kokusaihou Kenkyu [Tokyo Review of International Law]*, 7, pp. 81–114.

Kim and others v. Uzbekistan (2017). ICSID Case No. ARB/13/6, Decision on Jurisdiction.
Marcoux, J.-M. and Bjorklund, A. K. (2020). Foreign Investors' Responsibilities and Contributory Fault in Investment Arbitration. *International and Comparative Law Quarterly*, 69(4), pp. 877–905. Available at: http://dx.doi.org/10.1017/S0020589320000354
Occidental v. Ecuador (II) (2012). ICSID Case No. ARB/06/11, Award.
Shao, X. (2021). Environmental and Human Rights Counterclaims in International Investment Arbitration: At the Crossroads of Domestic and International Law. *Journal of International Economic Law*, 24(1), pp. 157–179. Available at: http://dx.doi.org/10.1093/jiel/jgab001
Söderlund, C. and Burova, E. (2018). Is There Such a Thing as Admissibility in Investment Arbitration? *ICSID Review – Foreign Investment Law Journal*, 33(2), pp. 525–559. Available at: http://dx.doi.org/10.1093/icsidreview/siy009
Urbaser and CABB v. Argentina (2016). ICSID Case No. ARB/07/26, Award.
Viñuales, J. E. (2017). Investor Diligence in Investment Arbitration: Sources and Arguments. *ICSID Review – Foreign Investment Law Journal*, 32(2), pp. 346–370. Available at: https://academic.oup.com/icsidreview/article-abstract/32/2/346/3100254

16 Transboundary Environmental Damage

Midori NARAZAKI

Introduction

In Japan, since the end of the 1950s, many pollution lawsuits have been filed due to health problems caused by environmental pollution, including the *Minamata* disease that led to stricter environmental control laws. In the 1980s, 'exportation of pollution', namely, relocating facilities to developing countries to avoid strict regulations of the home country, became a problem. A prominent example is the *Bukit Merah* radioactive pollution case (*Woon Tan Kan and Ors. v. Asian Rare Earth Sdn. Bhd*, 1992, 1993)) in Malaysia. The Malaysian-Japanese joint venture *Asian Rare Earth* (ARE) was established in Malaysia in 1979 by *Mitsubishi* Chemical Industries Ltd., with a 35% stake, to extract and refine rare earths such as yttrium. ARE dumped radioactive waste from its plant in Bukit Merah, Ipoh on adjacent land in 1982. The Ipoh High Court ordered the closure of the plant, but the Supreme Court of Malaysia accepted evidence that proved that the radiation levels at the site did not exceed the permissible standards and that the ARE plant was operating under a license issued by the Malaysian Ministry under the *Atomic Energy Licensing Act* (1984). The Supreme Court found that the legal requirements for an order to permanently enjoin the operation of the plant were not fulfilled (Ichihara and Harding, 1995; JETRO, 1994; Murase, 1993). In the 1990s, during which the Earth Summit in Rio de Janeiro and the Rio Declaration were held in 1992, Japan's Official Development Assistance (ODA) to Asian countries was questioned regarding its investment in development projects such as the construction of dams, which destroys the regional environment (Potter, 1994). Japan has been investing in the export of nuclear power plants and thermal power plants to other countries in a concerted effort by the public and private sectors, but it is not uncommon to encounter local residents who oppose the construction of such plants on the grounds of environmental pollution. For example, in the UK, a new nuclear power plant project of the Japanese company *Hitachi* got a huge loan from *Japan Bank for International Cooperation* (JBIC) and other Japanese megabanks and a governmental guarantee for the entire loan (Friends of the Earth Japan, 2018). In Asian countries, the *Joint-Venture in Energy Sector* (JERA) by *Tokyo Electric Power Co.* and the *Chubu Electric Power Co.* participated in the gas-fired power project in Taiwan and Bangladesh (Goso, 2020; Shimizu, 2021). Recently, the accident at

DOI: 10.4324/9781003193098-16

the *Fukushima Daiichi Nuclear Power Plant* (FNPP) in 2011 and the resulting environmental pollution have led to many disputes with neighboring countries. The Japanese government announced on 13 April 2021 the decision to release contaminated water used to cool the FNPP into the Pacific Ocean after treating it with the Advanced Liquid Processing System (ALPS). South Korea then protested and stated that it would file a complaint with the *International Tribunal for the Law of the Sea* (ITLOS) for provisional measures to stop the release of the water into the Pacific. Additionally, the export of international waste such as plastic waste from industrialized countries, including Japan, has also been questioned as a cause of environmental degradation in Asian countries (Kojima, 2020).

Four Modes of Transboundary Pollution Damage Involving Japan

In the past, transboundary environmental pollution had typically been modeled on the *Trail Smelter* case (*United States v. Canada*, 1938, 1941), where toxic emissions from land-based facilities flow into neighboring countries (Mode 1: Nuisance from Neighboring Sources). This mode of transboundary damage includes cases where the damage spreads to neighboring countries through fluids such as rivers.

Japan is surrounded by the sea. Transboundary pollution to neighboring countries may occur via ocean. This possibility has been examined as a form of nuclear damage in the wake of the FNPP accident in 2011 and also in Japan's accession in 2014 to the 1997 *Convention on Supplementary Compensation for Nuclear Damage* (CSC). A recent example of transboundary pollution via ocean, which led to civil damage litigation, is a case brought by Indonesians against a multinational enterprise that operates an oil platform, the *Montara* oil spill case (*Sanda v. PTTEP Australasia (Ashmore Cartier) Pty Ltd*, 2021). The class-action claimant alleged in an Australian court that gas and oil emissions from the *Montara* oil field accident in 2006 damaged seaweed farming in the Indonesian islands across the Timor Sea. The Federal Court of Australia ruled in favor of the victim's claim after a long-term hearing on the issues of the limitation period for filing a lawsuit and the causation with respect to the arrival of the spilled oil to the islands.

Next are cases of people who suffered damage after staying close to a source of contamination temporarily (Mode 2: Self-Approach and Return). A recent civil dispute involves a lawsuit filed by former soldiers who were on a US aircraft carrier, and they claimed that they were exposed to radiation from the *Fukushima* nuclear disaster. The *Cooper v. Tokyo Electric Power Co.* (2013–2020) was filed in the US State of California, and ultimately, the Court of Appeals withheld the US court's jurisdiction in the interest of international comity.

Other notable developments in civil litigation include cases where foreign investment causes environmental damage to the region (Mode 3: Damage From Facilities Built Using Foreign Investment). Following the *Bhopal* case *(In re Union Carbide Corp. Gas Plant Disaster at Bhopal, India*, 1986, 1987) where environmental damage was caused by production infrastructure and factories that relocated to developing countries to avoid tight environmental regulations in industrialized countries, the court's jurisdiction was denied for reasons such as *forum non-*

conveniens, even if the case was brought in the home country of the parent company. In recent years, however, the UK Supreme Court's judgments in *Lungowe v. Vedanta* (2019) and *Okpabi v. Royal Dutch Shell* (2021) recognize the jurisdiction of actions against parent companies in countries where the holding companies of multinational corporate groups or parent companies are based.

A more recent issue is the case where damage spreads to many countries due to transboundary movement, and transport and trading of goods and services risk spreading pollution (Mode 4: Spreading Pollution Through Trading). As the global spread of COVID-19 has shown, when a source of contamination is not known but the damage spreads diffusely, most countries tend to close themselves off, raise barriers against the outside world, and tackle the issue internally. Such a level of protection against high-risk foreign products is regarded as a trade barrier, and exporting countries may find this trade block a problem, which might lead to World Trade Organization (WTO) dispute settlement. An example is when Japan complained to the WTO about South Korea's ban on imports of Japanese marine products due to the risk of radioactive contamination from the FNPP accident (Korea – Radionuclides (Japan), 2019). In addition, oil pollution damages caused by shipping accidents, which can be categorized under Mode 4, are outside the scope of this chapter because most maritime nations are signatories to the 1969 *Convention on Civil Liability for Oil Pollution Damage* (CLC) and the 1971 *Convention on the Establishment of an International Fund for Compensation for Oil Pollution Damage* (FC), which provide the framework for the compensation and restoration obligations of shipowners and shippers to damage caused by shipping accidents.

Discussion

Assuming the worst-case scenario, first, the cooling water from the nuclear power plant released into the Pacific Ocean reaches the coast of one of the Korean islands and affects their seafood industry (Mode 1). Second, Korean fishing boats arrive at the waters around Japan, and after returning home, the crew develops radiation sickness (Mode 2). Third, a Japanese company that built a power plant in an Asian country with export guarantees and financial support from Japanese government agencies is sued before the Japanese court by the residents of this Asian country for damaging the local environment and violating their human rights (Mode 3). Fourth, unreleased cooling water from a nuclear power plant is chemically treated to have its composition change into that of plain water, loaded on a ship flagged by another country, and then exported by a foreign company with a global network for it to be dumped or released in waters belonging to other countries, with the prior consent of these importing countries. In this case, would a civil environmental group ask a Japanese court to order the foreign company to stop such trades because of the potential risk (Mode 4)?

Due Diligence of the State for Industrial Activities Under Its Jurisdiction or Control

In Mode 1, Japan will be questioned whether the government has taken sufficient measures to prevent pollution if *Tokyo Electric Power Co.*, the operator of the

Fukushima nuclear power plant, discharges water used to cool the plant into the Pacific Ocean.

The obligation of states in preventing transboundary pollution is set forth in Principle 7 of the 1992 *Rio Declaration on Environment and Development*; particularly regarding the marine environment, see Part XII of the *United Nations Convention on the Law of the Sea* (UNCLOS). Article 194 (2) of UNCLOS indicates that states have a duty to ensure that transboundary pollution caused by activities under their jurisdiction or control does not spread. These articles indicate the duty of states in control and therefore impose a duty of *due diligence* on such states. As part of *due diligence*, the obligation set forth in Article 194(2) of UNCLOS refers, according to the ITLOS (*International Tribunal for the Law of the Sea*) *Advisory Opinion on Seabed Activities* (2011), to the obligation of conduct to take all necessary measures to bring private persons under the jurisdiction of a state into compliance with their treaty obligations. The Japanese government is now being challenged by neighboring countries on its obligation to *due diligence* regarding the release of cooling water into the Pacific Ocean, which was stored for a long period since the FNPP accident. They are depending on the IAEA to conduct an environmental assessment and judge that the water is safe to be released.

Regarding compensation for damage, UNCLOS does not clearly establish the direct obligations of states but only notes that

> The member states shall ensure that prompt and adequate means of compensation and other remedies are available in accordance with their legal systems for damage caused by pollution of the marine environment by natural or legal persons under their jurisdiction.
>
> (UNCLOS, Art. 235(2))

UNCLOS also states that 'None of the provisions of the Convention shall affect the initiation of civil proceedings in respect of claims for loss or damage arising from pollution of the marine environment' (UNCLOS, Art. 229).

In the *Montara* oil spill case, in the early stages after the accident, the Indonesian government claimed compensation for civil damages collectively but did not call into question the Australian government's direct obligation to compensate (Lyons, 2015, p. 184; Prihandono and Dewanty, 2015).

Direct Responsibilities of Transboundary Damage of the State in Control

For nuclear damage liability, the *Paris Convention on Third Party Liability for Nuclear Energy* (Paris Convention, 1960), the *Vienna Convention on Civil Liability for Nuclear Damage* (Vienna Convention, 1963), and the CSC explicitly indicate the direct compensation obligation of a state that controls a nuclear facility that caused pollution damage to individuals. These conventions indicate that the majority of the liability falls on the operator of the nuclear facility and that the state in control is obliged to follow the rule of no-fault liability and has to set aside funds for compensation.

Japan acceded to the CSC in 2014 after the FNPP accident; the CSC applies to damage caused by nuclear accidents to a member state's nationals, ships, aircraft, or facilities. It is arguable whether the release of cooling water can be interpreted as a form of after-the-fact pollution caused by the FNPP accident. But in any case, since South Korea is not a signatory to any conventions for nuclear damage liability, including the CSC, these conventions do not apply to damage caused to South Korea.

In the nuclear energy, petroleum, chemical, and mineral industries, it is still difficult for an injured foreign nation to directly seek responsibility from a foreign state in civil damage litigation. The most important reason is that, in principle, a state is granted immunity from civil jurisdiction in foreign courts due to the privilege of sovereign immunity. Additionally, if a lawsuit against a foreign state involves highly political issues, the courts of the forum may avoid making a conclusion because it is not amenable to judicial review due to the principle of separation of powers. In *Cooper v. Tokyo Electric Powe Co.* (2013), a former soldier who worked on a US aircraft carrier that was sailing in the waters near *Fukushima* and carrying out disaster relief operations immediately after the *Fukushima* disaster was exposed to radioactive contamination. The initial petition alleged that the State of Japan and *Tokyo Electric Power Co.* had conspired to hide information about the radiation. In the second amended complaint, the allegation was changed to that of *Tokyo Electric Power Co.*'s negligence, because the US courts withheld judicial power to decide the political question of whether the foreign government has committed fraud against U.S. government (Dogauchi, 2019, p. 45).

Focus of International Jurisdiction in the Court at the Venue of the Accident

For a lawsuit seeking civil damages against a liable operator for transboundary damage, Japanese rules on international jurisdiction in *Code of Civil Procedure* (CPC, 1996) indicate that Japanese courts have jurisdiction over a tort if it occurred in Japan, except for cases when the consequences of a wrongful act committed in a foreign country have arisen in Japan but are deemed not possible to foresee them arising in Japan (CPC, Art. 3–3 (viii)). In actual lawsuits, when an action for a tort is brought against a liable facility operator of another country (outside where the damage occurred), the forum's jurisdiction is sometimes likely to be challenged. Particularly, for Mode 2, it is likely that the victim will file a lawsuit in their home country after returning there.

In *Cooper v. Tokyo Electric Power Co.* (2020), after several amendments to the complaint, the Federal Court of Appeals denied jurisdiction over the lawsuit filed in court in California, US because based on 'international comity', the interests of Japan were greater than those of the US.

In the conventions for nuclear damage liability, when an action for damages is brought against a member state or an operator, in principle, the state where the accident occurred has exclusive jurisdiction (CSC, Art. 13; Paris Convention, Art. 13a; Vienna Convention, Art. 11(1)). If the accident occurred outside the member states, namely, on the high seas or in the air, or if the location of the accident cannot be identified, the member state where the nuclear facility caused contamination or where the facility operator is located will have exclusive jurisdiction (the State 'in whose territory the nuclear installation of the operator liable is situated' (Paris Convention, Art. 13(b)) or 'the Installation State of the operator liable' (Vienna Convention, Art. 11(2)), or 'by which or under which the authority of the nuclear installation is operated' (Vienna Convention, Art. 11(2)) or 'by which or under which the nuclear installation is operated' (CSC, Art. 1(e) and Art. 13(3)). This kind of distribution of jurisdiction is inextricably linked to the obligation of a state to arrange compensation for all civil damages resulting from the facility under its control.

For Modes 1 and 2, South Korea is not a signatory to any conventions for nuclear damage liability, so Japanese courts do not have exclusive jurisdiction over damages incurred in South Korea. When a lawsuit is brought in Japan, discussions may be carried out to decide whether Japanese courts have international jurisdiction. According to the rules of international jurisdiction in the CPC, the courts have jurisdiction over the defendant's domicile (CPC, Art. 3–2) or jurisdiction over actions for a tort if the location where the harmful act or its damage occurred in Japan (CPC, Art. 3–3 (viii)). However, if there are 'special circumstances' in which a trial in Japan is deemed inappropriate from the standpoint of a proper and efficient administration of justice and the fairness between the parties to the dispute, Japanese courts may restrain the exercise of jurisdiction and dismiss the whole or part of the proceedings (CPC, Art. 3–9). For Modes 1 and 2, since the damage is caused by water discharged from Japan, the jurisdiction of Japanese courts would be recognized. Even if a lawsuit is filed in Korea, the Japanese defendant would contest the jurisdiction of the Korean court. In the field of nuclear damage, the Japanese government has insisted in its *amicus brief* filed with the US Court of Appeals in *Cooper v. Tokyo Electric Power Co.* (2017) that Japan has great interests in applying a uniform standard of compensation, even if the damage claim does not fall within the scope of nuclear damage convention. For Mode 3, it depends on the extent to which the Japanese parent company exercises *de facto* control over the local company and whether the jurisdiction in a tort (CPC, Art. 3–3 (viii)) would be recognized. Under Mode 4, if an action against a foreign company exporting from Japan were filed, then jurisdiction would not be admitted unless the action relates to the company's business in Japan (CPC, Art. 3–3 (v)).

Clarification of the Governing Law Based on the Choice of the Parties to the Dispute

The next question is which law is applicable. Regarding claims for damages based on tort liability, if the harmful act and the damage occurred at different places, then modern legislation for choice of law has regarded the law where the damage occurred as applicable, in order to protect the victim. *Japanese Act on General Rules on Application of Laws* (General Rules, 2006) has no special rules on environmental damage. For a tort action, Article 17 of the General Rules indicates that the law where the result of the wrongful act occurred shall apply to the claim for the tort. However, if the parties to the dispute agree to apply a different law to the claim (General Rules, Art. 21) or if there is a different law that is connected 'manifestly more closely' to the claim (General Rules, Art. 20), then this different law can be applied. In the *Kota Panjan* Dam case (*Indonesian Residents and Indonesian Environmental Forum WALHI v. Japanese Government*, 2009), filed in 2002 by 8,396 Indonesian residents against the Japanese government and its agencies, Tokyo District Court applied Japanese law as the governing law as agreed by the parties to the dispute. Moreover, recently, the Dutch Court of Appeal in the Hague in *Dooh and Milieudifensie v. Shell* (2021) applied Nigerian law and its legal source, English law, as the governing law chosen by the parties to the dispute, according to Article 6 of the *Dutch Tort Conflict of Law Act* and Article 14 Rome II.

Therefore, in all cases of Modes 1 to 4, Japanese law will be the governing law if the parties to the dispute agree or if it is recognized to be more closely related to the claim. The *Japanese Act on Compensation for Nuclear Damages* (1961) will be applied as part of the governing law. The Act adopts the rule of no-fault liability. If a causal relationship between the release of cooling water and the damage is recognized, then the lawsuit for damage could be approved.

However, even if the governing law is chosen by the parties in dispute, depending on how it is chosen, there may be a problem as to which location to choose the law from. In *Milieudefensie, et al. v. Royal Dutch Shell* (2021), a collective action brought by civil foundations on behalf of 17,379 individual claimants, the Hague District Court ordered *Royal Dutch Shell* to limit carbon dioxide emissions; in this case the plaintiffs chose the law of the 'place of the event giving rise to the damage' as the governing law according to the second sentence of Article 7 Rome II (2007). The Hague District Court held that the place where *Royal Dutch Shell* presented its corporate policies to all affiliated companies of the *Shell* group, that is, the Netherlands, was where the event giving rise to the damage occurred. Although such a decision may be questioned, it is important to clarify that the law of the home country of a parent company that controls a global supply chain is applied as the governing law in a lawsuit that seeks liability for damages caused by carbon dioxide emissions around the world and that this was chosen by the plaintiffs, especially for Modes 3 and 4.

Due Diligence of States and Corporations in the Global Value Chain

The recent decisions of the UK Supreme Court in *Lungowe v. Vedant*a (2019) and in *Okupabi v. Royal Dutch Shell* (2021), which challenged the jurisdiction of a claim against a liable parent company for damage caused to a third party by the conduct of its subsidiary, held that there must be a practical and general examination of the parent company's interference with the group as a whole in order for the parent company to be found liable. This includes not only control in the capital between the parent company and subsidiary but also *de facto* management seizure such as positive intervention measures to implement group policies issued by the parent company. Moreover, great attention will be given to the parent company's public statements, which could indicate that it takes responsibility for the conduct of its group subsidiaries and affiliates.

For Modes 3 and 4, it might be pointed out that the relationship between a state government and a business corporation is similar to that of parent-subsidiary corporations. The due diligence of states and businesses has recently started expanding, especially in terms of human rights. On 28 July 2022, the United Nations General Assembly adopted the resolution that the right to a clean, healthy, and sustainable environment is a universal human right. States are now expected to encourage companies residing in their territories or within their jurisdictions to protect the human rights of foreign residents by conducting business activities away from their regions.

In the *Kota Panjan* Dam case (2009), the Tokyo District Court held that the due care owed by the Japanese government to residents of foreign countries to which it provides development assistance cannot be directly derived from Japan's membership in international human rights treaties. In the last decade, the civil lawsuits for environmental damage have developed a preference for relying on international instruments such as the 2011 *UN Guiding Business and Human Rights* and the 2011 *OECD Guidelines for Multinational Enterprises*. On 26 May 2021, citing these references as support, the Hague District Court ordered *Royal Dutch Shell* to reduce carbon dioxide emissions from the global activities of production and transaction of the *Shell* group.

Fragmentation of Lawsuits for Pollution from Trading and Global Business Activities

As mentioned previously, a recent emerging issue is the global harmful impact of business activities conducted by a multinational corporate group through its overseas subsidiaries and other affiliates in foreign environments and the human rights of foreign residents living there. Although international treaties and soft laws have been drafted in order to regulate cross-border activities, the scope of each treaty is segmented into individual aspects of business activities.

For example, for Mode 4, if the export of processed water from Japan for release in the waters of other countries is considered an act of pollution of the sea, then UNCLOS indicates that for marine pollution originating from a ship, in principle, the flag state shall have jurisdiction over the pollution, followed by the coastal state and port state that will have some jurisdiction. Also, if processed water from Japan is considered as waste, the 1972 *Convention on the Prevention of Marine Pollution by Dumping of Wastes and Other Matter* (London Convention), the 1996 *London Protocol*, and the 1973 *International Convention for the Prevention of Pollution from Ship*, as amended by the 1978 *Protocol* (MARPOL73/78), obligate the member states to prohibit the dumping of waste from ships into the sea. Also regulating the cross-border movement of waste is the 1989 *Basel Convention on the Control of Transboundary Movements of Hazardous Wastes and their Disposal* (Basel Convention), which obliges exporting countries not to allow the export of waste without prior consent from the importing and/or transiting countries. For Mode 4, if chemically treated water is considered as waste or pollutive product defined in these treaties, then its transport or trading is subject to international regulations.

The scope of domestic litigation is also likely to be fragmented. The *Probo Koala* case has resulted in many national lawsuits that have failed to capture the whole harmful events caused by the multinational corporation *Trafigura*, such as the cleaning of crude naphtha on the ship, the transportation of the slop, the discharge and re-loading at the Port of Amsterdam, the outsourcing to local contractors in Côte d'Ivoire, and the dumping of the slop there (Dezulay, 2019; Enneking, 2018; MacManus, 2018). The lawsuit against Trafigura for the cleanup of the site where the waste was dumped in Abidjan is still ongoing in group litigation in *Stichting Union des Victimes de Déchets Toxiques D'Abidjan et Banlieues (VDTCI) v. Trafigura Beheer B.V.* (2022) in the Netherlands.

Nevertheless, it has become a subject of national lawsuits in countries with class action systems in place that the worldwide activities of multinational companies are causing global environmental pollution, such as climate change from the carbon dioxide emissions of *Shell* group in *Milieudefensie, et al. v. Royal Dutch Shell* (2021), the water pollution caused by plastic packaging of food products marketed by *Coca-Cola, PepsiCo, Nestle*, and others, as seen in the lawsuit of *Earth Island Institute v. Crystal Geyser Water Co. et al.* (2021). However, challenges remain as only a limited amount of damage is covered by such litigation. In the *Shell* carbon emissions lawsuit, the class action proceeding was held only for the damages suffered by the residents in the Netherlands and the Wadden provinces. The global damages caused by climate change due to carbon dioxide emissions vary from region to region; they do not fall under 'similar interests' covered by the class action. These procedural limitations lead to the current fragmentation of damages not covered by these lawsuits.

Conclusion

For Modes 1 and 2, international conventions provide that the national jurisdiction for preventing transboundary pollution shall be centralized in a specific state, especially the control state that has risk activities under its jurisdiction. In the field of nuclear damage, the judicial jurisdiction is concentrated in the state where the accident occurred or to which the installation belongs. For Modes 1 and 2, the governments of the states concerned tend to actively cooperate or intervene in the civil lawsuit for damages, even in the absence of bilateral treaties for accidental damage between them.

For Modes 3 and 4, jurisdiction for preventing transboundary pollution is not centralized in a specific state. The trend in Mode 3 is that lawsuits for civil damage are brought in the home country of the parent company of a corporate group, and the jurisdiction of the court is determined using the methods of the human rights due diligence, on the ground that the group holding company in control of its worldwide business value chain is responsible for the global pollution damage. However, for Modes 3 and 4, it is still not clear how the responsibility of business actors controlling worldwide business relations will be determined in civil litigation. In this regard, the due diligence of companies has only just begun to catch on, given the recent rush to address the responsibilities of corporate groups in global supply chains and the obligations to ensure appropriate corporate activities to protect human rights.

With respect to the governing law, in Modes 1 and 2 of the bilateral model, as transboundary environmental damages in a narrow sense, the victim should be able to choose either the law of the place where the harm action or causal event occurred or the law of the place where the damage or injury occurred. Such a ubiquity principle is adopted in the second sentence of Article 7 of the Rome II Regulation (2007).

In the trilateral model (Mode 3) and the multilateral model (Mode 4), actions of harm are committed in more than one or in many places, and in Mode 4, a series of such actions cause damage or injury in more than one place. In such cases, we have to create conflict of laws rules from a new perspective to pick one national law to govern and discipline these actions or outcomes. It would be preferred that the law of the country that is granted jurisdiction by international treaty to prevent pollution from spreading to other countries should be chosen as the applicable law in interpreting 'the law most closely related to the case' by synchronizing the applicable law with the international regulatory jurisdiction of the state, presumably because such countries must provide generous protection against intra- and extraterritorial damage in their national mandatory substantive laws.

References

All subsequent websites were last visited on 16 September 2022.

Act on Compensation for Nuclear Damages 1961 (JP).

Act on General Rules for Application of Laws 2006 (JP).

Atomic Energy Licensing Act 1984 (MA).

Bhopal Case (In re Union Carbide Corp. Gas Plant Disaster at Bhopal) (1986). United States Dist. Ct, S.D.N.Y., 634 F.Supp.842, and (1987) Court of Appeals, 2d Cir.,809 F.2d 195.

Code of Civil Procedure 1996 (JP).

Dezulay, S. (2019). By-passing Sovereignty: Trafigura Lawsuits (re Ivory Coast). In: Watt, H. M. *et al.* eds., *Global Private International Law: Adjudication Without Frontiers*. Northamptom: Edward Elgar, p. 92.

Dogauchi, M. (2019). Tomodachi Sakusen ni Tomonau Hōshasen-Hibaku wo Riyū to suru Soshō [Lawsuits in the US on the Grounds of Radiation Exposure Associated with Operation TOMODACHI]—Lindsay R. Cooper v. Tokyo Electric Power Company, Inc. In: *Japan Energy Law Institute. Report of the Study Group on Issues in Nuclear Damage Compensation Legislation for Fiscal Years 2015~2016*, pp. 43–70. Available at: www.jeli.gr.jp/img/file29.pdf

Dooh and Milieudifensie v. Shell (2021). Eric Barizaa Dooh and Milieudifensie v. Royal Dutch Shell and SPDC (case c) and Shell Petroleum NV and Shell Transport & Trading (case d), Netherlands Court of Appeal the Hague, Case Nr. 200.126.843 (case c); 200.126.848 (case d), ECLI:NL: GHDHA:2021:1827.

Earth Island Institute v. Crystal Geyser Water Co. et al. (2021). United States Dist. Ct, N.D. California, 2021.521 F. Supp.3d. 863.

Enneking, L. (2018). The Common Denominator of the Trafigura Case, Foreign Direct Liability Case and the Rome II Regulation. *European Review of Private Law*, 2, pp. 283–311.

Friends of the Earth Japan (2018). *Urgent Petition No to Japanese Nuclear Exports Using Public Money*. Available at: www.foejapan.org/en/energy/pdf/wylfa_petition_en.pdf

Goso, S. (2020). Bangladesh LNG Power Plant Backed by $645m in Japanese Lending: Public and Private Financing to Support Project Part-owned by JERA. *NIKKEI Asia*, 15 July.

Ichihara, M. and Harding, A. (1995). Human Rights, the Environment and Radioactive Waste: A Study of the Asian Rare Earth Case in Malaysia. *Review of European Community & International Environmental Law*, 4(1), pp. 1–14.

Indonesian Residents and Indonesian Environmental Forum WALHI v. Japanese Government (2009). Japan Tokyo Dist. Ct, 10 September, Case Nr. H14(WA)19276・H15(WA)6732・H16(WA)104. Affirmed by Tokyo High Court's Decision on 26 December 2012 and Supreme Court's decision (2nd Petty Bench) on 26 December 2015.

International Tribunal for the Law of the Sea (2011). Responsibilities and Obligations of States with Respect to Activities in the Area, Advisory Opinion. *ITLOS Report, 2011*, p. 10.

Japan External Trade Organization (JETRO) (1994). *Malaysian Eixian Rare Earth Sha Kōgai Soshō Hanketsu: Saikōsai・Kōsai Hanketsu* [Malaysian Asian Rare Earth Pollution Lawsuit Decision: Supreme Court and High Court Decisions]. Available at: https://doi.org/10.20561/00029065

Kojima, M. (2020). The Impact of Recyclable Waste Trade Restrictions on Producer Recycling Activities. *International Journal of Automation Technology*, 14(6), p. 873. Available at: www.jstage.jst.go.jp/article/ijat/14/6/14_873/_article/-char/ja/

Korea – Import Bans, and Testing and Certification Requirements for Radionuclides (Korea – Radionuclides (Japan)) (2019). WTO Panel Report, WT/DS495/R; WTO Appellate Body Report, WT/DS495/AB/R.

Lindsay R. Cooper v. Tokyo Electric Power Co., Inc. et al. (2013). United States Dist. Ct, S.D. California, 26 November, 990 F.Supp.2d 1035; (2017) Court of Appeals 9th Cir., 22 June 2017, 860 F.3d.1193; and (2020) Court of Appeals 9th Cir., 22. May 2020, 960 F. 3rd. 549.

Lungowe and others v. Vedanta Resources Plc and Konkola Copper Mines Plc. (2019). United Kingdom Sup. Ct, 2019 UKSC 20.

Lyons, Y. (2015). Transboundary Pollution from Offshore Activities: A Study of the Montara Offshore Oil Spill. In: Jayakumar, S. *et al.* eds., *Transboundary Pollution*. Northampton: Edward Elgar, p. 162.

MacManus, T. (2018). *State-Corporate Crime and the Commodification of Victimhood: The Toxic Legacy of Trafigura's Ship of Death*. London and New York: Routledge.

Milieudefensie, et al. v. Royal Dutch Shell (2021). The Hague Dist. Ct, 26 May, ECLI:NL:RBDHA:2021:5339, C/09/571932/HA ZA 19–379.

Murase, S. (1993). Country/Region Report (JAPAN). *Yearbook of International Environment Law*, 4, p. 435.

Okpabi and others v. Royal Dutch Shell Plc and another (2021). United Kingdom Sup. Ct, 2021 UKSC 3.

Paris Convention on Third Party Liability for Nuclear Energy (1960) [Paris Convention], in force 1 April 1968.

Potter, D. (1994). Assessing Japan's Environmental Aid Policy. *Pacific Affairs*, 67(2), pp. 200–215.

Prihandono, I. and Dewanty, H. (2015). Litigating Cross-Border Environmental Dispute in Indonesian Civil Court: The Montara Case. *Indonesia Law Review*, 5(1), pp. 14–32.

Regulation (EC) No 864/2007 on the Law Applicable to Non-contractual Obligations (Rome II) (2007). Official Journal L199, p. 40.

Sanda v. PTTEP Australasia (Ashmore Cartier) Pty Ltd (No 7) (2021). Federal Court of Australia, FCA 237.

Shimizu, K. (2021). Taiwan Chip Industry's Energy Appetite Draws Japan Investment: JERA and Partners to Spend $900m to Expand Gas-fired Power Plant. *NIKKEI Asia*, 18 August.

Stichting Union des Victimes de Déchets Toxiques D'Abidjan et Banlieues (Stichting VDTCI) v. Trafigura Beheer B.V. (2022). Hoge Raad (Dutch Sup. Ct), 11 February, ECLI:NL:HR:2022:165.

United Nations. General Assembly (2022). *Resolution on the Right to a Clean, Healthy and Sustainable Environment*, A/76/L.75. Available at: https://digitallibrary.un.org/record/3982508?ln=en

United States v. Canada (Trail Smelter case) (1938 and 1941). Arbitrational Tribunal (Constituted for That Case) United Nations. *Reports of International Arbitral Awards*, 1941, III, p. 1905.

Vienna Convention on Civil Liability for Nuclear Damage (1963) [Vienna Convention], in force 12 November 1977.

Woon Tan Kan and Ors. v. Asian Rare Earth Sdn. Bhd. (1992). Ipoh High Ct, Civil 1985. No. 185, 11 July, 4 CLJ 2207; (1993) Sup. Ct of Malaysia, No. 02–313–92, 23 December 1993. In: Japan External Trade Organization (JETRO), 1994.

17 COVID-19 and Compulsory Licensing

Akiko KATO

Introduction

The system for the protection of intellectual property rights (IPRs) aims to achieve certain policy objectives, such as industrial and cultural development, by giving private persons the exclusive right to control IPRs in exchange for public disclosure as an IP sharing system. Regarding this characteristic, the IP system is quite similar to industrial policy compared with property rights in general, based on human rights theory and built on instrumentalism in the sense that this system is clearly placed as a legal measure to achieve specific national and/or regional purposes (Peukert, 2017, p. 161). Accordingly, each national/regional IP system has some specific dimension in accordance with its domestic interests, and the balance between public and private interests regarding IPRs is recognized as a central issue.

The Agreement on Trade-Related Aspects of Intellectual Property Rights (TRIPS Agreement) drastically changed this phenomenon by establishing a minimum standard of IPR protection among 164 member states/regions. This agreement obliges members to protect not only patents, industrial designs, trademarks and copyrights, protected since the19th century by universal treaties, but also undisclosed information, geographical indications, and layout designs of integrated circuits, thus realizing their universal protection and privatization. In contrast, such global codification of private interests requires IP sharing to create an appropriate balance between global public and private interests on global concerns, such as public health, the environment, and human rights, as indicated by the Millenium Development Goals (MDGs) and Sustainable Development Goals (SDGs). To improve these global concerns, various public and private actors have accumulated efforts globally and locally, such as, but not limited to, public-private partnerships (PPPs) (UN Secretary-General's High-level Panel on Access to Medicines, 2016). Their efforts involve various types of IP sharing to be discussed later.

In the face of the COVID-19 pandemic, we also witness many cases of IP sharing. Our ability to control COVID-19 and the ensuing pandemic have been tested in the face of extreme disparity between developed and developing countries on access to therapeutic medicines and vaccines.

This chapter analyzes the relationship between governments' legal obligation on compulsory licensing and the previously mentioned responses of IP holders

DOI: 10.4324/9781003193098-17

and proposes a desirable texturization of IP sharing for the post-COVID-19 era. First, the chapter clarifies various schemes on IP sharing. Then, these are discussed in the context of COVID-19 along with whether they are available to address our urgent issues.

Various Schemes for IP Sharing

Public Disclosure of IPRs and IP Sharing

Many countries/regions have adopted the formality principle with the emergence of IPRs, especially industrial property rights such as patents and trademarks, in which the government is involved through review and registration. The applicant submits an application describing the required information on the subject matter of rights to the government authority, and the authority reviews the application based on the registration requirements and notifies the applicant of whether they are registered or not. Simultaneously, one and a half years after the application date, all the patent applications will be published and thus disclosed. In the case of the procedure on trademarks and industrial designs, they are published immediately after application. The system of public disclosure, as a type of IP sharing, coincides with the recognition of these IPRs as absolute exclusive rights. In contrast, the universal system of copyright protection by the Berne Convention adopts non-formality, and copyright is admitted as a relative exclusive right. The system of public disclosure has the merit of not only preventing duplication of IP creation and application but also realizing IP sharing worldwide. For developing countries, such IP pools are an important source to access leading IP and improve their technological knowledge. The PCT (Patent Cooperation Treaty) on patents, Madrid Agreement and Protocol on trademarks, Hague Agreement on industrial designs, UPOV (International Convention for the Protection of New Varieties of Plants) on plant varieties, and Lisbon Agreement on appellation of origin and geographical indication are all examples.

However, this IP sharing would not be fully functional unless there is sufficient ability and resources on the part of the government to gather, open, and make regulatory review of the IP or for the user to extract and exploit the IP. To fill these functional gaps, some intermediate entities are established by inter-/non-governmental organizations (IGOs/NGOs). For example, WIPO provides WIPO Re:Search that targets research and development (R&D) of medical products for neglected disease and WIPO Pat-INFORMED that targets low-molecule drugs aimed at collecting patent information and creating opportunities for matching IPR holders and users. Another instance is the Medicines Patent Pool (MPP) that gathers pharmaceutical patent information submitted to/granted by lower and middle income countries (LMICs) and negotiates with patent holders asking for voluntary licensing and with generic makers for sub-licensing. It is typical here that the IPR holder is a licensor, and a generic company, university, or public research institute is the licensee. This means that the IPR holder can use its IP independently of these IPR pools; therefore, incentivizing them to participate in pools is one issue.

Next, IPRs without formality are also to be shared with others. The creator, user, and government do not incur costs related to the emergence of copyrights; however, the user wishing to make secondary use of copyrighted works frequently faces difficulty in getting permission. In addition, today, everyone can become a creator or transmitter through universal communication. To address this gap, practical systems such as archives and collective right management and legal systems such as compulsory licensing and limitations to exclusive rights including fair use/dealing and the renumeration right have been discussed and realized.

Furthermore, undisclosed information is less compatible with IP sharing because its confidentiality is a core value to be protected. However, this incompatibility does not place undisclosed information outside the subject of the balance between public and private interests. At the level of private persons, it inevitably affects the movements and interactions of humans. At the national level, undisclosed information influences national competitiveness, technological transfer, and dissemination among countries. In view of these aspects, undisclosed information is protected under the objective conditions of secrecy, availability, and non-publicity and the subjective conditions on the holder.

Use of IPRs and IP Sharing

Obviously, IP holders can use their IPRs by themselves. First, through assignment or entrustment of IPRs or through the sale of a product implementing some form of IP, funds can be raised. Second, IP holders can grant voluntarily licenses to licensees. In either case, IP is shared between an assignor and assignee or between a licensor and licensee. Third, IP holders can permit unspecified potential users to use their IP, that is, make an express or implied declaration of non-enforcement of IPRs. Recently, not a few innovative pharmaceutical companies have declared not to make patent applications or enforce their patent rights in countries with no local manufacturing capacity or those facing national health emergency. In a similar way, authors can express unilaterally their reservation of not only all but also part of their copyrights using a system like the creative commons (CC) system. Under such declarations, IP sharing occurs among IP holders and unspecified persons; therefore, extension of the sharing is unclear. This is a scheme in which the IP holder voluntary enters into an IP sharing relationship with others. Fourth, the IP holder can be invited to enter an involuntary statutory licensing relationship with a third party who has used this IP before the IP holder or who created the IP during their labor under an employer. Also, unvoluntary licensing includes compulsory licenses or use by the government for the realization of public and/or private interests. In the case of this licensing scheme, IP would be shared between the IP holder and the private person or public authority that filed the application.

We can divide the previously mentioned types of IP sharing into two categories from the viewpoint of whether the IP holder can select its own trading partner, that is, whether the IP holder is entitled to freedom to engage in economic activities. Such a licensing scheme as described previously in which the IP holder enters into an agreement based on its own intention gives the IP holder the freedom to select its trading partner and control how the IP is handled; therefore, the IP holder has an incentive to realize the appropriate use of the IP and maintain its own brand power. On the contrary, if an IP holder does not have such freedom, then such incentive would not function, and as a result, the IP would not be sufficiently shared. For example, around 2008, the Thai government granted eight compulsory licenses on medicines for treating HIV/AIDS, cancer, and tuberculosis. However, licensed institutes in Thailand could not manufacture generic version of these medicines because of the lack of related know-how, and this invited the importation of only one generic medicine from India and even a patent holder's withdrawal from the Thai market (Thanitcul and Braslow, 2013, pp. 66–73).

Additionally, there is a *de facto* driving force toward IP sharing provided by civil society. Recently, IP sharing is required of IP holders as an element of CSR (Corporate Social Responsibility) as is providing information disclosure of one's own IPRs' status, projects to disseminate/donate their IPR-related products, and participation in PPPs. In addition, they are subject to indexing and ranking within their industry by third parties, such as the Access to Medicine Index that the Access to Medicine Foundation publishes every two years based on their research on and hearings with the pharmaceutical industry (Kato and Naiki, 2021). These activities have a certain influence on the reputation and investor relations of IP holders.

IP Sharing in the Case of COVID-19

We can also find the previously mentioned types of IP sharing under the COVID-19 pandemic, and there is variation in the responses from IP holders by product group. First, on the patents of several therapeutic medicines available for COVID-19, IP holders have concluded voluntary licensing agreements. Gilead Sciences has acquired around 140 patents on ARV Remdesivir in LMICs and simultaneously concluded licensing agreements with generic companies covering 126 countries. In addition, to treat COVID-19 patients, it concluded nonexclusive and royalty-free licensing agreements with ten generic medicine companies in Egypt, India, and Pakistan and permitted provision of their products to 127 countries until the declaration of the World Health Organization (WHO) regarding the end of the state of emergency or until the filing of a product that is more effective than their products, whichever comes first (Gilead, 2021). AbbVie, a licensee of the patent on the therapeutic medicine Kaletra, concluded a royalty-free licensing agreement with MPP for pediatric products destined for 102 countries in 2014 and destined for the African continent in 2015. In this pandemic, AbbVie has substantially declared non-enforcement of their patent worldwide (WIPO COVID-19 IP Policy Tracker, 2020). Another case was Merck that in October 2021 concluded a licensing agreement with MPP on the oral antiviral medicine Molnupiravir, announcing that they would not receive royalties until release of the state of emergency by the WHO. In January 2022, MPP reported that 27 generic manufacturers concluded sub-licensing agreements of Molnupiravir with MPP (MPP, 2022).

Second, IPRs relating to medical products for COVID-19 or contents consumed in the 'new normal' life have been increasingly opened through declarations by the IP holders. In 2020, global information technology (IT) companies established the 'Open COVID Pledge' (Open COVID Pledge, 2020), and over 30 companies in Europe, the US, and Japan have joined it. Concurrently, Japanese venture and major companies announced the 'OPEN COVID-19 DECLARATION' (GC Kyoto, 2020). Certainly, these declarations contribute to manufacturing IPR-relating products without fear of being sued by IP holders, and they fill the gap between huge demand and provision. At the same time, it is uncertain what will happen when the pandemic is declared 'over'. Furthermore, the status of manufacturers is also uncertain in the sense that an IP holder's declaration might be withdrawn at any time based on their own discretion.

The global arrangement has also delivered results such as the COVID-19 Technology Access Pool (C-TAP) and MPP concluding their first licensing agreement in November 2021 with the Spanish National Research Council (CSIC) for a COVID-19 serological antibody test. The test effectively checks for the presence of anti-SARS-CoV-2 antibodies developed either in response to a COVID-19 infection or to a vaccine (WHO, 2021a). C-TAP is a global IP pool specific to the COVID-19 pandemic, established in May 2020 by the WHO in partnership with the Government of Costa Rica, under a global 'Solidarity Call to Action' endorsed by nearly 40 Member States and implementing partners such as MPP, Open COVID Pledge, UN Technology Bank, and Unitaid. However, the International Federation of Pharmaceutical Manufacturers and Associations (IFPMA), representing innovative pharmaceutical industries worldwide, immediately provided a counterstatement on C-TAP (IFPMA, 2020), and the few companies and countries in which these companies have their base have joined this IP pool. Therefore, the previous agreement represents the first transparent, global, and non-exclusive license for a COVID-19 health tool and the first test license signed by MPP and included in the Pool.

Furthermore, IP sharing is quite limited for COVID-19 vaccines. All of the vaccine developers have reinforced their own manufacturing capacity and given voluntary licensing to a few carefully selected partners. Especially, the mRNA vaccine by Pfizer and Moderna is based on patented technology and know-how and requires expertise, technique, and infrastructure to duplicate. Moderna declared earlier in October 2020 their non-enforcement until the end of the pandemic and stated that the best practice is the reinforcement of its own manufacturing capacity and that they will not share know-how on their vaccine with others (Moderna, 2020). Finally, at the end of August 2022, Moderna sued Pfizer and BioNTech for the infringement of patent rights regarding mRNA technology (Reed, 2022).

Furthermore, the regional scarcity and distributive inequity of COVID-19 vaccines are apparent. The WHO has a target to vaccinate 70% of the population of every country, with a focus on the most at-risk groups. However, as of 22 May 2022, almost one billion people in lower-income countries remain unvaccinated. Only 57 countries have vaccinated 70% of their population – almost all of them high-income countries (WHO, 2022).

To address this global access issue, the most straightforward way is reinforcing manufacturing capacity and increasing supply. In July 2021, the WHO established 'the mRNA technology transfer hub' in South Africa to boost vaccine production and provide training necessary to treat vaccines on the Africa continent within several years (MPP, 2021). Furthermore, at a special session of the World Health Assembly (WHA) held at the end of November 2021, strengthening local production was supported by over 100 Member States (WHO, 2022).

Here, a prerequisite for these efforts is IP sharing, but at the same time, a prominent issue is the difficulty in identifying the IPRs to be licensed to manufacture IPR-related products. For example, since June 2021, MPP has provided a patent database, 'VaxPal', that focuses on patent information regarding COVID-19 vaccines. Despite the previously mentioned reservations by pharmaceutical companies to acquire or enforce their IPRs related to COVID-19, the database shows a certain thicket of patents (as of 6 July 2021; Kianzad and Wested, 2021, pp. 86–87), including over 650 patent families (as of 8 February 2022).

To address this issue, several measures on both the national and global fronts have been proposed. First, in the early stage of the pandemic, some developed countries amended or enacted national law to make it possible for their governments to grant compulsory licenses to themselves (so-called 'government use') on the IPRs available for the immunization, prevention, and treatment of COVID-19, parallel to the provision to grant compulsory licenses to private persons (e.g., Loi no, 2020–290; Gesetz zum Schutz der Bevölkerung bei einer epidemischen Lage von nationaler Tragweite, 2020; COVID-19 Emergency Response Act 2020). However, few LMICs has taken such measures. These diverse responses may be caused partially by legal self-restraint on the part of governments in their authority to limit the effectiveness of IPRs by concluding free trade agreements (FTAs)/ economic partnership agreements (EPAs) with trade partners or by an expectation for various efforts by which IGOs or NGOs would establish schemes to improve access for all people to medical products (e.g., COVAX Facility).

Second, several schemes to share IPRs relating to the struggle with the pandemic, such as the C-TAP and the mRNA technology transfer hub, were realized. However, and regrettably, it is hard to say that they have functioned well enough to improve the access issue.

Finally, to break this deadlock, in October 2020, India and South Africa proposed to the World Trade Organization (WTO) TRIPS Council to submit a draft resolution to the General Council to admit waiving the obligations of Members to protect and enforce a part of IPRs according to the TRIPS Agreement for 'X' years from the decision of the General Council (WTO, 2020). This means that WTO members will not be obliged to protect patents, copyrights, industrial designs, and undisclosed information and that IP holders will not be able to take measures such as civil litigation, petitions for import injunction, or criminal complaints toward third parties' use of their IPRs. Many pros and cons have been discussed on this proposal, as is mentioned later. This proposal was partly revised and resubmitted in May 2021 with over 60 Member countries joining as co-sponsors (WTO, 2021a). In the same period, the US Biden Administration expressed its approval of the proposal, and in June, the European Union (EU) submitted another draft decision and its explanatory communication that emphasized the necessity to eliminate national/regional export restrictions on medical products and to fully exploit existing compulsory licensing schemes within national patent law and the TRIPS Agreement (WTO, 2021b, 2021c). This debate resulted in the adoption of the Decision on the TRIPS Agreement and COVID-19 at the 12th Ministerial Conference in June 2022 (WTO, 2022). The Decision makes it possible for developing countries to use the patented innovation addressed and specified to the manufacture and procurement of COVID-19 vaccines and states that the WTO Members will continue the negotiation to expand the scope of the waiver to other IPRs and medical products. In parallel, the WHO decided to start negotiations toward a global pandemic treaty in the coming years (WHO, 2021b).

Discussion

As Thambisetty *et al.* (2021, pp. 12–14) described, it should be clearly recognized that the COVAX Facilities are a mix that assemble various functions of various actors that have contributed access to medicine issues over the past decades, and they represent a type of collective procurement system of vaccines as products; hence, there is no relation with the IPRs regarding vaccines. This scheme suffered due to capital shortage in the early times and a shortage of products subsequently. Product shortage, which is caused by export restrictions of producer countries, buyout-contracts between developed countries and vaccine developers, and acceleration of booster immunizations to their nationals by countries that already have access in the face of new variants coincide with overwhelming inequality in access to vaccines.

Here, it is worth noting that compulsory licensing is available to resolve the shortage of IPR-related products *within limited areas*. In this context, countries/regions can control and limit IPRs, and by licensing, they can access the products through their own use or importation. However, in a global pandemic such as COVID-19, compulsory licensing granted by a country/region for fulfilling its national demand may induce an absolute shortage and uneven distribution worldwide. Therefore, the urgent issue is worldwide reinforcement of production and distribution to make the pie larger.

It has also been repeatedly pointed out that manufacturing IPR-related products is not usually possible by granting a compulsory license alone (e.g., Owoeye, 2019, Ch.3). This is especially the case with COVID-19 vaccines that use new, innovative technology (Gurgula and Hull, 2021). Because of this 'twist of the patent-trade secret duopoly' (Thambisetty *et al.*, 2021, p. 17), without sufficient local manufacturing capacity, compulsory licensing will not solve the access issue (Sepúlveda and Ocampos, 2021) and will culminate in importation from another country/region.

However, the TRIPS Agreement obliges Members to fulfill a number of conditions according to Article 31 in granting third parties the use of a patent right without the permission of the IP holder, for example, in compulsory licensing and government use; however, there is no mention of compulsory licensing of know-how in Article 39 or the other clauses. In the hope to manufacture a COVID-19 vaccine, several generic pharmaceutical companies in both developed and developing countries have offered manufacturing capacity for vaccines but were rebuffed and/or were unable to obtain a license (Thambisetty *et al.*, 2021, p. 38). Gurgula and Hull analyze that compulsory licensing of know-how is also possible and feasible in this pandemic, subject to sufficient government involvement and support such as maintaining secrecy and the implementation of patented technology, and that a further issue is another IP citing data exclusivity that prevents obtaining marketing approval for a vaccine (Gurgula and Hull, 2021). In other words, this scheme would be characterized as a type of technology transfer for government use. Then, the government should be obliged to provide support by giving economic interest to IP holders and potential users. The interest may be monetary support through royalty payments or any measure to improve their brand power to the public including an exclusion of counterfeits and/or low-quality goods.

That is, Article 31 bis of the TRIPS Agreement provides a scheme for trade among WTO Members under granting compulsory licensing, waiving Article 31(b), and so on. In February 2021, Bolivia, and in May 2021, Antigua and Barbuda submitted notifications of the intention to use this scheme as importing members (WTO, 2021d, 2021e). Parallel to these submissions, Bolivia concluded a buyout agreement with Canadian pharmaceutical company Biolyse Pharma, which estimated to be able to produce up to approximately 200,000 doses of vaccine per week. Biolyse has made an application and tried to persuade the Canadian government to grant compulsory licensing on the patent of Jonson & Johnson (Bruce, 2021), but it has not yet succeeded. This shows a part of a great number of the non-availabilities of this scheme (Kianzad and Wested, 2021, pp. 82–84; Thambisetty *et al.*, 2021, pp. 28–29).

Here, could the waiver be an appropriate measure to improve access to vaccines? Alongside the innovative pharmaceutical industry, many commentators have pointed out concerns about it (e.g., Baachus, J., 2020; Christoph A. *et al.*, 2021; Hilty, R. *et al.*, 2021). Here, the core issue to be addressed is that compulsory licensing and waiver are different from each other in terms of the mode of IP sharing and whether IP holders would recognize and have any control over the use of their IPRs by others or not. Voluntary licensing makes it possible for IP holders to select their trading partner and set all the conditions on the use, while compulsory licensing makes it impossible to do so; however, at least the licensees are identified. In contrast, waiver makes it impossible to recognize who intends to use the IPRs. At the same time, it provides no incentive to IP holders to consider voluntary licensing, to provide IPR-related know-how, or to state non-enforcement by one's own intention. Furthermore, the risk of free-riding (in the waiver case, this is not 'counterfeited') or manufacturing low-quality or even dangerous products would increase worldwide, and countries/regions might have few legal measures against them. Does this not also amount to a waiver of governments' obligation to protect the right to health?

As mentioned previously, under the COVID-19 pandemic, to rely on usual compulsory licensing schemes is difficult and risky. National governments should positively involve the use of IPRs not permitted by IP holders, namely, through government use, through matching IP holders and users with technology transfer, paying appropriate royalties, and even publicly praising or ranking IP holders to incentivize them and contribute to their brand power. New negotiations at the WHO on the pandemic treaty might be meaningful if they would oblige Members to make such efforts.

In addition, it is apparent that the products resulting from other uses should be distributed and provided worldwide and that local manufacturing capacity should be built in various places.

Conclusion

The continuation of the pandemic and appearance of new virus strains one after another have brought us to the situation of 'No one is safe until everyone is safe'. The extreme inequality of access to COVID-19 vaccines represents long-standing stagnation in carving out a path for substantial technology transfer. Discrete compulsory licensing by each country/region results in a scramble for vital products; therefore, this should be replaced with concerted governmental action. This requires revisiting governments' obligations to fulfill health needs and protect the right to health of not only their nationals but also people around the globe. If governments prioritize first immunization of the people in LMICs and put off the booster immunization of their own nationals, then they could necessitate and rely on the concept of the global public good. IP sharing is an element of the concept, and its style needs to be well discussed.

Note: This article was funded by JSPS KAKENHI Grant Number JP20K01429, JP20H04424 and JPJSJRP 20211703.

References

All subsequent websites were last visited on 19 September 2022.

Baachus, J. (2020). An Unnecessary Proposal: A WTO Waiver of Intellectual Property Rights for COVID-19 Vaccines. *CATO Institute Free Trade Bulletin*, 78, pp. 1–5.

Bruce, F. (2021). *Canadian Government Slammed Over 'Intransigence' on Compulsory Licensing*. Available at: https://pink.pharmaintelligence.informa.com/PS144533/Canadian-Government-Slammed-Over-Intransigence-On-Compulsory-Licensing

Christoph, A. *et al.* (2021). *The Waiving of Intellectual Property: A Poor Response to a Real Problem*. Available at: http://dx.doi.org/10.2139/ssrn.3850550

COVID-19 Emergency Response Act 2020 (CA) Available at: https://laws-lois.justice.gc.ca/eng/AnnualStatutes/2020_5/FullText.html

GC Kyoto (2020). *Open COVID-19 Declaration*. Available at: www.gckyoto.com/covid19

Gesetz zum Schutz der Bevölkerung bei einer epidemischen Lage von nationaler Tragweite vom 27. März 2020 (DE). Available at: www.bundesgesundheitsministerium.de/fileadmin/Dateien/3_Downloads/Gesetze_und_Verordnungen/GuV/B/3._BevSchG_BGBl.pdf

Gilead (2021). *Gilead's Response to COVID-19*. Available at: www.gilead.com/purpose/advancing-global-health/covid-19/voluntary-licensing-agreements-for-remdesivir

Gurgula, O. and Hull, J. (2021). Compulsory Licensing of Trade Secrets: Ensuring Access to COVID-19 Vaccines Via Involuntary Technology Transfer. *Journal of Intellectual Property Law & Practice*, 16(11), pp. 1242–1261.

Hilty, R. *et al.* (2021). *COVID-19 and the Role of Intellectual Property: Position Statement of the Max Planck Institute for Innovation and Competition of 7 May 2021*. Available at: http://dx.doi.org/10.2139/ssrn.3841549

IFPMA (2020). *IFPMA Statement on the 'Solidarity Call to Action to Realize Equitable Global Access to COVID-19 Health Technologies Through Pooling of Knowledge, Intellectual Property and Data*. Available at: www.ifpma.org/resource-centre/ifpma-statement-on-the-solidarity-call-to-action-to-realize-equitable-global-access-to-covid-19-health-technologies-through-pooling-of-knowledge-intellectual-property-and-data/#:~:text=IFPMA%20Statement%20on%20the%20%E2%80%9CSolidarity%20Call%20to%20Action,health%2C%20social%20and%20economic%20impact%20around%20the%20world

Kato, A. and Naiki, Y. (2021). The Access to Medicine index: How Ranking Pharmaceutical Companies Encourages Polycentric Health Governance. *Health Policy*, 125(11), pp. 1399–1405. Available at: https://doi.org/10.1016/j.healthpol.2021.09.002

Kianzad, B. and Wested, J. (2021). 'No-one Is Safe Until Everyone Is Safe' – Patent Waiver, Compulsory Licensing and COVID-19. *European Pharmaceutical Law Review*, 5(2), pp. 71–91. Available at: https://doi.org/10.21552/eplr/2021/2/4

Loi no 2020–290 du 23 mars 2020 d'urgence pour faire face à l'épidémie de covid-19 2020 (FR). Available at: www.legifrance.gouv.fr/jorf/id/JORFTEXT000041746313

Medicines Patent Pool (2021). *The mRNA Vaccine Technology Transfer Hub: A Need for Equity in Access to COVID-19 Vaccines*. Available at: https://medicinespatentpool.org/covid-19/technology-transfer-hub#:~:text=The%20mRNA%20vaccine%20Technology%20Transfer%20Hub%20A%20need,in%20low-%20and%20middle-income%20countries%2C%20especially%20in%20Africa

Medicines Patent Pool (2022). *27 Generic Manufacturers Sign Agreements with MPP to Produce Low-cost Versions of COVID-19 Antiviral Medication Molnupiravir for Supply in 105 Low-and-middle-income Countries*. Available at: https://medicinespatentpool.org/news-publications-post/27-generic-manufacturers-sign-agreements-with-mpp-to-produce-molnupiravir

Moderna (2020). *Statement by Moderna on Intellectual Property Matters During the COVID-19 Pandemic*. Available at: https://investors.modernatx.com/Statements – Perspectives/Statements – Perspectives-Details/2020/Statement-by-Moderna-on-Intellectual-Property-Matters-during-the-COVID-19-Pandemic/default.aspx

Owoeye, O. (2019). *Intellectual Property and Access to Medicines in Africa: A Regional Framework for Access*. London and New York: Routledge.

Peukert, A. (2017). Vereinheitlichung des Immaterialgüterrechts: Strukturen, Akteure, Zwecke. *RabelsZ*, 81, pp. 158–193.

Reed, J. (2022). Moderna Suing Pfizer Over Covid Vaccine Technology. *BBC News*, 26 August. Available at: www.bbc.com/news/health

Sepúlveda, C. I. and Ocampos, J. A. (2021). International Technology Transfer to Promote Access and Innovation in Times of Global Crisis. *les Nouvelles – Journal of the Licensing Executives Society*, LVI(1). Available at: https://papers.ssrn.com/sol3/papers.cfm?abstract_id=3771482

Thambisetty, S. *et al.* (2021). The TRIPS Intellectual Property Waiver Proposal: Creating the Right Incentives in Patent Law and Politics to End the COVID-19 Pandemic. *LSE Law, Society and Economy Working Papers*, 06/2021. Available at: http://dx.doi.org/10.2139/ssrn.3851737

Thanitcul, S. and Braslow, L. M. (2013). Compulsory Licensing of Chronic Disease Pharmaceuticals in Thailand. *Thai Journal of Pharmaceutical Sciences*, 37, pp. 61–83.

UN Secretary-General's High-level Panel on Access to Medicines (2016). *Promoting Innovation and Access to Health Technologies*. Available at: www.unsgaccessmeds.org/final-report.

WHO (2021a). *WHO and MPP Announce the First Transparent, Global, Non-exclusive Licence for a COVID-19 Technology; CSIC Offers Serological Test to C-TAP*. Available at: www.who.int/news/item/23-11-2021-who-and-mpp-announce-the-first-transparent-global-non-exclusive-licence-for-a-covid-19-technology

WHO (2021b). *The World Together: Establishment of an Intergovernmental Negotiating Body to Strengthen Pandemic Prevention, Preparedness and Response*, SSA2(5). Available at: https://apps.who.int/gb/ebwha/pdf_files/WHASSA2/SSA2(5)-en.pdf

WHO (2022). *COVID-19 Vaccines*. Available at: www.who.int/emergencies/diseases/novel-coronavirus-2019/covid-19-vaccines

WIPO (2020). *COVID-19 IP Policy Tracker*. Available at: www.wipo.int/covid19-policy-tracker/#/covid19-policy-tracker/ipo-operations

WTO (2020). *Waiver from Certain Provisions of the TRIPS Agreement for the Prevention, Containment and Treatment of COVID-19: Communication from India and South Africa*, IP/C/W/669. Available at: https://docs.wto.org/dol2fe/Pages/SS/directdoc.aspx?filename=q:/IP/C/W669R1.pdf&Open=True

WTO (2021a). *Waiver from Certain Provisions of the TRIPS Agreement for the Prevention, Containment and Treatment of COVID-19*, IP/C/W/669. Available at: https://docs.wto.org/dol2fe/Pages/SS/directdoc.aspx?filename=q:/IP/C/W669R1.pdf&Open=True

WTO (2021b). *Urgent Trade Policy Responses to the COVID-19 Crisis: Intellectual Property: Communication from the European Union to the Council for TRIPS*, IP/C/W/680. Available at: https://trade.ec.europa.eu/doclib/docs/2021/june/tradoc_159606.pdf

WTO (2021c). *Draft General Council Declaration on the TRIPS Agreement and Public Health in the Circumstances of a Pandemic: Communication from the European Union to the Council for TRIPS*, IP/C/W/681. Available at: www.tralac.org/documents/resources/covid-19/4473-draft-wto-general-council-declaration-on-the-trips-agreement-and-public-health-covid-19-pandemic-communication-eu-18-june-2021/file.html

WTO (2021d). *Notification Under the Amended TRIPS Agreement: Notification of Intention to Use the Special Compulsory Licensing System as an Importing Member: Plurinational State of Bolivia*, IP/N/8/BOL/1. Available at: www.wto.org/english/tratop_e/trips_e/public_health_notif_import_e.htm

WTO (2021e). *Notification Under the Amended TRIPS Agreement: Notification of Intention to Use the Special Compulsory Licensing System as an Importing Member*, IP/N/8/ATG/1. Available at: https://docs.wto.org/dol2fe/Pages/SS/directdoc.aspx?filename=q:/IP/N/8ATG1.pdf&Open=True

WTO (2022). *Ministerial Decision on the TRIPS Agreement*, WT/MIN(22)/30, WT/L/1141. Available at: https://docs.wto.org/dol2fe/Pages/SS/directdoc.aspx?filename=q:/WT/MIN22/30.pdf&Open=True

Index

For Product Safety Concerns and Information please contact our EU representative GPSR@taylorandfrancis.com
Taylor & Francis Verlag GmbH, Kaufingerstraße 24, 80331 München, Germany

www.ingramcontent.com/pod-product-compliance
Ingram Content Group UK Ltd.
Pitfield, Milton Keynes, MK11 3LW, UK
UKHW020009200926
475702UK00015B/2559

9781032044149